PREFACE TO CHRISTIAN STUDIES

PREFACE TO CHRISTIAN STUDIES

Edited by

F. G. HEALEY

Barbour Professor of Systematic Theology
Westminster and Cheshunt Colleges
Cambridge

LUTTERWORTH PRESS LONDON

First published 1971
Lutterworth Press, 4 Bouverie Street, London, E.C.4

ISBN 0 7188 1713 3

Printed in Great Britain
by Ebenezer Baylis and Son Ltd.
The Trinity Press, Worcester, and London

Contents

5

Foreword

THIS BOOK is intended especially, but not exclusively, for the growing number of those who are taking up the study of Christian beliefs, practices and institutions. It is remarkable that, even in countries where membership of Christian churches and the enrolment of candidates for their ordained ministry have fallen, there has been a marked increase in the number of schools, colleges and universities which offer courses in religious studies and in Christian theology.

There are good reasons for this. Current moral attitudes and social practices challenge traditional Christian precepts and standards. The intellectual climate of our time encourages the radical questioning of what Christians believe. The meaningfulness of all religious language is in dispute. In societies that are more and more multi-racial, where the expression and practice of non-Christian faiths become even in so-called Christian countries part of the domestic scene, Christian claims to uniqueness and finality are more forcibly called in question than before. The result is a wider interest and a greater liveliness in the discussion of religion in general and of Christian beliefs in particular.

The chapters which follow provide a view of Christian theology as a whole, and an introduction to the main features of each of its parts. Not only those who come fresh to the subject, but also those who have studied theology already and want to know how its various branches appear in the light of more recent discussion, will find the book of use. In these days of open discussion, moreover, it is hoped that in addition to professing

Christians, whether Protestant or Catholic, members of the Jewish faith and other religious faiths will read with interest what a group of Christian scholars have to say at the present time about the studies in which they are specially engaged.

The Editor wishes to express his warmest thanks to the contributors to this volume who have generously made time to write its various chapters, and to the publishers who sponsored the undertaking. The note on language study in connection with theological studies has been kindly supplied by Professor Ackroyd.

The Bounds,   F. G. HEALEY
Westminster College, Cambridge

I

CHRISTIAN THEOLOGY: ITS NATURE AND SCOPE

F. G. HEALEY

Christian Theology: Its Nature and Scope

CHRISTIAN THEOLOGY comprises a number of inter-related studies which constitute an organic whole. The present chapter is concerned with the general character of Christian theology, and why it makes necessary the particular enquiries which fall within its scope. We shall see that the general character of Christian theology also demands studies not strictly theological, such as scientific studies of religion and its organized forms, and philosophical study of religious language and concepts. Later chapters will deal in turn with particular fields of enquiry which, because they are constituent parts of Christian theology or because of their intimate relationships to it, may together be designated Christian studies.

I

There are four main ways of dealing with the question, What is theology? The first is to trace back the word itself as far as possible to its original form and usage. A definition based on such work is called etymological. The second is to state, not merely how the word was originally used, but in what way it is generally employed at present—its conventional use. Technically the result is called a reportive definition. The third way is taken by those who declare how they intend to use or understand the term, no matter how it is used or understood by others. Such declaration is technically called a stipulative definition. A fourth kind of definition consists in setting out the problems with which theology is concerned.

Difficulties arise with all such definitions taken by themselves.

If the etymological road is followed, the Greek words *theologia* and *theologos* are studied in the ancient writers. As we shall see, this is useful and interesting. Nevertheless, scholarly research leaves room for defensible differences of opinion as to the exact significance of those terms at the first. We are left with such diverse explications of 'theology' as sayings about the gods, and ordered discourse concerning the gods, or God, or things divine. The student should be on his guard against accepting uncritically the kind of statement which boldly implies (often in brackets) that the word 'theology' originally meant 'the science of God'. So far as the second way of describing theology is concerned, there is no generally accepted reportive definition today. On the third way we shall comment in a moment. The fourth kind of definition is attractive. It conceals however this difficulty: Which problems are to be included? If they are put down as though they were the problems generally regarded as belonging to theology, we have in effect a reportive definition. The question then arises whether the report is accurate. In the light of present as well as past discussion, it is only fair to say that no such report is credible. On the other hand, if a writer or a group of writers has decided despite the views of others which problems comprise the task of theology, we are being offered in effect a stipulative definition.

As etymological answers to the questions are not by themselves very helpful and a unanimous reportive reply is at present impossible, it looks as if we were shut up to a stipulative definition of theology. About this kind of definition one or two comments must be made. In the first place, it is often concealed. The beginner needs to be cautious about interpreting declarations, especially in manuals and short articles, that theology *is* such and such, or (with a more authoritative ring) theology *proper* is so-and-so. More often than not such sentences should be taken to read: "I am going to use the term theology as if it meant..." Secondly, in the case of responsible authors at any rate, a stipulative definition is not just an arbitrary choice. There is more to it than in the oft-quoted remark of Humpty-Dumpty: "When I use a word, it means just what I choose it to mean—neither more nor less." A stipulative definition usually rests on grounds that have been carefully considered, even if they are not fully displayed. In the third place, a stipulative definition competes for attention with others. The fact that there are several candidates in the field need not trouble the student unduly at first, so long as what is offered really helps him to find his way around the subject and its various parts. Nevertheless, fourthly, it is hardly satisfactory to be asked to accept a definition merely on trust. Is it too broad, or too narrow, or otherwise inadequate? What are the reasons for making this choice rather than that about the subject-matter of theology, or its starting point, or its methods? The difficulty for anyone who is entering on this study is that he is in no position to reply. He has to master much of the subject before he can exercise the informed judgement which the answering of these questions demands. One thing at least can be done to help the student, and that is to review in outline some of the more important ways in which Christian theology has been regarded in the past.

II

When Christians began to reflect in orderly fashion upon their faith the word theology was already available as a convenient term for what they were doing. So far as its pre-Christian usage is concerned, it will be enough to mention three writers only. In the works of Plato (c. 427–347 B.C.) 'theology' was used in connection with statements, especially those found in the poets, about the gods. Plato and his master Socrates often criticized some of these statements as unworthy of divine beings, and as having pernicious moral effects. Aristotle (384–322 B.C.) used the word in a similar way but, more important, also used it as an alternative name for his metaphysics, or 'first philosophy'. As such it described an undertaking which finds the rational explanation of all that is, in terms of a Supreme Mind. This usage was influential although, to avoid confusion with other subsequent uses of 'theology', more modern writers tended to use in the same general sense another term, theism. Varro (116–27 B.C.), a contemporary of Cicero and renowned as the most learned of the Romans, discriminated between three kinds of theology. The first he called fabulous or mythical theology. By this he meant what was expressed by those statements about the gods and their relationships with one another and with men which are found in poetry and plays. The second kind he called civil theology, notions about the gods or the divine which were made manifest in civic ceremonies and festivals. The third he named natural theology (*theologia physica*). This term became of immense significance later, although its interpretation has varied a great deal. Augustine (354–430) was influential in putting it into circulation among Christians. What Varro himself appears to have had in mind was the work of philosophers who were concerned to identify the ultimate power underlying and activating natural phenomena. For his part he taught that God was the 'soul' of the universe[1].

Although Christians had this convenient term 'theology' to hand, they seem to have been rather chary of using it at first, perhaps because of its pagan associations. In any case they have used it since in a wide variety of ways. We shall not attempt to trace the long history of the use of the word itself. It is more profitable to try and make plain the chief kinds of questions the answering of which has been taken at one period or another to be the essential task of theology. Whether the word was generally applied to such work at the time, or whether this was done only at a later period, is for our purpose not of great account. In order to keep the survey within bounds, references to names will be few and brief[2]. To give it shape, a roughly chronological order will be followed. It should be borne in mind however that earlier views about theology reappear later, while views which became prominent at a later stage can also be found in earlier writers.

Theology was at one time used by Christians to designate discussion of the deity of Jesus Christ or the doctrine of the Trinity. Athanasius (*c.* 296–373) and Gregory of Nazianzus (329–389) for example were called theologians mainly because of their part in the debating of such matters. A much later instance (indeed after a lengthy period during which the word theology had again largely fallen out of use in the Western Church) is found in the title of two books by Abelard (1079–1142), *Introduction to Theology* and *Christian Theology*. Both are treatises on trinitarian doctrine.

No one nowadays would restrict theology to the consideration of such themes, momentous as they are. In the fourth and fifth centuries a wider view, though not unknown before, gained ground. We may put it this way. Theology supplies the answer to the question, What is it that every priest should know? Chrysostom (died 407) for example, after exalting the office and responsibilities of priests, went on to say that they should be, not only virtuous as angels, but also proficient in knowledge of authoritative church teachings. That meant knowledge of the contents of Scripture, knowledge of extra-Scriptural tradition (regarded as stemming from, or implied in, and in any case agreeable to apostolic practice and teaching), and knowledge of church decisions as to how the Scriptures and tradition were to be interpreted.

If such knowledge was essential for ministers of the Church, it had long been recognized that other knowledge too is a help. This was urged by Augustine, a contemporary of Chrysostom, when he wrote a book for preachers called *On Christian Doctrine*. Those who interpreted the Scriptures should acquire, not only mastery of the original biblical languages and the techniques of reasoning and persuasion, but also knowledge of subjects like history, natural science, the mechanical arts, and numbers. In the sixth century this was carried further. The conviction had already been fostered that the study of theology was more than a course of instruction for priest and preacher. It was valuable also as an aid to the religious life—a conviction which sometimes falters in the mind of modern students. A Roman senator, Cassiodorus (*c.* 485–580), on retiring from public office established two monasteries, and himself became a monk. He played an important part in creating the great (and continuing) monastic tradition of scholarship. In addition to practical pursuits, he included in his curriculum such studies as natural science, grammar, mathematics, and music[3].

It is easy to understand that enquiring minds would want to

relate such other learning to the discussion of teaching authoritatively promulgated by the Church. Some of the early Fathers had already pressed the philosophical work of non-Christians into the service of Christian apologetic. From now on, however, theology became more generally than before, not only the exposition of Church teaching, but also an enquiry as to how far, and in what ways, such teaching is supportable by human reasoning alone. This stance was succinctly expressed for example by Anselm (1033–1109), when he described the purpose of some of his work as faith seeking an understanding of itself (*fides quaerens intellectum*). In this connection Hugh of St. Vincent (1096–c. 1141) is of interest because he was a mystic. He regarded discursive thinking as the first stage on the way to the blissful contemplation of God. For him Christian doctrine is certainly above reason (*supra rationem*), but it is assuredly also congruent with reason (*secundum rationem*). This kind of attitude made it possible for the greatest of the scholastic theologians, Thomas Aquinas (*c.* 1227–1274), to make full and brilliant use of the works of Aristotle, both philosophical and scientific (by then more fully available than ever before), in the service of theology.

The genius of scholars like Albertus Magnus (*c.* 1200–1280) and Thomas Aquinas could not prevent this enlargement of the scope of theology, nor the scholastic way of doing theology, from deteriorating for a time into arid intellectualism. An early reaction within the Roman Catholic Church against this, as well as against immorality among the clergy, is found in Roger Bacon (*c.* 1212–1292). He exemplifies a recognizably different view of theology, which among others has persisted to this day. For him the essential and paramount concern of theology is with biblical teaching. The Bible is the sole authoritative source-book of Christian doctrine. He was ready to admit that some wisdom is to be found in other writers, but why should theologians turn elsewhere when wisdom in its fullness is to be found in the Bible alone? This appeal to the Bible alone (*sola scriptura*) has sometimes been carried to absurd lengths,[4] but short of that a similar general attitude to the task of theology was widely adopted by theologians of the Reformation. Purely as a theologian (i.e. without making comparisons in other respects with such men as Luther) the greatest of them was Calvin (1509–1564). He quoted pagan writers and early Fathers of the Church, but for him all non-biblical writings are to be tested by the truth to be apprehended, with the aid of the internal testimony of the Holy Spirit, in sacred Scripture.

By sacred Scripture Calvin did not mean, or at any rate did not consistently mean, that every word in the text of the Bible as we have it was divinely given. He used some curious figures of speech in writing about the origin of Scripture, but his commentaries reveal a freedom to criticize and amend the actual current text which does not accord with any theory of its verbal inerrancy. Nevertheless, for him 'the Bible' had divine authority (that is to say, was entitled to be unquestionably believed and obeyed), as for others 'the Church' had divine authority. In the late seventeenth and especially in the eighteenth century, views about the nature of theology were deeply affected by a revolt against all such unquestionable authorities. A number of influential thinkers regarded theology as essentially an engagement with the question, What by reasoning can a rational person find out as to the truth concerning God, the world and man? The titles of some of the English theological books of the period show the shift in interest and point of view.[5] This movement of thought, philosophical as well as theological, is sometimes designated English Deism and, as it is more widely known on the Continent, the Enlightenment. It was stimulated by the obvious and rapidly growing success of the 'scientific method' in enlarging man's knowledge. Such knowledge raised serious difficulties about statements in church and biblical teaching based upon pre-scientific opinions. Those difficulties in turn encouraged scepticism about other statements not amenable to testing by the methods and the results obtaining in the natural sciences. Free thinkers, as the sceptics were coming more generally to be called, condemned traditional theology for being merely a deductive exercise, that is to say essentially a drawing of conclusions from uncriticizable presuppositions.

It was not long before this largely negative criticism was seen to be inadequate. The result was a further important turning-point in the history of Christian theology. The key figure is Schleiermacher (1768–1824). He was acutely conscious that many educated persons had become apathetic towards the organized Church and critical of its doctrinal teaching. He was convinced that their attitude could be changed only as they came to recognize and share in first-hand religious experience. Religious experience is experiencing of what he variously described as the Infinite, or the All, or God. What is so experienced provides the data from which alone sound theological work can proceed. In taking up this position, Schleiermacher was urging that theology should become a systematic empirical undertaking. Its starting point should be, not a set of doctrines taken on trust as divinely given and therefore indubitably true, but actual experience of divine reality. If that is the starting-point of theology, its task is to identify such experience, reflect upon it, and in an orderly and critical way expound both what it is and what it implies. So far as specifically Christian theology is concerned, its primary datum also is a fact of experience; namely, that Christians in community as well as individually have shared and do now share in Christ's awareness of God. The task of Christian theology is to identify such awareness and in systematic fashion to expound it, drawing out also its implications for both the thought and conduct of members of the Christian community. The application of theology provides sound guidance and ensures good government for the organized Church.[6]

While earlier views persisted, this revolutionary attitude to theology greatly stimulated theological activity and profoundly affected its development in the nineteenth and early twentieth centuries, especially among Protestant thinkers. Subsequent statements about Christian theology, at least those which take account of its historical development, imply even if they do not explicitly say so a judgement on the strength and the weakness of Schleiermacher's general position.

One result of that position was to direct more attention to questions about the nature and 'truth' of religion in general.

This tendency went along with a striking enlargement in knowledge of religions other than Christianity (see p. 179). Such knowledge was made possible by greatly improved facilities for travel, and by the growing mastery on the part of European scholars of ancient as well as many living languages imperfectly known, or quite unknown, before. Christianity was still generally regarded in the Western world as supreme among all forms of religion, but the fresh interest taken by theologians in points of similarity as well as difference between it and them was bound to call in question its radical uniqueness and finality. To some this latest development in the history of theology seemed like a betrayal of Christian convictions. The flaccidity of the organized churches in face of political and other social upheavals during and after the first world war gave countenance to the view that the Christian message had been weakened. Best known among those who vigorously criticized the change which had taken place in theology was Karl Barth (1886–1968). For him and those associated with him the concern of theology was solely with the statement and exposition of the authentic proclamation (*kerygma*) given to the Christian community by God, and the critical application of God's self-revelation in his Word to the preaching, teaching and practices of the contemporary Church.[7]

In so summary a review as this it is not possible to do justice to a point of view of which Karl Barth was the chief exponent. It largely dominated Protestant theology until the middle of the present century, it is still influential, and it has made its mark on Roman Catholic thinking as well. At present however many theologians would regard it as too narrow. They are very sensitive to and appreciative of current criticism of the Christian message. Some objections arise from greatly extended knowledge of the natural order, and its application to human affairs. Some spring from philosophical discussion, particularly in connection with the uses and abuses of language. To confine theology to expounding what the Christian Church has been given to proclaim, and to the consequent self-criticism in which the Church should engage, is for many modern theologians (despite Barth's monumental volumes) unduly to restrict its scope. Theology, they would say, must also wrestle with questions about the meaningfulness or otherwise to contemporary persons of the statements in which that proclamation is expressed, and with questions concerning its truth. Present-day theology is moving in a number of new directions, as well as along former paths, and struggling with old questions posed in new ways. Later chapters will illustrate these facts.

III

The foregoing survey, brief as it is, helps to substantiate the statement (p. 12) that no generally acceptable reportive account of Christian theology is possible today. In other words, there is no such thing as a 'correct' definition: past and present usage sanction too many. We have to make do with a working description. It should take into account the history of the concept of theology. It cannot be put forward as the only justifiable definition. Its usefulness, like that of any alternative statement, resides not least in the way it helps a student to see both the inter-relatedness and also the essential unity of the kind of studies which are introduced in the rest of this volume. Within those limitations, and subject to the fuller explanations which follow, Christian theology may be described as systematic study of beliefs, practices and institutions which articulate Christian faith.

Before enlarging on this description, we should mention two features of theological study in the modern period which have some bearing upon it. First, for generations Christian theology has been taught and studied in seminaries, monasteries, colleges and universities founded by Christian benefactors for the education of Christians, particularly those who were to become priests and ministers of the Church. While that is still done, Christian theology is also taught and studied today in schools, colleges and universities having no direct link with ecclesiastical bodies. It claims, as one writer puts it, "parity of esteem in academic communities" with other subjects in the curriculum, and its place in a general syllabus for higher education is justified, in the words of another, as "helping to complete the circle of university studies". It is no longer assumed, as once it was, that theology can be taught only where all the students are of one religious persuasion, or where religious belief is a matter of complete indifference.[8] Nevertheless, claims to academic esteem for the teaching and study of Christian theology can only be upheld if standards of intellectual integrity are as conscientiously maintained and respected there as in the teaching and study of other subjects— maintained and respected not least in the conflicts of discussion which take place on the borders between theology and some related studies (see below p. 22).

Second, as noted already (p. 18), during the modern period there has been a tendency to use the term theology in relation to orderly reflection upon religion in general, and in connection with beliefs found in the various organized religions of the world. That tendency has now become widespread. It is no longer possible to confine the word to studies of Christianity. More important than that, however, Christian theology itself is bound to take serious account of non-Christian theology. Some forms of non-Christian theology are live options for educated persons in the Western world today, as well as elsewhere. Students of Christian theology must take account of them, however, not merely with a view to defending distinctively Christian convictions. The Christian scholar has something to learn, as well as to offer, in encounters with alien faith and alien religious thought.

I. We have now to consider more fully our description of Christian theology. The first term to be explained is *systematic study*. Systematic study in any field of enquiry has four characteristics. It is concerned, for one thing, to discriminate what is essential to the subject-matter from what is irrelevant, or merely associated with it. In the systematic study of Rembrandt as an artist, for example, it is essential to know when and where he lived. It is interesting, but not essential, to know the colour of his eyes. Christians hold beliefs, do things, and are involved in institutions, which do not articulate Christian faith. Failure to discriminate between what does and what does not express Christian faith has led to many misunderstandings (both within and outside the Christian churches), and sometimes to bitter dissension. Secondly, systematic study aims at a comprehensive investigation of what thus properly falls to be examined. How comprehensive it is possible to be depends upon the subject-matter, as well as upon the resources of enquirers. In the study of any subject, however, progress is often due to the discovery that something essential has been overlooked by previous workers, or was not available to them. In the natural sciences this is constantly happening. In the field of historical science the contribution of Karl Marx, despite its exaggerations, might be cited as another example. An example in the field of New Testament studies is the finding of the Qumran Scrolls. Thirdly, systematic study is rigorously self-critical. That is to say, it is a sustained attempt to express its problems and the results of its enquiries in as clear and precise and orderly a fashion as possible. The degree of clarity, precision and orderliness which is attainable depends to some extent on the subject-matter which is being studied. It is higher in the biological sciences, for example, than in aesthetics. Fourthly, systematic study involves the effort to relate the results of enquiry into its particular subject-matter to the results obtained from enquiries into those other areas of knowledge which border upon its own.

This last point calls for further comment. It implies that whatever is to be studied systematically has to do with what is real, or at any rate with what is claimed to be real. By real is here meant what makes a difference to man's experience. Statements about 'reality' embody truth claims. But claims to truth about reality are testable in part by their coherence with other claims to truth about reality. Now the subject-matter of theology, as we shall see, embodies claims as to what really is the case with regard to God, the universe, and man. Theological study therefore cannot be separated entirely from the study of other subjects: for instance, philosophy, natural sciences, ethics, sociology, history, psychology, and so on. Studies like these include in their field of concern matters which have little or nothing to do with theology, but each of them deals also with matters which are relevant to one or more parts of the total theological task. The necessity for taking them into account does not arise from their usefulness in illustrating church or biblical teaching. It arises from the claims of theology, so far as they go, to be stating and discussing what is true. One consequence of describing Christian theology as systematic study is declaring it to be an 'open-ended' enterprise. It has a centre, which we have yet to consider, but it has no rigidly circumscribed area[9].

All this will show itself more clearly as we turn to the subject-matter of Christian theology. It was described as beliefs, practices and institutions which articulate Christian faith. One difficulty about explaining the key words in this description cannot be avoided. Some statements have to be made, and some terms used, which it is an important part of the theological task to explicate, to discuss and to justify. One obvious example is the term 'God'. When Thomas Aquinas was setting out his famous five ways of proving the existence of God, he was able to conclude an argument with the words, "This everyone understands to be God", or "This all men speak of as God". Even if 'everyone' or 'all men' signified 'every Christian' no such statement would pass unchallenged today. The student can only be assured that the questions he might, indeed should, want to raise are not just being brushed aside at this point, or overlooked. Any adequate treatment of them, however, not least the refinement and discussion of expressions beyond what can be done in a general introductory essay, falls within one or other department of the total work of theologizing.

II. What has just been said needs particularly to be borne in mind as we move on to the term Christian faith. The word *faith* is currently used in a bewildering variety of ways.[10] What it signifies in our description of theology is awareness or recognition of the presence of God and worshipful response to God in trust and obedience, or to use a term currently more popular, commitment. It has cognitive, affective and volitional aspects. It is not merely either intellectual conviction, or an emotional attitude, or venturesome commitment, but combines something of them all. What then is meant by distinctively *Christian* faith? It is related to Jesus of Nazareth who suffered under Pontius Pilate, that is to say a person geographically and historically locatable, who is acknowledged and worshipfully responded to by his followers now, as by others before them, as the Lord Jesus Christ. The expressions Christ and Lord have to be studied carefully in the light of biblical and other studies in order to bring out the full significance of their traditional usage. The main point however is that when they are applied to Jesus of Nazareth they link him intimately with the living God as believed in by Jews. That is why we can speak of Christian faith, and not merely Christian admiration. The history and development of Jewish beliefs falls to be discussed elsewhere (see especially Chapters 3 and 4), but what 'God' had come mainly to signify by the time that Jesus appeared may be set out broadly as follows. God is the only God; creator and ruler of the universe, and of mankind; transcendent over all, yet a self-disclosing God who in part makes known to human beings his presence, his power and his purposes; all this God makes known to some extent through the natural order and the course of human history, but most clearly in the formation, discipline and enlightenment of the people of Israel; and who is yet to manifest himself more fully in carrying through to completion his sovereign will for the world and mankind. When the early Christians used 'Christ' (or its Semitic equivalent 'Messiah') of Jesus it was primarily to designate him the 'anointed' one through whom God was so to manifest himself and his will more fully. That by itself was not sufficient, however, to express what they found and acknowledged Jesus to be. They declared 'Jesus is Lord'. In the documentary evidence we have about the early Christians, the significance of the use of this title seems to vary. What is most significant however is the implication that Jesus is so related to God that those accustomed to address, and speak of, God, as Lord could now also speak of Jesus, and address him, after his resurrection as Lord.[11] Some writers indeed called him 'Immanuel', or 'God with us'.

Reflection on all this gave rise to intense theological activity, which has continued ever since. We have already said (p.23) that Christian theology has a centre but no hard and fast circumference. This can now be specified. At the centre of Christian theology are affirmations about distinctively Christian faith. Such faith is acknowledgement of, trust in, and worshipful devotion to the living Lord Jesus Christ—that is to say, a historical person who lived, died and was buried in Palestine, who rose again from the dead, who is so uniquely revelatory of and so uniquely related to the living God that he alone is describable as Christ and Lord in the developed New Testament sense of those titles (see also p. 52 below).

To complete what should be said in even the most concise explication of Christian faith, four additional points must be made. First, present-day Christian faith is, or at any rate claims to be, continuous with that faith which is characteristic of Christians from New Testament times. This point is important, as we shall see, for any attempt to show the organic inter-relatedness of theological studies. The claim itself can be substantiated only when testimony to Christian faith today has been shown to be confessedly, and in essentials recognizably, in accord with what can be learned from those testimonies to Christian faith which are examined in New Testament studies (see p. 35).

Second, religious faith which is predicable of individuals is characteristic of individuals who are in some way related to a religious community. The beginnings of religion as such are beyond the scope of historical investigation. In any known situation, however, the religious community, whether separate from the social group as a whole or indistinguishable from it, is prior to religious individuals. That is one reason why, in the case of Christianity, some theologians would make the Church the starting-point of distinctively Christian theology. While not quarrelling with this preference as a matter of procedure, there seem to be good reasons for setting out the matter otherwise. 'Church' is used in quite as many diverse ways as 'faith', and is apt to have associated with it even more misleading notions. More important, the Church in one sense of the term (as found for example in the Apostles' Creed) itself signifies a matter of faith—a recognition and response to God disclosing and giving himself in and through the religious community as 'the mystical Body of Christ'. In another sense, namely as an organized body of Christians, a church is an expression of faith.

That last phrase leads on to the third point. We have been careful to avoid saying that Christian theology is the study of Christian faith. The reason for this should now be clear. Theology as systematic study (see p. 21 above) is a 'public' enterprise. In the sense already described, Christian faith (like any other kind of faith) is not *directly* amenable to public enquiry. It is personal experiencing and a personal disposition, and all that can be discussed publicly is the expression of faith in words and in non-verbal manifestations of it. Fourth, while such expressions of faith are certainly distinguishable from faith itself, they are hardly separable from it. The two points made in this paragraph will be amplified as now we go on to consider further key words in the description of Christian theology.

III. The next term to be examined is *beliefs*. Beliefs are statements in which faith, or aspects of faith, or implications of the fact of faith are expressed. Although beliefs are thus distinguishable from faith, it is of great importance to emphasize and expand what has just been said: faith and beliefs are intimately conjoined. For one thing, faith as acknowledgement, or recognition, of the presence of divinity always presupposes beliefs of some sort, however rudimentary, about divine reality. This seems to land us in the familiar theoretical quandary as to which comes first, the chicken or the egg, so far as the order of coming to know (*ordo cognoscendi*) is concerned. There is no escape from the quandary, so long as the question is about the beginnings of religion in general (see also p. 25 above). Faith, it may be argued, presupposes some sort of beliefs about divine reality, and beliefs about divine reality presuppose some degree of faith which gave rise to them. This much however can also be said: in any known situation an individual in whom faith is evoked has already acquired some knowledge of the beliefs of others. Secondly, faith as experiencing of the divine presence may lead to the modification of antecedent beliefs. On the other hand, thirdly, antecedently accepted beliefs may be a powerful factor affecting the present range of an individual's experiencing of divine reality. The significance of both these last points is perhaps best brought out by examples. Many examples are to be found in the biblical records, in the past history of the Christian Church, and in our own time.[12]

The intimate relationship between faith and beliefs is by no means just an individualistic affair. As already stated (p. 25) faith is an experience of individuals in community, that is to say, of individuals who are members of a religious community or individuals who have been influenced to some extent by a religious community even if they were not, at the time of consciously 'coming to faith', members of it. At this juncture further aspects of that truth come into view. The great importance of Christian communities (to confine ourselves to them) for both the faith and the beliefs of individual Christians is obvious. The faith and beliefs of any Christian presuppose the faith and beliefs of others. However, there is more to be taken into the reckoning than that. Religious education of both the young and the more mature members of the Christian community rests on the well-grounded assumption that, at any stage, an individual's experience of God may be enlarged, and his beliefs corrected, by the beliefs and faith found in the community as a whole. On the other hand it sometimes happens that the faith and beliefs of an individual may lead to a change in the faith and beliefs of the community to which he belongs.[13] We shall shortly have to note also (see p. 28 below) that the faith and beliefs of a whole Christian community may be modified by encounter with those of another Christian community.

IV. Systematic study of beliefs which articulate faith, or aspects of faith, or implications of the fact of faith, constitutes a major part of theology, but not the whole. Some elements in religious faith, as also for example in human love or friendship, can only be 'lived through' (*erlebt*) and are not expressible in words. If there are aspects of religious experience which cannot be expressed in any way whatsoever, as is sometimes said, then of course they cannot be studied. Some aspects of faith however which are inexpressible in words can be articulated, and commonly are, in non-verbal ways. Non-verbal expressions, moreover, may supplement and help to remove some of the inadequacies of verbal articulations. For example, Christian sacraments whatever else they are express in actions more than words can do. A particular manner of organizing and administering a church and church affairs, in so far as such administration is not only intended but also actually exercised as an expression of faith, declares something over and above what will go into even the most comprehensive document on ecclesiastical order. In our description of theology the words 'practices and institutions' are meant to cover such non-verbal expressions of faith. The kind of matters so included will be set out more fully in our account of the scope of Christian theology.

Non-verbal expressions of faith, however, do not merely co-exist with beliefs. In any lively Christian community they interact. Each supplements the other, but also each in part tests the other. Practices and institutions may disclose the shortcomings of some currently accepted beliefs, and some beliefs make plain the errors or inadequacies implicit in accepted practices and institutions. Nor is this so merely within one particular community. The beliefs, practices and institutions of any Christian community, or group of like-minded communities (churches, denominations, confessional bodies), confront those which characterize another. In the past such confrontation did not always lead to reasoned or even amicable discussion, and does not always do so now. Far too often it has issued in vilification and persecution. One of the laudable results of the modern 'ecumenical movement' is a greater willingness on the part of representatives of differing ways and convictions to reckon seriously and reasonably with one another's practices and beliefs. Indeed there is a wider, though as yet far from universal, appreciation of the fact that every church or group of churches has something to learn from the rest.[14]

We have now explained the way in which key words in our description of the nature of Christian theology as a whole are to be understood: systematic study, Christian faith, beliefs, practices and institutions. Further explanation of that description, and also an important test of its adequacy, is to be got by considering how far it allows the organic inter-relatedness of theological studies to appear. To that and a brief outline of the scope of Christian theology we now turn.

IV

Christian theology, we have suggested, is describable as systematic study of the articulations of that faith which is professed today in Christian communities. Christian communities today however, claim to share in faith which is continuous with such faith as characterized the early disciples of Jesus Christ. How can such a claim be examined? Only by comparing present-day testimony to Christian faith with the evidences we have concerning Christian faith at the first. The primary written evidence available is to be found in the documents which make up the New Testament. Yet the New Testament itself cannot be adequately understood, nor its witness to Christian faith at the first properly interpreted, apart from studies of the Old Testament and a corpus of writings usually referred to as Inter-testamental Literature.

One part of organic theology then may be called Biblical Studies, so long as we understand by that not only the study of what is in the Bible but the study also of whatever material enables us to understand it. Biblical Studies in that sense include (a) study of the languages in which the Bible and the supplementary material were written; (b) textual criticism—this is necessary because there is no original copy of any biblical documents extant, but only copies of copies which to some extent vary from one another; (c) literary criticism, or study of the problems concerning date, authorship, manner of composition or compilation, and the historical setting, of each book; (d) studies of the geography, chronology, customs and cultures referred to in the Bible, or bearing upon it; (e) an enquiry into the way the Bible as we have it now came to be —the problem of the Canon, as it is called; and (f), making use of all the other studies, the work of exegesis and interpretation.

If Biblical Studies so understood provide evidence about Christian faith at the first, they are organically linked with a second part of theology, Church History. As a theological discipline Church History may be regarded as study of the evidence to continuing Christian faith and its multifarious articulations in the centuries between New Testament times and the present. This does not of course exclude study of the evidence to the weakening or even absence of Christian faith among professed Christians, nor study of expressions of faith which appear to us bizarre or sometimes horrifying. Church History is a complex of studies, including the history of Christian missionary outreach; the development of forms of worship, church organization and administration; changes in relationships between Christian communities and civil society; the relations between various churches; and the history of Christian doctrine. In connection with the history of Christian doctrine, special importance attaches to the formulation of creeds and confessions of faith. The more specialized study of their formulation, significance and use is sometimes marked with the technical term Symbolics (see p. 126).

It is on what has been described in rather broad terms as Biblical Studies and Church History that a third major part of Christian theology is based, namely, Systematic Theology. This is the contemporary, comprehensive, coherent and critical study of Christian doctrine. The aim of Systematic Theology is to expound and discuss Christian teaching in the light of two main problems. These problems are always arising, but they present themselves from time to time in rather different guise. They have to be faced as they appear in the present age. The first problem springs from the fact that some churches or groups of churches, and even parties within one church, hold beliefs at variance with the beliefs of others. That part of Systematic Theology which expounds and discusses Christian teaching more particularly in view of this problem is technically called Dogmatic Theology, or Dogmatics.[15] Distinguishable from this first problem, but never entirely separable from it, is a second problem. The varieties of

Christian beliefs rest in part on considerations which are not specifically Christian. The systematic study of differences in the articulation of Christian faith makes plain divergent understanding of and attitudes to advances in scientific knowledge and philosophical discussion. Scientific and philosophical studies are distinguishable from theological studies, but they are highly relevant in some respects to the student of theology because they raise questions which cannot be ignored—questions such as the validity of religious faith and the truth-claims of fundamental Christian beliefs. As examples of such studies, later chapters introduce the reader to scientific studies of religion and to philosophical concern with religious concepts and religious language. That part of Systematic Theology which treats more directly with the problem that Christian convictions are seriously doubted or denied by non-Christians on scientific or philosophical grounds used to be, and sometimes still is, called Christian Apologetics. The name Apologetics—'apology' meaning not some expression of regret, but 'giving an answer'—seems to be coming back into use, after a period in which it was disliked. If it should come to be used more widely, however, it ought always to be understood as a dialogue in which Christians listen to and learn from non-Christians, as well as make answers.

Christian doctrine, then, has to be systematized and discussed in the face of contemporary questioning and in contemporary terms. But it has also to be applied. This is implicit in the concept of faith as response to the continuing self-disclosure and self-giving of God in Christ. We have already drawn attention to the mutual inter-action of beliefs and non-verbal expressions of faith. We can now go further and say that there are two main fields in which questions of the application of doctrine have to be discussed. One is the manner and forms of the worship, organization, life and work of the Christian community itself. The other covers the problems of individual conduct, and the social and international issues, which confront its members. The part of theology, thus closely linked with the rest, which is concerned with such problems is sometimes called Practical Theology, but more clearly as

Applied Theology (see pp. 219f.). It has a number of sections the names of which tend to vary with different writers. For the purpose of this survey it is enough to say that the subjects discussed include (a) the principles and practice of Christian ministering within the Church—e.g. worship, preaching, religious education, counselling and otherwise caring for persons in need, church order and discipline, inter-church or ecumenical relations; (b) the principles and practice of the Church's mission to individuals who are not members of the Church, and to the society in which it is set; and (c), related to both those groups of subjects in part, Christian ethics. Although the fields of Applied Theology can be discriminated in this way, it is important to note how much they overlap (see for example pp. 223ff).

The kinds of subject which fall within the general field of Christian theology, and also their inter-relatedness, have now been indicated. All this was not intended to daunt the student, but neither should he be deceived. In theology, as in every other branch of learning, its parts become more and more the object of specialized attention. It is not possible to be master of them all, and even to master one of them is an ambitious undertaking. Apart from those who desire to specialize in some branch of theology, however, anyone may become theologically educated by acquiring (i) an understanding of the mutual connections between the different parts of theology; (ii) knowledge of what may be called the 'internal organization' of each part, and of the leading topics it includes; and (iii) acquaintance with the sources of help from which he may gain whatever information he needs. It is hoped that the material in this volume will be of some assistance in all those respects.

2

THE NEW TESTAMENT

C. F. D. MOULE
Lady Margaret's Professor of Divinity, University of Cambridge

2

The New Testament

IF THEOLOGY means an articulated system, it will not be
found in the Bible. But theological study of the New
Testament certainly begins, as soon as you take that small
volume in your hands and ask, Where did it come from, and
how did it come by its name? The attempt to account for the
N.T. is, at every turn, bound up with essentially theological
questions, and it is impossible to treat the disciplines of literary
criticism, historical research, and theological evaluation as
independent of one another (see p. 24 above). Even the most
primitive beginnings of critical investigation in the early
Church were occasioned by theological questions; and when
the era of what may be called 'scientific' or 'scholarly' work on
the N.T. began (effectively, not until the nineteenth century),[1]
literary and historical matters were quickly found to be
inseparable from theological. This is, after all, exactly what one
would expect, if Christianity is, in a special sense, a historical
religion. So, too, the very collecting of the documents is a
matter of theological import.

Thus, the introductory questions of the 'whence?' and the
'why?' are inseparable from theology. Even more directly
theological is the interpretation of the documents and their
evaluation, and the study of subsequent phases of Christian
thought, from the sub-apostolic period to the present day—a
study which, in its turn, helps to illuminate the N.T.[2] The
most manifestly theological activity of all, taking the student
through and beyond the N.T. field, is the study of the relation
of Jesus himself to the Christian Church: and central to this is
the evaluation of the Christian conviction that Jesus had been

raised from death to absolute life. An attempt will therefore be made here—necessarily in only the briefest sketches—to indicate the direction of research in the chief fields of N.T. study, and to show their interconnection.

THE DEVELOPMENT OF NEW TESTAMENT THOUGHT

What, for a start, may be said about the development and variety of thought within the N.T.? No doubt, if verbal inspiration were presupposed, it would leave no room for development or change (unless it be an artificial development, decreed by God's economy for didactic purposes). But such a theory, which receives scant support from the N.T. itself or from observed facts outside it, will not be pursued here. On any other presupposition, an obvious approach to the under-standing of N.T. thought is by trying to trace an evolutionary sequence. This is commonly done; and it certainly corresponds, in some measure, to the facts. But it needs much qualification. For instance, it has been suggested that the Christian estimate of Jesus evolved from the idea that he was a man who became divine (a so-called 'adoptionist' Christology) to the idea that he existed eternally as fully divine (a pre-existence Christology). This would be an evolution from, let us say, the 'declared Son of God' of Rom. 1: 4, through the judgement-scene of Matt. 25: 31, to the pre-existence Christology of Col. 1: 15 ff. and of John 1: 1 ff., and so to the confession, 'My Lord and my God' of John 20: 28. This sort of evolutionary theory, it is to be observed, tends to lean not only on chronological sequence but also on the idea that there were distinct communities in the early Church, each with its characteristic theological emphasis: the primitive, Palestinian type, using human terms, whose ultimate offspring is the so-called 'Ebionite' Christianity, with its reduced Christology; the Jerusalem Hellenists, with the beginnings of a more theological understanding; the pre-Pauline Hellenism of the dispersion outside Palestine, with gnostic tendencies (see p. 44 below); then Paul's own develop-ments; and finally, perhaps, the cosmopolitan syncretism of Johannine Ephesus.

Now, it is likely enough that the Christological level of different communities did vary, and that there were distinct phases: to be convinced of this, one only needs to consider side by side the Epistle of James, the Epistle to the Romans and I John. But it does not necessarily follow that there was a straight evolution from 'low' to 'high', or that a high Christology is not a true description of Jesus as he was from the beginning, or that one particular type came from one particular quarter. It is possible, within the Pauline epistles, to recognize a variation of emphasis matching changes in circumstance rather than chronological sequence; and there is no intrinsic reason why a 'high' Christology should necessarily be the climax of an evolutionary process.

In the same way an evolutionary sequence has been suggested for eschatology (that is, the interpretation of the ultimate and absolute in religion, and of how God's purposes are brought to their completion). It is possible to devise a tidy pattern, and to imagine that, starting from the expectation that Jesus would return the day after tomorrow, to wind up history and declare the Kingdom of God, the Christians had gradually to learn to adjust themselves to delay; and that a doctrine of the Holy Spirit's temporary presence was evolved to compensate for the apparent absence of the Lord, until, ultimately, a Johannine climax was reached in which it was realized that the expected future coming of the Lord was to be identified with the coming of the Spirit which had already taken place. This is a theoretically intelligible sequence, but is not close to the facts of the N.T. For instance, the Pauline epistles reflect a highly developed doctrine of the Holy Spirit's presence, yet this appears side by side with an ardent expectation of the return of Christ, and with a deep conviction of the Church's continued life in Christ. These are not, in Paul at least, successive phases at all, but different facets of a single, complex and very rich experience. And the so-called 'realized eschatology' of St. John's Gospel (that is, the affirmations that the end has already come with the coming of the Paraclete) turns out, on examination, to be confined mainly to the experience of individuals, while the collective purpose of God

37

for his people as a whole is still couched, even in John, in futurist terms.[3] Much the same applies to the widely held theory that, whereas authentic Christian existence is necessarily a tension between 'the already' and 'the not yet'—between the fact that 'the new age' has come, and yet 'the old age' has not yet been left behind—Luke–Acts has resolved the authentic tension by finding for the Church a recognized era in which it belongs and into which it can fit, in the sequence of events, without being torn by the Christian tension.[4]

Evolutionary theories can similarly be applied to other aspects of N.T. thought—about the Church, for instance—and similarly criticized. It is certainly no safe axiom that the least theological is the most primitive and authentic—or, for that matter, that the most ecclesiastical is the most decadent. Perhaps a more fruitful method of tracing sequences is to examine the use of the O.T. by the N.T. writers, and use the application of one and the same O.T. passage in different ways and in different contexts as an index to successive stages in the elaboration of Christian apologetic.[5]

Thus, while it is undoubtedly right to investigate the extent of growth and development in Christian thought and of the influence of one set of ideas upon another, the realities are likely to be too complicated to be reduced to a mechanical principle or squeezed into some hypothetical scheme.

If this essay were an exposition of N.T. thought, rather than an introduction to the study of it, the great themes of eschatology, Christology, the doctrine of the Holy Spirit, salvation, and so forth would have to be investigated. As it is, the reader need, at this point, only be reminded of these and many areas of study, and of the available literature.[6]

SOURCE-CRITICISM

The evolutionary theories just described depend, of course, not only upon assumptions about how thought grows, but also upon some knowledge of the forces shaping thought at the time, and some measure of confidence about the chronological order of the documents. This latter, on any showing, it is desirable to determine. Before we either accept or reject a theory which detects a development of thought from genuinely Pauline epistles through deutero-Pauline (i.e. those springing from Paul's disciples or his imitators) to the Synoptic Gospels, the Acts, the Johannine writings, and, perhaps, later epistles, we need to know whether this, in fact, is a plausible order. Thus we are brought to the elaborate disciplines more or less comprised under the term 'source-criticism'.[7]

Long and complicated is the story of the critical investigation of the letters attributed to St Paul. Which are genuinely Pauline? The Tübingen school, in the nineteenth century, said only Romans, the Corinthian epistles, and Galatians; and a similar conclusion has been reached by A. Q. Morton through statistical tests of style.[8] However, a number of scholars, believing the determining factors to be too complex to be amenable to the sort of test applied whether by the old Tübingenian assumptions or by computer analysis, are ready to allow to Paul some or all of the group comprising the Thessalonian epistles, Colossians and Philemon, and Philippians. About Ephesians there is considerably more doubt; and the non-Pauline character of at least parts of the so-called Pastoral Epistles, addressed to Timothy and Titus, is widely held.[9] The Epistle to the Hebrews contains no internal attribution to Paul, and ought never to have been ascribed to him. None of this implies, in itself, any judgement in respect of religious or theological value; but it might greatly affect conclusions about the apostle's own development and the sequence of phases in Christian thought. If the latter group is 'deutero-Pauline', obviously an important chronological consideration is introduced. Also, the question of pseudonymity is raised.[10] In modern times, it would be dishonest to write a letter under a false name. Were these ancient letters, if not by the master, intended to deceive? This is not a simple question, and debate about it continues. The line between the very words of Paul and the work of 'Paulinists' may turn out to be difficult to draw with precision.

More important, theologically, is the investigation of the setting and purpose of each epistle. Most of them are evidently addressed to quite specific situations, and the interpretation of their meaning depends not a little on that of their setting. The reason why Paul's teaching on 'justification by faith' is virtually limited to Galatians and Romans is clearly that, in these epistles, he was replying to a legalistic type of religion. A defence of the uniqueness of Christ and of the unity of God occurs in 1 Corinthians and Colossians, where the dangers addressed are connected with pagan ideas and polytheism. The more developed doctrine of the Church in Ephesians (whether this is Pauline or not) seems to be due to the growth of gentile congregations and their need to be given a status *vis-à-vis* Israel. But here we are encroaching on the study of background, which must be postponed for a while.

If we turn to the source-criticism of the Synoptic Gospels we find that the beginning of modern research into them is generally associated with Lachmann, who, by comparing the three, reached the celebrated conclusion that, behind them all, lay a common source to which Mark approximated the most closely.[11] Subsequent research tended to eliminate the common source by identifying it with Mark itself, or with an earlier version of Mark. Further, comparison between the non-Marcan parts of Matthew and Luke led to the conclusion that, as well as both using Mark, they had another source in common. This was labelled 'Q';[12] and it is this 'two-document hypo-thesis'—the belief that Matthew and Luke used Mark and 'Q'—that has been the foundation of nearly all subsequent investigation. B. H. Streeter attempted to give some definition and locality, further, to the special sources which he detected behind Matthew and Luke respectively ('M' and 'L'), thus building a 'four-document hypothesis'.[13] For some time, the only serious challenge to this scheme came from Roman Catholic scholars, who defended the priority of Matthew, or at least of a Semitic 'original Matthew' behind the present Greek gospel.[14] But the defence of Matthean priority has also been taken up by Protestant scholars, especially W. R. Farmer.[15] Obviously, a decision on this question must have decisive effects on the understanding of the development of the thought of the Gospels.

As for the remainder of the N.T., it is the Johannine writings which present the major enigma in source-criticism.[16] 'The disciple whom Jesus loved' is apparently declared, in Jo. 21 : 24, to be the author of this Gospel;[17] and, until the 'critical era', he was usually identified with the apostle John. Doubt was thrown on this by the observation that St. John's Gospel differed, in a multitude of respects, from the Synoptists—in its chronology, in its portrait of Jesus, in the emphasis and manner of its teaching, and in countless details. On the assumption that Mark was nearest to the authentic facts, it seemed natural to deduce that John, by contrast, stood at the end of a long period of doctrinal development. It was known that this Gospel was slow to be fully accepted and recognized among the canonical writings, and had affinities, in language if not in thought, with what in its later manifestations we now call Gnosticism (see below, p. 44). Accordingly, it came to be regarded as a freely-contrived, late, reflective meditation on the meaning of Jesus, with only a tenuous attachment to the original facts: an outpost of the N.T. period and at the threshold of the sub-apostolic age. Certain traditions in Irenaeus, Clement of Alexandria, and Eusebius associated the aged John with Ephesus, and seemed also to be naming another John, likewise belonging to the Ephesian Church. It seemed plausible to conclude that, if there was anything Johannine about this Gospel, one must look not to the apostle but to another of the name for its origin; and that, if there were reliable traditions about the beginnings of Christianity anywhere, they were certainly not to be found here. A very considerable swing of the pendulum in more recent years has, however, led some scholars to believe that, whether or not the document as we have it is late, it embodies a great deal that is early and authentic, and indeed preferable, historically, to some of the synoptic material. The debate continues, about its date, its relation to the Synoptists, its historical content, and its theological significance: is it truly incarnational or 'docetic' in Christology? Is it anti-sacramental, or subtly sacramental? At the same time, the other N.T. documents associated with the name of John—the three epistles and the Apocalypse (or the

Revelation)—have been both approximated to and divorced from the Gospel by different theories. The writer of the Apocalypse calls himself John but does not indicate much more about his identity. Everybody recognizes that this document, with its wholly different (and often barbarous) Greek, its apocalyptic eschatology, its kaleidoscopic imagery, and its difference of outlook, is unlike the Gospel; and it is usually held to be by a different author. The Johannine Epistles, on the other hand, are attributed by many to the writer (or ultimate editor) of the Gospel. But, on any showing, there are interesting differences in emphasis between the Epistles and the Gospel, which might point, if only their chronological relation may be determined, to an important development of thought or, at least, change of setting and purpose. Clearly the Johannine *corpus* is a mixture within itself, and also, as a whole, distinctive over against the rest of the N.T.: a theological enigma of the first importance for the student of N.T. thought.[18]

Over and above the Pauline (or 'Paulinistic') epistles, the Synoptic Gospels, and the Johannine writing, there are other epistles and the Acts, all of which are studied with close attention to their sources, origin, and theological outlook. The two volumes Luke and Acts together are elaborately investigated in respect of their composition, outlook, and theological leanings; and Acts is a storm-centre of debate. Is it an early and reasonably trustworthy account of the early years of the Church? May Paul's letters be fitted into its framework? Or is it a late romance, tendentious and of small value for their elucidation? The complexities of these problems cannot be unfolded here. Perhaps this sketch is enough to indicate the type of problem belonging to the discipline broadly known as source-criticism.

BACKGROUND—HISTORICAL, CULTURAL, SOCIOLOGICAL

So closely bound up with this, however, as to be virtually overlapping is the kind of investigation that comes under the heading of 'background'.[19] The understanding of the N.T. is, in large measure, dependent on a knowledge of the historical and cultural setting in which it took shape. The comparison of Christianity with other ancient religions and cults is an obviously important method of study—so important that it affords a name to a whole 'school' of research—*die religions-geschichtliche Schule*, the school of thought proceeding by way of the history of religions.[20] The setting of Christianity in its milieu, side by side with the mystery religions and other cults and the ethical systems of the time, is an obvious way of study. The sources for such knowledge range from the archaeological evidence of sites, buildings, and inscriptions, through the masses of non-literary papyri—business documents, occasional letters, spells and incantations, and so forth, mainly from the hot, dry sands of Egypt—to literary writings. The volume of papyrus and other such material already available is so enormous that it has not yet all been even sorted and examined; and there is likely to be much yet to be discovered. Only in about 1945 a new trove of Coptic papyri came to light at Nag Hammadi on the Nile, representing the first considerable collection of gnostic writings to become available.[21] Until then, Gnosticism had been known mainly through antagonistic references by orthodox writers such as Irenaeus. It was about the same time (about 1947) that the discovery began, in caves at Qumran near the Dead Sea, of the now famous scrolls, mostly in Hebrew or Aramaic on leather (see p. 87 below). Half a century earlier, in a Cairo *geniza* (i.e. a chamber for the storage of old sacred writings), important documents had been found, including the so-called Zadokite or Damascus Document, which appears to be closely associated with the Qumran documents, and other writings, especially targumic, throwing light on Bible-reading, interpretation, and language in Palestine.[23]

Study of the non-literary papyri helps to illuminate the language, idioms, and customs of the ordinary world of the N.T. period;[24] study of the Qumran scrolls and kindred literature is throwing a flood of light on the beliefs of sectarian Judaism, almost certainly shortly before the time of Christ.

But the Coptic documents of Nag Hammadi are later than the N.T., and such importance as they have for N.T. study is a reflex one. And this raises an important issue—perhaps the biggest issue facing the present-day representatives of the history-of-religions school: How far is Gnosticism relevant to the N.T.? The very definition of Gnosticism is still debated, and confusion is caused by imprecise application of the term. 'Gnosis' is simply the Greek for 'knowledge'. But, as a technical term, it came to stand for a tendency to regard salvation as the possession of esoteric knowledge, which often went hand in hand with a dualistic outlook. An attempt is beginning to be made at greater precision in the use of the term. It has been usefully suggested that the term 'gnosis' should be used for an outlook in which quite unsystematized dualistic tendencies are evident, in distinction from 'Gnosticism', which should be reserved for an articulated system of dualistic beliefs. To be observed also is the basic distinction between, on the one hand, a moral and metaphorical dualism (as between light and darkness, truth and falsehood)—a dualism inevitable in almost any ethical context—and, on the other hand, a genuinely metaphysical dualism of spirit and matter. There is no evidence, to date, of a systematized Gnosticism as early as the N.T., and this justifies the view, held by some scholars, that Gnosticism is a Christian heresy, springing from and dependent on an antecedent Christian belief. On the other hand, gnosis, in the much broader, looser sense of a tendency to associate the created world with evil and to drive lines of demarcation between the elect and the reprobate—this is demonstrably present in the religious thought of all sorts of areas and civilizations (including, indeed, the Old Testament) long before the N.T., and such tendencies, even if comparatively slight and muted, do appear here and there in the N.T., not least in St. John's Gospel. Thus, one of the most urgent tasks in N.T. research is to give more precise definition to the gnostic problem.[25] How 'gnostic' is the N.T.? Without some precision, it is all too easy to make sweeping assertions about the influence of Gnosticism on (for example) the Corinthian Epistles, or to use supposed gnostic tendencies as a criterion of the provenance of a document, whereas what is really being observed need only be 'gnosis' in the sense defined above,

44

namely, such dualistic language (in the looser sense) as may be found in almost any context, or reflections of systematic tendencies towards what is more strictly dualistic, such as may crop up in religious thought of almost any period.

The gnostic problem thus sharpens the need to distinguish clearly between sources positively known to be earlier than or contemporary with the N.T. documents, and sources which are definitely later or cannot certainly be dated earlier.

This applies also to the use of evidence from Jewish sources such as the Mishnah and the Targums, which took shape later, so that great care has to be exercised in determining what parts represent material early enough to be relevant to the interpretation of N.T. thought.[26] The relevant documents securely datable as prior to or contemporary with the N.T. are comparatively few. Unless one includes all the ancient literature that is indirectly relevant as contributing in some sense to the general background, the most obvious are the voluminous works of Philo of Alexandria (c. 20 B.C.—c. A.D. 50); the writings of Josephus (c. A.D. 37–100); such papyri as are demonstrably early enough; the Qumran scrolls (almost certainly early enough); and the books of the O.T. 'canon' with such of the Jewish apocrypha and pseudepigrapha as fall in the period.[27]

Another important debate concerns the relation between Jewish and Greek ways of life and thought—or, rather, the definition of these adjectives. A sharp contrast between Hebrew-Jewish modes of thought and Hellenic modes is sometimes irresponsibly drawn. There are, no doubt, important tendencies of thought characteristic of the bulk of the O.T. in contrast to—for instance—the Platonic dialogues, and these do indeed set a characteristic stamp on the whole Christian gospel; but to generalize from this contrast, and to ignore the scope of Semitic and Hellenic thought respectively and the degree of their mutual interpenetration is to distort the facts.[28]

Other relevant considerations of background, over and above philosophical trends and religious thought and practice, include political, social, economic, and civic conditions. Such considerations are particularly important, for instance, in the assessment of Luke–Acts. In particular, to study the relation of the Roman imperial government, and of the local government in various provinces, to Judaism and Christianity is important for the understanding of the N.T. Jewish-Christian relations need to be studied in the light of Roman-Jewish relations, for tension between the government and Judaism reacted on the relations between Christians and Jews.[29] Degrees and phases of persecution afford a sinister background to much of the N.T.—the disciplining or persecution of Christians by Jews, and the beginnings of persecution of Christians by the Roman Empire for refusing to conform to gestures of Emperor-worship, with all the attendant horrors of informers and intrigue.[30] (The one horror mercifully missing from this period, so far as evidence goes, is the persecution of Jews by Christians.) Equally, the varying economic circumstances are not without their relevance—famine or plenty, harsh taxation or leniency; and so are the social structures of various sections of life under the Emperors, involving slaves, women, disfranchised persons, Roman citizens, and so forth.[31]

FORM-CRITICISM

If the dating of the N.T. documents and the reconstruction of the larger thought-world and the circumstances in which they grew up are of obvious importance for any attempt to trace the genesis and development of their thought—and it is these considerations which led to this digression to sketch such studies—it is clear that enquiry into the activities and circumstances obtaining within the Christian communities themselves comes even closer to the text of the N.T. A very important discipline is thus introduced, which, in English-speaking countries, goes by the infelicitous label of 'form-criticism', a rough-and-ready equivalent for *die formgeschichtliche Methode*—a method of research, that is, which proceeds by classifying units of tradition according to their 'shape', and tracing the history of the successive changes in shape which a unit assumes as it passes from mouth to mouth and from one context to another.[32]

The method had been used by O.T. scholars before it became usual in the N.T. field (see pp. 72f below). But the strict limits of this technique were quickly overstepped, and, in effect, it became far more than the mere classification of units of tradition according to their forms. It became an examination of all aspects of the mode of transmission prior to the writing of the documents, and an enquiry into the living context or setting *(Sitz im Leben)* in which each unit of tradition was used. Following, as it did, a period when the closest scrutiny had been devoted to the documents and a false emphasis thereby given to the literary aspects of early Christianity, form-criticism let in a great deal of daylight on the character of the primitive Church. It brought home what, after all, could have been obvious all along, that it was not a backward-looking, anti-quarian society with an anxious concern for archives. Anchored though they were in what they believed to be a great *fait accompli* of the past—what God, in Jesus Christ, had done—the early Christians lived in the present and the future—lived enthusiastically, in the confidence that a new era of prophetic inspiration had begun, that the living Lord was among them and speaking through them, and that his visible return and acclamation were soon to follow. Why should such persons worry about the precise preservation of annals? Rather, their traditions must have been treated as living[33] and contemporary, and freely adapted to successive needs—the needs of worship, preaching and evangelizing, instructing, and defending their position against criticism and attack. It is in such living contexts, and not on the (anachronous!) study-tables of early scholars and historians, that—so form-criticism discerned—the processes of transmission must be understood. This led to radical conclusions. The Synoptic Gospels were not the chronological narratives they had seemed, but, rather, collections of isolated pearls loosely strung on a thread of the evangelist's own spinning. And who could say whether the pearls themselves were not counterfeit? We all know how easy it is to embellish or even invent stories in the process of time. It is demonstrable that the N.T. writers like to see what seemed to be predictions in the O.T. fulfilled in Christ:[34] is it possible,

then, that narratives were sometimes invented on the basis of
O.T. passages? The view of a Scandinavian school of thought
represented by H. Riesenfeld and B. Gerhardsson, that Jesus
caused his disciples to memorize his sayings and deeds, in the
manner of rabbinic teachers, is—although their research
undoubtedly illuminates rabbinic procedure—difficult to
maintain in the face of the demonstrable discrepancies between
the Synoptic Gospels.[35]

At any rate, the result of form-criticism was a focusing of
attention on the circumstances, needs, and intentions of the
oral period, rather than the literary history of the documents.
The parables offer special scope for such exercises, since two
or three versions of a parable in different Gospels may be
compared, and conclusions drawn.[36]

Thus, once more, an evolutionary conception of Christian
thought comes to the fore: a development was traced, from the
message of Jesus, mainly addressed to the Jewish authorities
menaced by the crisis of the Jewish war, to its adaptation to
the Church authorities under the expectation of the return of
Christ, or, perhaps, to Christians generally, suffering from
hope deferred. Hand in hand with this close attention to the
various circumstances of early Christian life went a new stress
on the importance of the apostolic 'proclamation' or 'kerygma'.
The Christian announcement about what God had done in
Jesus Christ came to be contrasted with the mere story of the life
of Jesus. The latter, even if it could be reconstructed (which
was doubtful), was not the saving proclamation of the Gospel.
The liberal Protestant zeal for retrieving the Jesus of history and
his teachings was left far behind in a concern for the apostolic
'kerygma' or proclamation of the Gospel of what God had done
in Jesus, crucified and living.[37]

The form-critical picture of the early Church's way of
using its traditions is well in line with the much-quoted remark
of Papias,[38] that Peter produced his teachings simply as need
arose, and that Mark wrote them down, but not in order.
Mark's concern, said Papias, was to get them right and get them
all. He could not arrange them chronologically, for that was
not how Peter had produced them. And another witness,

probably Clement of Alexandria, seems to endorse the pragmatic purpose of the Gospel, when he says that Mark wrote down the reminiscences of Peter for the benefit of catechumens. From the N.T. itself come other indications of the various purposes to which tradition about Jesus was put. For instance, 1 Cor. 7: 10 (contrast verses 11 f.) appeals to words of Jesus for ethical purposes, to meet problems arising from the marriage of Christian believers with unbelievers. 1 Tim. 5: 18 may contain another saying of Jesus applied to a current problem. Acts 20: 35 represents Paul as clinching his farewell message to the Church leaders of Ephesus with a remembered saying of Jesus: "It is more blessed to give than to receive." Again, a great deal in the N.T. points to a setting in worship (see also p. 243 below): one overhears liturgical language in such passages as 2 Cor. 1: 20, Eph. 1: 3 ff., 5: 14, 1 Tim. 3: 16, 1 Pet. 1: 3 ff.; and baptism is often reflected. A great deal also points to polemic: Matthew appears to contain much material that was used in debate with antagonistic Jewish (possibly Pharisaic) neighbours;[39] the same is almost certainly true of parts of John;[40] and all the Gospels contain units that could have been used in disputes over the sabbath laws.

What the form-critical method had, perhaps, been too slow to concede is that the early Church was capable of discriminating between past fact and present interpretation. No doubt Christians were practical persons living in the present, not academic antiquarians. No doubt it is true that Christian prophets sincerely (and often rightly) believed that they were interpreting the will of the Lord and speaking with his contemporary voice.[41] No doubt there was a sense in which the risen Lord was his own tradition. But the very fact that St. Paul, in 1 Cor. 7: 10 ff., does expressly contrast the authentic sayings of Jesus with his own opinion, and that the prologue to St Luke's Gospel declares its purpose to be to give the facts, should warn against a wholesale assumption that the early Church had no concern to retain the story of its own beginings and no capacity for distinguishing documentary narration from preaching. This is a question which vitally affects the interpretation of the purpose of the Gospels. In a zeal for the apostolic proclamation

two grave mistakes are often made: first, it is supposed that the
Gospels had no other purpose than proclaiming the post-
resurrection message of Christ, alive from among the dead. This
is to ignore the possibility that, on the contrary, the Gospels
may be an attempt (even if not uniformly successful) to
authenticate that proclamation, by looking back and telling
the story of what led up to this conviction, and how it all
happened.[42] After all, the only Gospels that do declare their
purpose say that it was to provide knowledge (Lk. 1: 4) and
lead to faith (John 20: 31). Secondly, it is assumed that,
because the epistles make scant allusion to the story of Jesus,
Paul and the others were not interested in it. This is to ignore
the elementary fact that the epistles—which, after all, are
addressed, in the face of special needs, to those who had
already been evangelized—had no occasion for retelling this
story. In any case, there are, in fact, more echoes of the sayings
of Jesus in the epistles than is sometimes supposed.[43]

REDACTION-CRITICISM

Thus, the form-critical concern with the oral period has had
important theological repercussions. Redaction-criticism, more
recently (again, a poor word for a German term, *Redak-
tionsgeschichte*—the history of editorial work), has concentrated
on what each Evangelist has made of his material and what
it is that he wants to say through it.[44] Analysis of the way in
which a given writer selects, modifies, and arranges his matter—
which can often be achieved with some measure of objectivity
by comparison between the Gospels—may lead to valuable
insights into his outlook, his theological interests, his special
message, and his purposes. It is unfortunately true that, so far,
there is not much unanimity about the results. Luke has been
depicted by some (cf. p. 38 above) as the evangelist who
opened the door to a late and decadent period by turning
the story of God's decisive act in Jesus into a human martyr-tale
and resolving the authentic eschatological tension of the
'already but not yet', in which the original gospel hope was
held, in favour of a neatly divided sequence, helping the

Church to acquiesce in an interim era. This is not wholly fair to the two volumes, Luke and Acts. If Luke is superior in artistic delineation, this does not necessarily mean that he sells the pass to a rationalistic conception of Jesus. As for Matthew, it is apparently an anthology of traditions which, though not uniform, are arranged with brilliant success for the teaching, perhaps, of enquirers, and for the equipment of Christians to counter hostile criticism from non-Christian Pharisaism. Mark is very variously characterized as a martyr gospel, a Pauline gospel, a Galilean eschatological document, a gospel of the hidden Messiah, a collection of readings for a lectionary, an elaborately allusive and subtly structured theological document, full of ingenious numerical groupings, prefigurings, and hints. Most of these theories are difficult to substantiate; and, as for the martyr-theme, that is part of any Gospel. What Mark does seem to do is to present reasons for believing that Jesus, who goes about proclaiming the Kingdom of God and healing illnesses, is the centre of God's martyr-people, Daniel's 'human figure' or 'Son of Man', destined to be vindicated, through suffering, as Son of God.

Returning for a moment to the techniques of form-criticism and redaction-criticism, these can be, and have been, applied not only to the Gospels but to other parts of the N.T.[45] At every point it is right to ask what was the 'setting' *(Sitz im Leben)* of this writing, or from what 'settings' did its component parts spring, and why has it been put together like this? Such questions often reveal the decidedly 'situational' character of N.T. ethics.[46] If we are able rightly to reconstruct the situation at Corinth which Paul was addressing, it may become clear that while adhering indeed to constant basic principles, he was advocating, as an actual course of action, something that was only appropriate in those particular circumstances, and that it is a mistake to try to generalize from them. Some would say that this is the explanation of the injunction, in Rom. 13, to obey all governmental authority as God's appointment. Taken as a generalization rather than an injunction intended for a particular situation, it presents acute moral problems.

THE CANON

In short, attention is now paid, more than ever before, to the *raison d'être* of each part of the N.T., both in its present form and in the successive stages behind it. But the whole N.T. also, as a collection, has to be understood in its total setting. What led to this selection of documents being set apart from others? Many other Christian writings have actually survived to our own day; still more were available then. Alexandrine Judaism apparently got on quite happily without a closed collection of scriptures. What led to the belief that the books now called the N.T. were alone 'normative' (the word 'canon' means a norm or measuring rod)? The answer is complicated, and subject to much further research.[47] And, within the story, there are complex problems relating to the formation of the smaller component parts of the whole collection—for instance, the Pauline *corpus*[48] and the Four Gospels canon.[49] But, to put it briefly, Christianity—unless it is to lose all its distinctiveness—stands or falls by the conviction that a man Jesus, who actually lived at a known time and in a known place, is, in a unique sense, one with God—God's own Son, the expression of God's final word in human character (see p. 25 above). And if so, then the historical roots of this faith have to be presented. It is not enough to tell an unauthenticated story—a legend or even a good myth—and say that it is a true story because it truly portrays human destiny or represents the meaning of human existence: it is necessary to ask whether it is a true story in the sense also that it actually happened. Consequently, when teachers, such as those alluded to or implied in 1 John 4: 2 f., 5: 5 ff., talked about Jesus as though he were divine but had never been truly human, or, conversely, when teachers proclaimed a truly human person as an example of the good life, but without the apostolic witness to his aliveness after death, it was necessary to indicate where authentic, eye-witness evidence for the faith from its early days could be found. Thus the need to specify the authoritative books arose. Before the need did arise, a good many of these books had established themselves already, for teaching and for use in worship, by long acceptance in influential congregations; others by their convincing excellence and their trueness to the apostolic Gospel as it was understood and maintained in the communities. Even if and when the attribution of a document to an actual apostle was mistaken, something in the collective instinct of the Church detected whether or not it was true to the apostolic essentials. And, although certain writings floated about on the perimeter, sometimes inside the circle and sometimes outside, it is questionable whether, as a matter of fact, there were many which rivalled the ultimately canonical books in antiquity, let alone in essential soundness. The story of the canon throws much light on the nature of authority. It shows the historical character of Christian beginnings, such that the initial facts determine the Church's existence; and it shows the work of God's Spirit in the Church which, in its turn, perceives what is essential and selects and defines. Although the Church, in a sense, made the traditions, the Church is itself made by what the traditions attest. Study of the canon also brings home the wide diversity which came to be included within normative Christianity, from the epistle of James, where the name of Jesus occurs only twice, and where conduct rather than belief seems dominant, to 2 Peter, with its special eschatology and its apparent affinity with Hellenistic divinizing cults (2 Pet. 1 : 4).[50] But all through, it is devotion to Jesus (even in James) which seems to be the unifying force.[51]

TEXTUAL STUDY AND PHILOLOGY

Two more disciplines—textual criticism[52] and linguistic studies[53] —contribute their share to the understanding of the N.T. Textual criticism of the N.T. is more elaborate than in any other writings of antiquity, because of the vastly greater number of manuscripts and the extreme complexity of their variants. It need, however, only be said here that there are only comparatively few of the countless variants which at all seriously affect the meaning. The vast majority represent only trends in interpretation or stages in corruption, and, while presenting fascinating puzzles, cannot be said greatly to affect theological judgements. The text determined, the interpreter needs to ask the precise meaning of the words; and a huge literature has grown up on the grammar, syntax, idioms, and philology of N.T. Greek. It is not true that N.T. Greek is nothing more than the Greek of the market place and the law courts, and it has become clear that a definite stamp has been set on it by Semitic influence, especially from the Greek O.T., not to mention the creative power of the Christian experience itself. But the diligent lexicographers of the papyri have thrown much light on the meaning of the words and idioms of Christian discourse; and the great Theological Dictionary edited by G. Kittel and G. Friedrich (see note 6) has redressed the balance by its careful attention to all stages of a word's development.

INTERPRETATION

The establishing of textual and philological detail, like the reconstruction of the background and all the other disciplines, is a means to an end—that of understanding N.T. thought and how it developed. But this, in its turn, is a means to a further end. The main question for any student with more than purely historical concerns is, How does Jesus come to be contemporary with us, as Christians believe him to be?[54] This takes us beyond the study of the theology of the N.T. itself to the study of its implications in dogmatic and philosophical theology. It takes us to 'hermeneutic' in the sense of interpreting the meaning of the N.T. *for us*; and this belongs to other sections of this book.[55] But something must be said, very briefly, about the link between the past and present. The resurrection of Jesus and all that that implies is the heart of the problem, not only for the study of the Gospels, but for the entire N.T. Determined attempts have been made, from time to time (especially from the mid-nineteenth to the early twentieth century), to find, in Jesus, a rationally intelligible figure of past history, a great prophet and teacher who lived and died, and only in the imagination of his followers was raised and deified. If so, he is important for us only in so far as we can translate his message into modern terms. Albert Schweitzer's famous *The Quest of the Historical Jesus* tells the story of such attempts.[56] At the opposite extreme to this 'Liberal Protestant' quest for the intelligible man is the view that what matters is faith in the risen, transcendental Lord preached by the early Church, and that it is neither possible nor desirable to authenticate, by historical research, what is essentially a decision of faith. By some, it has been deemed possible to 'demythologize' this value-judgement of faith, so as to interpret it as a pronouncement on human existence and a call to decision (cf. p. 275). Remove the mythical apparatus (three-tier universe, angels, demons, resurrection, ascension), and the resurrection of Jesus, demy-thologized, becomes a creative insight into the death of Jesus as bringing man to the end of himself and of his own resources, and so to a new kind of life.

Now, the former approach—the rationalized biography—yields only good advice and a fine example, not the power of God leading to salvation. But is not the logic of the latter approach to detach Christianity from its historical roots and make it into no more than a symbol or myth of human existence? It is round this approach that the demythologizing debate (associated with the name of Rudolf Bultmann) has raged. More recently, a new phase has supervened—the 'hermeneutic' or interpretation of the words of the Gospels as a means of bringing the reader into the self-understanding of Jesus himself: responded to, the words become an 'event of speech' by which the attitude of Jesus is reproduced.[57]

But is there no alternative to these procedures? The writer of this essay (who at this point must speak personally) is one who believes that faith in Jesus Christ, crucified and alive, does depend on a character-sketch conveying an impression of Jesus, and on historical authentication of the Christian inter-pretation of the sequel to his death, so far as history can take us. It is true that history can only point us across the frontier to certain value-judgements. History cannot take us all the way to the value judgement which says 'Jesus is Lord'. But it can point us there; and it may even say that it is flying in the face of the facts to interpret Jesus in any other way. It can show us that the first disciples' conviction that Jesus was alive needs to be reckoned with and is difficult to escape. Is, then, my faith in Jesus, whom I know as alive and as my Lord, vulnerable to the researches of scholars? Could critical scholarship discover something that might render that faith impossible or null? The answer seems to be: Theoretically, yes. For perhaps (theoretically) critical scholarship could discover conclusive evidence that the disciples were led to their conviction by a trick or a deliberately contrived falsehood, or by a subjectivism such as would provide no basis for the sharing of their faith by subsequent generations. Highly improbable as it is that evidence of such a character as to be conclusive could be found, it nevertheless is a theoretical possibility. What can, however, be said is this: Those who, through the apostolic witness and in the Christian Church, know Christ as Saviour and Lord, are sufficiently sure of him now to be convinced that, in fact, such a thing will not happen.[58]

For further reading

In the following list, and in the notes, no reference is made to books and articles in foreign languages which have not yet been translated into English.

References to most of the relevant literature will be found under the appropriate headings in standard Introductions, such as the following.

The fullest and best documented available in English is W. G. Kümmel, *Introduction to the New Testament*, S.C.M., London, 1966.

Note also:
R. M. Grant, *A Historical Introduction to the New Testament*, Collins, London, 1963.
D. Guthrie, *New Testament Introduction*, 3 vols. Tyndale, London, 1961–.
A. F. J. Klijn, *An Introduction to the New Testament*, Brill, Leiden, 1967.
J. Moffatt, *Introduction to the Literature of the New Testament*, T. and T. Clark, Edinburgh, 1912.
A. Wikenhauser, *New Testament Introduction*, Nelson, Edinburgh, 1958.

Of the New Testament Theologies, the following may be mentioned:
A popular and very scholarly introduction to the thought of the N.T. is W. D. Davies, *Invitation to the New Testament*, Darton, Longman and Todd, London, 1967.

Fuller and more systematic are:

J. Bonsirven, *Theology of the New Testament*, Burns and Oates, London, 1963.

R. Bultmann, *The Theology of the New Testament*, 2 vols. S.C.M., London, 1952–55.

H. Conzelmann, *An Outline of the Theology of the New Testament*, S.C.M., London, 1969.

F. C. Grant, *An Introduction to New Testament Thought*, Abingdon-Cokesbury, New York, 1950.

A. Richardson, *An Introduction to the Theology of the New Testament*, S.C.M., London, 1958

E. Stauffer, *New Testament Theology*, S.C.M., London, 1955.

3

THE OLD TESTAMENT

P. R. ACKROYD

*Samuel Davidson Professor of the Old Testament, King's College,
University of London*

3

The Old Testament

To study the Old Testament adequately, we need to know what it is; to know what it is, we have to engage in its study. That is the kind of difficulty which has to be faced by those who approach it, perhaps for the first time, with a desire to penetrate behind the façade and to meet its problems with something more than an impatient rejection of the Old Testament as consisting far too much of 'old, unhappy, far-off things, and battles long ago'. It is easy enough to raise a cheap laugh by pointing to Old Testament passages which by their unsatisfactory morality or by their narrowness contradict what are accepted as normal, decent standards, let alone Christian ones. It is also relatively easy to appeal for the use of an expurgated text which will not offend the simple. It is tempting to use the Old Testament selectively and so to avoid—apparently—the problems it presents, to concentrate upon its high moments and to write off as sub-standard the imprecatory psalms or the vituperative utterances of Jeremiah or the nationalism of Esther or the cynicism of Ecclesiastes. But to do so must always be recognized as somewhat less than honest; and, as Marcion was clear-sighted enough to recognize, the process of expurgation once begun cannot be held in check and limited to the Old Testament; it will carry with it a similar questioning of not a little that belongs to the New Testament.

THE CONTEXT OF THE OLD TESTAMENT

We may begin with a consideration of the context—or more accurately, contexts—in which the Old Testament is to be seen.

Here we may distinguish three relationships which are of particular significance.

(i) It is natural that, in the consideration of the study of theology, and primarily of Christian theology, the first and most important context is that of Christian faith. Within this context, we recognize that the Old Testament stands in a particular relation to the New Testament (see p. 29 above). To Jesus himself and to the whole community of the early Church as it emerges in the New Testament period, the Old Testament, more or less precisely defined, constituted the sacred writings to which recourse was had. Faced with the affirmation of Christian experience, new converts were found "examining the scriptures daily to see if these things were so" (Acts 17: 11). The development and canonization of the New Testament clarified the perspective in which what now became the Old Testament was viewed. Subsequent exegesis and discussion of the function of the whole Bible in relation to dogmatic state-ment, to belief and to conduct, produced a very great variety of estimates of the precise way in which biblical material should be used. This is a continuing discussion (cf. Chapter 7, especially pp. 162 to 164). It is rightly influenced by the understanding of the Old Testament which the development of scholarship brings about in each generation, and this leads us on into the discussion of the other contexts in which the Old Testament belongs. In particular, however, we may observe that there is a continuing tension between various types of approach. At one extreme, emphasis on the absolute distinctiveness and newness of Christian experience and statement inevitably leads to an assessment of the Old Testament as outdated; the contrast is often expressed in terms of 'law' and 'gospel', though an adequate definition of both these terms makes it clear that neither is simply applicable to either Testament. At the other extreme, the emphasis on the integral character of scripture can lead to an oversimple use of Old Testament material because there are so many matters on which, with its larger span, it provides evidence. At worst, this makes for a totally uncritical handling of the Old Testament all at one level; at its best and most useful, it provides the illumination of what is implicit in the New Testament, where so much rests upon the presuppositions of Old Testament thought.

(ii) No consideration of the Christian theological context of the Old Testament can be adequately undertaken without the wider religious context being taken into account. The Old Testament is the sacred scripture of Judaism; it also has a revered place in the traditions of Islam. From both these religious developments, and particularly from the former, insights into its nature and interpretation are to be obtained. But in a much broader sense, the Old Testament provides the record of a religion, an account of the religious experience of one particular community. It is true that in many respects the Old Testament does not provide the detail which would be necessary for a full description of the religion and of the attitudes of those who adhered to it. Any account of their worship remains incomplete because so much is not mentioned or is taken for granted. What the devout member of the community thought can often be only inferred rather than stated precisely. The complexity is increased by the fact that the literature itself which enshrines the expression of this religious experience has come down to us after centuries of use within the Old Testament period itself, so that the layers of interpretation due to the use of the material in different periods make precise definition again very difficult and often hypothetical. Nevertheless, particularly with the aids now available for the understanding of the world of the ancient Near East to which the Old Testament belongs, the reading of the text provides a cumulative picture of a rich religious tradition, of faithful members of a community practising their religion, and expressing, either directly or through their use of already existing forms, the nature of their faith, their response to what they understood to be the nature and action of God.

(iii) But such understanding of the text must avoid the risk of reading back into it the attitudes of our contemporary situation. The depicting of Old Testament characters in the costume of Renaissance Italy often results in good art; but it creates an impression of remoteness if no due allowance is made for the degree of transfer which has to be made. We may ask wrong questions about the nature of ancient religious experience if we approach it with the conditioning of our contemporary understanding. An emphasis on sincerity, or on right belief, may obscure the nature of religious obedience as then understood. It may be that the Jewish emphasis on right practice is nearer to a proper appreciation. For the correction of anachronistic misunderstanding an adequate knowledge of the ancient world in general is essential, and it is this which provides the third general context for the Old Testament. Whatever it may have become, it remains a part also of that ancient culture and must be understood in the light of our increasing knowledge of that ancient world. The Old Testament is a document of primary importance for the history of the ancient world, though it does not set out to be history in any narrow sense. It provides a rich body of literary material, comparable with the other ancient literatures while having its own particular characteristics and problems of interpretation. Above all, because of its profoundly religious basis, it enables us to have a picture of a religious system and life which may be placed alongside other such, itself illuminated by comparison just as it provides clues to the understanding of the religious phenomena evinced by other cultures of that ancient world. The greatest problem here is the one which makes the Old Testament much more difficult to interpret: it is the fact that virtually all the other religious systems of the ancient world are known only through now dead records, documents cut off from us by time and space, accounts of dead systems whose aftermath may be detected in later periods only with very great difficulty. The texts from Ras Shamra-Ugarit, dated from before 1400 B.C., provide us with a wealth of religious literature from one ancient community, closely linked with Canaan. They provide a 'fossilized' account, though the later forms of the related religious cultures of Phoenicia, of Carthage and of the Israelite area give us a variety of clues to the way in which the same or similar ideas were further developed. The Old Testament stands for us in a continuous and continuing tradition, in a living relationship with contemporary religious experience; it is therefore both alive in the sense that it continues, and also the more difficult to understand because of our involvement with it.

COMPARABILITY AND UNIQUENESS

This raises one of the basic questions about the Old Testament. Where does it stand in relation to the Near Eastern context in which it belongs? It is clear that it can no longer be read—as it formerly was—as if it were the only literature from the area and period. The literary forms much studied in recent years are not unique to the Old Testament. The psalms find their direct counterparts in Mesopotamia and Egypt. The wisdom sayings and the larger structures of the wisdom books cannot be adequately understood without a recognition of the wealth of comparable literature in the same areas. The forms of its poetry may be paralleled. It is one literature among many.

Nor is the comparability simply at the literary level. The customs and laws which govern the life of Israel are often to be understood fully only as we discover more of the life of the area to which it belongs. Recent years have brought from Mari and Nuzu in particular a fresh light on the social life which underlies the stories of the patriarchs in Genesis, and on aspects of the social life of later periods too. The legal heritage of Israel has for long been known to be related to that of the whole area; the earlier comparisons with the laws of Hammurabi are enriched with knowledge of a much larger legal tradition in which those laws themselves belong. With all the proper allowance for the differences due to a different type of culture, there is still clear evidence of community of custom and of legal practice. The phenomenon of prophecy, paralleled tentatively by reference to various types of religious ecstasy in other cultures, now finds its clearer counterpart in prophets in the Egyptian story of Wen-Amon and in the prophetic pronouncements in the Mari texts. More important still, the recognition must be made that the religion of the Old Testament finds its counterparts in the neighbouring cultures. The interrelationship between Israelite and Canaanite religion, already detected within the Old Testament in prophetic and legal strictures on practices viewed as alien to Israel's true spirit, is now more fully clarified as the religion of Canaan comes to be better understood in the texts which depict it. The interpretation of God's relationship with Israel in terms of historic intervention— an element so markedly central to much Old Testament material—is found to be characteristic of many other religious systems, the Moabite Stone providing the nearest example; the too simple discrimination between religions of the natural order and religions of historic experience breaks down.

The areas in which comparison has been made have become increasingly large. It has become more and more evident that no part of the Old Testament can be understood in isolation. The effect of this has often seemed to be that nothing distinctive remains. When a particular literary feature appears to stand out, it is always with the question left open that some new discovery may show that other communities too had developed such a style. The belief that this or that characteristic of theological presentation is unique has also again and again been met with the sobering recognition that similar material is to be found elsewhere.

Is it then improper to think of uniqueness at all? Or, if such a term is used, must it be used only in the sense that each and every religious community is unique, represents a particular combination of elements which, however much they may be paralleled individually, nevertheless present a unique configuration? Such a definition of uniqueness is not, in fact, so deficient as might at first sight appear. The quality of the Old Testament, its particular literature, its particular thought, are to be seen as the expression of the life of a real community, one which embodied in this literature a statement of its faith. This statement is not in the form of a well-ordered document setting out precise beliefs; it is in the form of a collection of works, belonging to many periods and to many groups and individuals, handed down and elaborated and reinterpreted over centuries, and in the end coming to occupy a position of authority because expressive of that community's faith. The validity of its claims lies not in anything external to itself, as if one could prove the truth of the claim by some reference to another authority. It lies in the material itself, in the response to a divine activity to which it testifies, a response which reveals all the strengths and weaknesses of the community which made it over the centuries.

But further, the special quality of the Old Testament belongs with the continuity of its use and influence. When all the comparisons have been made, the Old Testament is by reason of this continuity unlike a document or collection of documents dug up in an archaeological investigation. Rooted as it is in the past and therefore to be understood only within its ancient environment, its interpretation has been a continuous process, and its influence on theological thinking in the circles in which it has been handed down has been unbroken. The modern reader, however much he may see it as ancient and in some respects alien because of the differences of the life to which it witnesses, stands in a direct line not simply with his immediate predecessors in interpretation, as each generation learns from and builds upon the last, but also with those who within the Old Testament itself can be found to be at work in the process of reapplying older words to new situations.

THE OLD TESTAMENT CANON AND TEXT

This leads into the question of what writings have this special quality, and it is clear that in so far as it is this continuity of tradition and interpretation which marks them out, the limits of the canon as commonly accepted denote a line of demarcation between writings belonging to or associated with the Old Testament community which have not been accorded such a status and those which have (cf. pp. 52 ff. above). Such a definition is a matter of historical fact, though the precise process involved and the exact limits may be less easily indicated. On the one hand, the existence of a canon provides a demarcation line over against other ancient writings which either still exist or which may be supposed to have existed which have not passed through the process which made them the vehicle of Israel's own faith. Thus it distinguishes psalms which are canonical—within the Psalter or elsewhere in the Old

Testament—and psalms which exist or which may be postu-
lated as the earlier patterns from which Old Testament
psalmody derives. The common elements between Hebrew
and Canaanite poetry make it natural to see that Israel took
over already existing religious poetry. We may see in Ps. 29,
for example, relics of an earlier, non-Israelite, religious background, and observe that that part of the psalm which reappears
in Ps. 96 has undergone a further refinement and reinterpretation. But the hypothetical Canaanite psalm underlying Ps. 29
has not enjoyed the process by which that psalm itself became
the vehicle of Israel's own faith. If the borderline is narrow,
it is nevertheless real. On the other hand, the existence of a
canon provides a line of demarcation over against writings of
a later date, of which many examples in fragmentary form have
come from the Qumran area (see p. 87). Forming a part of the
religious literature of a particular group, they did not find a
final place in that tradition which belonged to the Jewish and
Christian communities as they became more precisely defined.
Here, it is evident, the line of demarcation is clear historically
but less readily explicable. Within Christian (and Jewish)
tradition, the point at which the line has been drawn has not
always been exactly agreed. The writings which make up the
Old Testament as this is found in the Hebrew Bible (the
threefold canon of Judaism, the *Tanak*) is generally accepted;
but marked differences of church tradition are found in regard
to what is rather inappropriately termed the Apocrypha,
regarding whose status there has often been debate. Still wider
differences are to be found in regard to a further range of
writings, some of which, for example the book of Enoch, were
highly regarded in outlying Christian communities such as that
of Ethiopia. If the central core of the canon is clear, the outer
edges are less precise. A line has been drawn historically, and
it is a line which must be respected because it is within this
limit that the main development of interpretation has been
confined; but for the understanding of the material itself, and
for a full appreciation of the life and thought of the community
from which it derives, the line has to be crossed and due
account taken of the wider range of literature (see Chapter 4.)

The history of the Old Testament text, bound up as it is with principles of textual development which it shares with other ancient manuscript traditions, is itself part of this whole process of interpretation. One important aspect of the study is the more purely mechanical; it is the attempt at discovering the best readings, tracing and accounting for the obvious errors of transmission. But this passes over at once into the wider question of interpretation, for while accidental error may account for a proportion of textual problems, much more of the difficulty of textual history arises out of interpretation. Within the transmission of the Hebrew text itself, and already within the Old Testament, there is a diversity of material which raises problems which are both textual and interpretative. The existence of the considerable parallel texts of Samuel/Kings and Chronicles shows the way in which the same material may be presented in often sharply divergent forms within two different theological traditions. Every example of a duplicate text is of importance not only for the light it may shed on particular readings, but also for alternative ways of understanding. To this must be added the evidence of the ancient translations, the Versions. These, in their proper place, contribute substantially to the resolving of textual problems; but they also provide insights into the ways in which particular communities of Jews and then of Christians could understand the text. The Qumran biblical texts have taken further back our direct knowledge of actual Hebrew manuscripts; they have also provided direct evidence of the diversity of traditions which existed already at an early date (cf. pp. 43 and 87). Textual history and the history of interpretation are not separable activities, but closely interrelated, for even an apparently inadvertent miscopying of a text may shed light on the theological or cultural atmosphere in which the scribe operated, and thus in turn provide evidence of the way in which he understood what he copied.

New textual knowledge has been matched by new linguistic information, with the discovery of Ugaritic as a whole new language close to Hebrew as the most important of many such sources of understanding. As in other spheres, such new material makes the study more and not less complex. The resources of language study—knowledge of the language itself, its ancient and more modern cognates, the meanings given to words and phrases in ancient translations and in later tradition—must all be brought to bear upon particular points of interpretation. A precise separation between purely philological questions and exegetical cannot be made; the interpretation of the text must be linguistically sound, but the choice between alternative possible meanings of a passage or of a word will be the result of a combination of linguistic and exegetical considerations.

THE LITERATURE AND ITS STRUCTURE

Questions concerning canon and text bring us to the nature of the literature itself, and again there is a measure of overlap. Clearly, any discussion of the literature must begin from the canon and text as it is, hypotheses about the earlier stages being inevitably dependent upon what we actually have at our disposal. Ultimately any hypothesis about what underlies the present material must include a satisfying explanation of the development from the earlier stage to the later. Here too the existence of more than one form of the same material may provide a starting point, or may raise questions about the nature of the material being handled. For example, the book of Jeremiah is known to us in two quite markedly distinct forms, the Hebrew and the Greek, and fragmentary Qumran texts provide evidence pointing towards both. The differences in points of detail are substantial, the Greek lacking many short phrases or single words, and also lacking some considerably longer sections; here is a problem which is one of textual criticism and of interpretation. In addition, the Hebrew has the considerable collection of foreign nation oracles as chapters 46–51, whereas in the Greek form of the book substantially the same collection appears in a different order in the middle of chapter 25. This major difference raises questions about the literary history of the book, the processes by which a collection of such oracles came together, the order in which they are arranged, and the position which they come to occupy in relation to other material. Again the elements which make up the first chapter of the book of Judges are in large measure found as scattered fragments in the latter part of the book of Joshua. The textual and interpretative questions raised by such double occurrences have already been mentioned; they have a further significance in the investigation of the literature. So too, double occurrences of psalms (e.g. 14 and 53) provide some evidence of how the Psalter came to be formed, presumably out of already existing but independent smaller collections.

From such a recognition of alternative forms of the same material, it is only a further step to the analysis of the literature with a recognition of the occurrence of duplicate forms of the same narrative in which more substantial differences occur. This is to be found repeatedly in a comparison of the Kings/Chronicles texts: thus, 2 Kings 16 offers a quite different construction of the reign of Ahaz of Judah from that which is provided in the overlapping but distinct 2 Chron. 28. The existence of alternative traditions like those of David's sparing of Saul in 1 Sam. 24 and 26 introduces a new feature, that of alternatives which both make the same point but where the actual narrative is different. The two creation narratives in Gen. 1: 1—2: 4a and 2: 4b–25 (and its sequel in chapter 3) provide fewer points of overlap, and profounder differences of theological interpretation. Many such examples occur and provide a basis for the literary analysis of the books of the Old Testament, giving clues to the existence of earlier sources upon which the later and more elaborate structures were built. At many points, it can be recognized that two or more earlier traditions—whether documentary or oral is a point of less immediate importance—have been interwoven, as in the now composite narrative of the flood in Gen. 6–8 and in the accounts of the plagues in Egypt in Exod. 5–11. It may be that one form of a narrative has been expanded with elements from an alternative tradition.

For the last two hundred years and more, such literary analysis has been a major preoccupation of Old Testament scholarship. With wide differences of opinion about detail, there has come to be no doubt that the present books derive from earlier forms of the material. Where the term 'document' has been commonly used for these earlier forms, there has been an increasing tendency in recent years to speak of 'traditions', with the recognition that there may be both written sources, forms of the material shaped by authors, interpreters of the narratives, and that there may also be living oral transmission which may influence the development of the written works. In the prophetic books, it may be seen that the spoken word of the prophet has been transmitted in part through his own use of it and that a message once spoken may be applied to new situations (cf. e.g. Isa. 28 and Jer. 36). It also owes much to associates, perhaps disciples, and circles in which the message of a prophet was kept alive and reapplied and amplified in the light of new experience. The prophetic material of the eighth century shows considerable signs of such reapplication in the exilic age, and the subsequent period also left its mark on the transmission of the prophetic oracles both in more precise applications and in the arrangement of them in more elaborate complexes.

But whereas much of the literary analysis concentrates on finding earlier sources within the existing material, the emphasis has shifted increasingly to the study on the one hand of the nature of the units of the material and on the other hand to the processes by which the material came together in more complex structures. Both these types of study lay much greater stress on the relationship between the literature and the life of the community in which it took its shape. Thus the study of the smaller units is in part the recognition that particular types of material are shaped in particular stereotyped ways. Small narrative units—such for example as a legend relating the origin of a sanctuary—follow a pattern. Psalms, whether laments or hymns, have an observably regular structure and a typical phraseology; in considerable measure these features may be traced in other ancient Near Eastern psalmody. The analysis of the prophetic books reveals types of oracular utterance, oracles of judgement, diatribes, pronouncements related to legal formulae, or words of salvation comparable to priestly blessings and promises. In some cases the smaller units may be seen to be built upon what we should term 'secular' patterns, though the dividing line between sacred and secular would be differently drawn in the Old Testament; harvest songs, wedding poetry, victory songs, and the like, occur to only a limited extent in their original context, but much more frequently in new forms adapted to a new theological application.

This type of study, termed form-criticism (see p. 46 above) in fact offers only one approach to the understanding of the present form of the material. It draws attention to features which belong to a convention; it illuminates the kind of material with which we are dealing. But these forms appear in the Old Testament re-used and re-interpreted, the result of processes which we may term 'redaction' (cf. p. 50), but which really need to be described so as to indicate the living handling of the tradition by those who carried it further. The prophet who uses the watchman's song (cf. Isa. 21) may in fact be aware that he is describing his own function in terms which belong to those of the secular activity; but it is an analogy in which the important element lies in the way in which he presents warning and encouragement in a specific situation requiring theological comment. The narrator of an ancient story concerning one of the ancestors of Israel (e.g. in Gen. 22) may be entirely unaware of the nature of the story he is using; for him it is the vehicle of interpretation, of comment on the ways of God with men at a place ultimately to be linked (so 2 Chron. 3: 1) with the building of a temple at Jerusalem. The description of the whole process—for which terms such as traditio-history and redaction-history have been used (with different emphasis)—is an attempt to give greater precision to the fact that throughout the long period of the growth of the literature to the point at which we meet it, there has been repeated handling and rehandling, the addition of new elements, the elaboration of new modes of understanding. Such a description of the process includes the recognition of sources, whether as oral traditions or as written documents. The discovery of these sources is in many cases a hypothesis only, based upon the analysis of the present form of the material, and particularly in regard to the Pentateuch, source-analysis has been a fruitful approach to understanding though sometimes deficient in recognizing the real nature of an ancient literature. In other cases, source-analysis is more tangibly based, as in the study of the relationship between the writings of the Chronicler and those of his predecessors in the Pentateuch, in Samuel and Kings, so that the existence and use of earlier sources cannot be ruled out for other parts of the material too. This last example also makes it clear that a writer who uses already known and in some measure fixed sources can be just as much a creative artist as the one who, supposedly, operates without such a basis. Shakespeare is not the less creative because he used Holinshed.

HISTORY, LIFE AND THOUGHT

The investigation of the literature thus runs alongside the wider study of the whole history of the people from which it stems. Behind its present form lie centuries of change; the different levels within it reflect, if we could but know precisely, many facets of a rich and variegated life. The study of the Old Testament therefore involves discovering how men lived, how they thought, how the experiences of their history shaped their life and thought, and how their recounting of historic experience, or what was believed to be historic experience, was itself affected by the way in which it was viewed in the perspective of later situations. Part of the source material for the broader study is to be found in the results of archaeological activity, which provides a continual check on the material aspects of life. Precise correlation with events described in the Old Testament is relatively rare; the date for the capture of Jerusalem by Nebuchadnezzar in March 597 B.C., stands out. Much more often ancient non-biblical texts and other evidence create as many problems of historical assessment as they appear to solve. This may be seen for example in the examination of the evidence, biblical and extra-biblical, for the period of Hezekiah and Sennacherib, around 700 B.C. But much is gained in the understanding of the general level of culture, the detail of layout of buildings and towns, evidence of periods of occupation and of destruction, as well as many points at which particular questions of interpretation of texts may be illuminated (as for example the mention of the *pim* weight in 1 Sam. 13: 21, now known from factual discoveries but previously much debated).

In such an introductory survey as this, it would be inappropriate to devote space to a historical outline which can be found readily in many books both more elementary and more advanced; nor do the many difficult problems of chronology and interpretation of particular periods need to be more than mentioned. It is more important to stress the necessity of seeing the literature and the thought always in the context of an understanding of the period and situation to which it belongs, recognizing the inevitable degree of abstraction which affects the study of ancient texts for which precise historical correlation is not available. It cannot be too often stressed that the Old Testament comes to us from the real life of a real people; our fuller understanding of it goes hand in hand with such fuller understanding of the nature of that life as becomes available.

OLD TESTAMENT RELIGION AND THEOLOGY

In view of the nature of the study of the Old Testament in which we are concerned, it is clear that the religious thought of its people will be the central point of interest in the consideration of its life and thought in general. Equally clearly, this religious thought must never be isolated, since the ways in which men formulate their religious apprehensions are intimately linked with the conventions of their own time. The nature of God as conceived in one period will be as inevitably linked with the type of political and social organization which prevails as the concept of creation will be tied into the understanding of what the world is and how it operates.

The distinction between religion and theology suggested by the title of this section is not intended to be in any way a precise one, but rather a convenient indication of two elements. On the one hand, our concern must be with practices and beliefs which can be shown to exist at any given moment; the task here is primarily descriptive, sorting out from the biblical and non-biblical material available the precise nature of religious practice—sacrifices and other types of worship, religious buildings, liturgical forms and the like—and the concepts of God and man and of the interrelationship between them which belong to a particular moment. Religion is in so many respects a conservative type of activity, that it is not easy in such matters to discriminate between the continuing and only gradually changing external forms and the nature of the interpretation which is placed upon them. The use and re-use of the same religious texts over many years, even centuries—as for example particularly clearly in the psalms—makes precision in such a descriptive process very difficult to attain. Nevertheless, the broad outlines of religious change can be traced, and the appearance of a number of fuller surveys of this kind in recent years shows that while much diversity of interpretation remains there is a recognizable correlation observable between historical and social changes and those which affect religious practice and belief.

On the other hand, an attempt must be made to evaluate the theology, to make some assessment of the meaning of belief and practices, to see the changing patterns of thought not just as evidence of development and modification but as expressions of the underlying reality which is thereby affirmed. For the position of those who approach the Old Testament in the context of theology in general is that the claims which it makes about the nature and activity of God and about the human response to that nature and activity are not just of antiquarian interest but of lasting significance. Here we are dealing again with questions raised at the outset of this discussion (p. 62). At the very least, we have here a self-contained body of evidence regarding men's statements of their faith and practice; and this is to be taken seriously in the whole context of religious experience in the broadest sense. In the relationship between Old Testament and subsequent Christian theology there is to be seen an organic connection which makes the Old Testament affirmations about the nature and purpose of God of particular value, for it was in their context that the Christian affirmations are themselves made (cf. p. 29). The evaluation of the latter is intimately linked with the evaluation of the former. The description of Old Testament theological developments and their evaluation is part of a broader theological task, dependent on the establishment of the general validity of theological judgement but at the same time an important contributory factor to the exposition of that validity.

Whereas the variety of religious ideas which the Old Testament contains is evident and accepted, Old Testament scholars and theologians more generally have supposed that there is a clear unity of theology. In the past this was in some measure dictated by the use of Old Testament material—interpreted according to some accepted scheme, often typological or allegorical—in the formulation of Christian doctrine; the weight and authority accorded to the whole Bible made it naturally desirable to see a clear unity here, an economy of salvation, a discernible pattern, within which every part could occupy its proper place. More historical approaches to biblical criticism made less easy the acceptance of such patterns, and a fuller understanding of the origins of particular works suggested that they must be accorded different levels of importance in their use for doctrinal purposes. Some parts of the Old Testament, viewed from a Christian standpoint, even seemed to have little or nothing to contribute to a full theological statement. But any selective use inevitably raises the kind of questions touched on at the outset; the biblical canon is there as a historic fact, and its place within the evolution of Christian doctrine is fixed. Some more adequate approach must be found.

Attempts at delineating the unity of Old Testament theology have been made in various ways in recent years. In some, the approach suggested by the older dogmatic in which a Christian theological scheme was imposed on the Old Testament, has seemed to offer a sufficient recognition of unity while avoiding a mere projection of more recent constructions. In others, the attempt has been made of looking at Old Testament theology from within, seeing it as 'recital', as Israel's own confessions, presented in a variety of ways and forming a rich pattern not to be simply subsumed under one overriding idea. In yet others, the attempt has been made of taking a central biblical concept—such as 'covenant'—and showing the interrelationship of the various aspects of the material to this. All these approaches, and others which form in some measure variants upon them, have contributed to our appreciation of the very great richness of the material. In very recent days, there has been a certain turning away again from the idea of producing an overall Old Testament theology, and a greater recognition of the need for the more specific and detailed study of parts of the material.

Whatever the approach, it may be recognized that there is an underlying unity which belongs to the people which produced the Old Testament and was also itself produced or at least moulded by it; this is no uniformity since the people, known primarily through its most oustanding figures but sensed as a continuum behind them, is itself not uniform. The ideal of one people, unmixed with other peoples which might contaminate its faith, is one which develops only gradually in the Old Testament; rooted ultimately in ancient concepts of tribe and kinship which hedge a community about with laws and taboos particularly as regards marriage, it emerges eventually as an ideal conception, projecting into the past a picture of unity but recognizing at the same time that the history testifies to a large measure of divisiveness and of outside influence. As an ideal, it is a potent factor; but within the reality there was a richness of difference of approach. This is evident if we consider the great prophetic figures, who belong together and are yet identifiable individually; it is clear as we look at the major presentations of the people's history, in the Tetrateuch (the so-called 'Priestly Work', Genesis to Numbers), the Deuteronomic History (Deuteronomy to 2 Kings), and the Chronicler (Chronicles, Ezra, Nehemiah); it is clear also when we try to set the wisdom literature (Proverbs and Job and Ecclesiastes and their counterparts outside the Old Testament canon in the narrower sense) in relation to other aspects of Israel's thought. In every case there is community of thought, of basic presupposition; but there is also diversity of interpretation and a resultant richness of material.

Unity may also, and rightly, be defined in relation to the God whom the people acknowledge in their literature. The study of the religion, the detailed examination of the documents, makes it clear that many different ideas jostle one another as to what kind of God he is, and how he acts, and what response it is right for man to make. But equally there is continuity of understanding. The confession of faith which identifies Yahweh of the Exodus events with the God of Abraham, Isaac and Jacob—an identification which raises many problems of interpretation—is nevertheless a right recognition that there is no break within the people's experience of God. Through its experience the people testifies to the reality of God and it is in this testimony that it knows itself to be what it is: *You shall be my people and I will be your God.* The concepts of covenant, of election, of divine-human enounter, are here drawn together.

For further reading

Introductory volumes:
J. Bowden, *What about the Old Testament*, S.C.M., London, 1969
The volumes of the *New Clarendon Bible, Old Testament*, O.U.P., London, 1966.

General Works:
A Companion to the Bible, 2nd ed., ed. by H. H. Rowley, T. and T. Clark, Edinburgh, 1963.
Dictionary of the Bible, 2nd ed., ed. F. C. Grant and H. H. Rowley, T. and T. Clark, Edinburgh, 1963.
The Interpreter's Dictionary of the Bible, 4 vols. ed. by G. A. Buttrick, Abingdon, Nashville, 1962.

Commentaries

One volume works:
Peake's Commentary, rev. ed., Nelson, London, 1962.
Jerome Biblical Commentary, Chapman, London, 1968.
New Catholic Commentary, rev. ed., Nelson, London, 1969.

Series:
Torch, S.C.M.; *Cambridge Bible Commentary*, C.U.P., 1971.
Old Testament Library, S.C.M., *Anchor Bible*, Doubleday, New York.
International Critical Commentary, T. and T. Clark.

Text:
E. Würthwein, *The Text of the Old Testament*, Blackwell, Oxford, 1957.

The Literature:
G. W. Anderson, *A Critical Introduction to the Old Testament,*
Duckworth, London, 1959.
O. Eissfeldt, *The Old Testament: an Introduction,* Blackwell,
Oxford, 1965.

History, Institutions and Archaeology:
M. Noth, *History of Israel,* rev. ed., A. and C. Black, London,
1960.
J. Bright, *History of Israel,* S.C.M., 1960.
R. de Vaux, *Ancient Israel; its life and institutions,* Darton,
Longman and Todd, London, 1961.
Archaeology and Old Testament Study, ed. by D. Winton Thomas,
O.U.P., London, 1967.

Religion and Theology:
H. Ringgren, *Israelite Religions,* S.P.C.K., London, 1966.
G. von Rad, *Old Testament Theology,* 2 volumes, Oliver and
Boyd, Edinburgh, 1962, 1965.
W. Eichrodt, *Theology of the Old Testament,* 2 volumes, S.C.M.,
London, 1961, 1967.

Most of the volumes listed above contain lists of books for
further reading.

4

INTER-TESTAMENTAL LITERATURE

F. F. BRUCE

*Rylands Professor of Biblical Criticism and Exegesis,
University of Manchester*

4

Inter-testamental Literature

I. BETWEEN THE TESTAMENTS

SOME ACQUAINTANCE with political, cultural and religious developments in the last three centuries B.C. is simply indispensable if we are to understand the thought of the New Testament. By the thought of the New Testament we mean not only the good news brought by Jesus and the teaching of his followers (diversified as their teaching was) but also the many facets of belief and practice in the Judaism of their day, the positions, for example, of the Sadducees and Pharisees, whom we meet in the New Testament narrative, and of other parties and movements which receive no explicit mention there but are not at all irrelevant to the origins of Christianity.

By inter-testamental literature is meant Jewish literature produced between the end of the Persian Empire (331 B.C.) and the fall of the second Temple (A.D. 70)—that is to say, during a period of four hundred years—both in Palestine and in the Dispersion. But these chronological limits cannot be applied absolutely: a few documents in the Hebrew canon are to be dated fairly certainly in the Hellenistic period, and if *Tobit* is included in the inter-testamental literature (which no one would dispute), it is difficult to exclude the story of *Ahiqar* from our purview simply because it was current in the fifth century B.C.

The period in which the inter-testamental literature appeared witnessed the overthrow of the Persian Empire by Alexander the Great and the incorporation of Judaea within his empire— an incorporation which was even more important culturally than it was politically. Henceforth, under Alexander (331–323 B.C.) and his successors (the Ptolemies until 198 B.C. and the Seleucids after them), as under the independent Hasmonaean regime which was established in 142 B.C. after the successful struggle against Antiochus Epiphanes and his heirs, and even under the Romans who brought Jewish independence to an end in 63 B.C., Judaea was part of the Hellenistic world. The vicissitudes of those centuries are reflected in the inter-testamental literature and in the religious development to which this literature bears witness. Whether Hellenism was accepted as a boon or resisted as a threat to everything that was of value in Israel's heritage, its influence was inescapable.

2. VARIETIES OF LITERATURE

The inter-testamental literature is as varied in its range as the canonical literature. Prophecy has disappeared, but its place is taken by 'apocalyptic' (see next section), the beginnings of which appear in the Hebrew Bible. The literary genres embrace also narrative (both historical and fictitious), 'wisdom' collections, psalmody and other liturgical documents, rewriting of biblical texts so as to apply them to new situations or make them teach new lessons, commentaries, manuals of right conduct, and so forth. At least passing mention must be made of the voluminous writings of Philo of Alexandria (c. 20 B.C.–A.D. 50), in which he allegorizes the Pentateuchal narratives and laws so as to bring them into line with Platonic philosophy, although space forbids their further treatment here. A century or so earlier the *Letter of Aristeas,* purporting to tell of the origins of the Greek (Septuagint) version of the Old Testament, is actually a good sample of Jewish propaganda among the Greeks, especially in Alexandria.

Of the other works referred to, some are relatively well known as the 'apocryphal' or deutero-canonical books; but there is no need to keep them apart from the mass of pseudepigrapha (works published under the names of ancient prophets and righteous men), which has come down from the same period. Sayings attributed to leading rabbis of the period may also be considered, even if they were not written down until well after the New Testament age. Above all, close attention must be given to the amazing access of inter-testamental literature which the discoveries in the Qumran caves in 1947 and the years following have brought to light. The Qumran manuscripts, evidently the surviving portions of the library of an ascetic Jewish community which had its headquarters in that region, north-west of the Dead Sea, during the two centuries preceding A.D. 70, represent some 400 literary compositions. Of these about 100 are books of Hebrew scripture (some of the biblical books being represented several times over); the remainder comprise a wide variety of texts. Some of these belong to the category of apocrypha and pseudepigrapha, both previously known and unknown. Among those already known, fragments in the original Hebrew or Aramaic have occasionally come to light for the first time, such as *Tobit* in both these languages, *Jubilees* in Hebrew, *First Enoch* in Aramaic, the *Testament of Levi* in Aramaic and the *Testament of Naphtali* in Hebrew. Works previously unknown which have been found in whole or (more often) in part include many documents relating to the faith, life and worship of the community, commentaries on biblical books and, in the category of apocrypha and pseudepigrapha, portions of one or more *Daniel* cycles unrepresented in the canonical or deutero-canonical literature, a *Genesis Apocryphon,* the *Vision of Amran,* the *Sayings of Moses,* the *Psalms of Joshua,* the *Book of Mysteries* and (apparently a favourite, to judge by the number of copies) the *Apocalypse of the New Jerusalem.*

3. APOCALYPTIC WRITINGS

Some of the most distinctive and important inter-testamental texts belong to the apocalyptic genre. These works record visions of the unseen—either of the remoter universe or (more frequently) of the allegedly distant future, usually published in the name of some hero of the past (such as Enoch, Noah, Moses or Ezra). The persecution under Antiochus Epiphanes (*c.* 168–164 B.C.), the oppression of the godly under the later

Hasmonaeans, especially Alexander Jannaeus (103–76 B.C.) and the period following the Roman occupation of Judaea (63 B.C.), situations from which the pious could see no way out except by direct divine intervention, encouraged the production of such works, in which the cataclysmic termination of the 'era of wickedness' and inauguration of the age of righteousness are confidently and picturesquely forecast.

4. WISDOM TEACHING

The wisdom literature of the period includes further 'success stories' of the Joseph and Daniel type, of the pious Jew who, exiled among pagans, triumphs over adversity and attains a position of trust and honour. This kind of theme appears in *Tobit*, where the piety of Tobit in Nineveh is rewarded by the prosperity won by his dutiful but rather simple-minded son, and even more so in the story of the Jew *Aḥiqar* at the court of Sennacherib, to which reference is made by Tobit.[1]

The later wisdom books have a narrower religious outlook than those in the Hebrew Bible, which are more internationally minded than anything else in the canon. Ben Sira and the author of *Baruch* identify Wisdom with the Torah;[2] in the so-called *Wisdom of Solomon* the history of Israel is seen to have been directed by Wisdom, in contrast to the pagan neighbours of Israel, especially the Egyptians, who are involved in disaster because it was not among them that Wisdom made her abode.[3]

The near-hypostatization of the Word of Yahweh which begins in the Old Testament (where on occasion it acts as his messenger)[4] is developed in the inter-testamental period, the best known instance being the picture in *Wisdom* of God's 'all-powerful word' (*logos*) leaping down from his heavenly throne into the doomed land of Egypt to kill the first-born—"a stern warrior carrying the sharp sword of thy authentic command".[5]

5. GOD AND PROVIDENCE

There is an increasing emphasis on God as transcendent and

'wholly other'. This appears, for example, in the deliberate avoidance of the older anthropomorphic language about God (for example, the substitution in the Septuagint of "Enoch pleased God" for "Enoch walked with God",[6] or of "they saw the place where the God of Israel stood"—still an anthropomorphism, but rather less direct—for "they saw the God of Israel"[7]). It appears also in the avoidance of the term 'God' (comparable to the earlier avoidance of the name Yahweh: see p. 318). The one allusion to God in the Hebrew *Esther* describes help from him as "relief and deliverance ... from another quarter".[8] In the books of *Maccabees* there is a tendency to say 'Heaven' instead of God—especially marked in the rather secularly minded *First Maccabees* but also to be recognized in the religiously orientated *Second Maccabees*.[9]

At the same time God's fatherly relation to his people is acknowledged:

> The Lord shall rejoice in his children
> And be well pleased in his beloved ones for ever.[10]

Even if the rabbinical designation of God as "your Father who is in heaven" is not attested in our period,[11] its common use indicates that it was pre-Christian. It is not this designation, but the single word *Abba,* that was so distinctive on the lips of Jesus.[12]

On the degree to which the fortunes of men were determined by divine providence the main schools of Jewish thought disagreed. The Essenes, according to Josephus, were thoroughly predestinarian:[13] a similar doctrine is taught in the Qumran literature, where human beings are apportioned in advance between the Prince of lights and the angel of darkness.[14] The Sadducees, at the opposite extreme, believed in complete freedom of choice.[15] The Pharisees found that life gives evidence of both divine foreordination and human free will[16] (as one of them put it later, "Everything is foreseen, and freedom of choice is given");[17] but they believed that God's will would triumph in the end—a belief reflected in Gamaliel's advice to the Sanhedrin, as reported by Luke.[18]

6. ETHICS

The ideal of Israel as "the people of the book", encouraged by the work of Ezra and his associates, was cherished in the Hellenistic age by the *hasidim,* the pious groups who sought to strengthen one another's hands in the study and practice of the Law.[19] This ideal was increasingly threatened by the attraction of the Hellenistic way of life. It triumphed however largely because of the heroism of its devotees under Antiochus Epiphanes, who inaugurated a deliberate policy of abolishing everything that was distinctive of Judaism. Thereafter, even among those who did not attempt to live up to the ideal themselves, it was venerated as the true way of God. Among the heirs of the *hasidim,* some carried devotion to the ideal so far as to withdraw to the wilderness to prepare the way of the Lord, like the community of Qumran and similar groups. The majority, living among their fellow-Israelites, formed themselves into brotherhoods for mutual encouragement in law-abiding piety: such were the Pharisees, first emerging towards the end of the second century B.C., whose scrupulousness in observing the laws of purity and tithing imposed on them a degree of separatism which probably explains their name. The rank and file of the population, "the people of the land", could not hope to approach such a standard.[20]

The supremacy of the law is manifested not only in the tendency to invoke the authority of Sinai[21] for the "tradition of the elders"[22] as well as for the written law which that tradition interpreted and amplified, but also in the tendency, expressed most clearly in *Jubilees,* to trace the practice of the Mosaic law back to the Creation:[23] the Law, in fact, is eternal; it is (as a later rabbi said) the instrument by which the world was created.[24]

The essence of morality, then, is the keeping of the Law. In the *Testaments of the Twelve Patriarchs* the Law is summed up in terms of love:

> love the Lord and your neighbour;
> have compassion on the poor and weak.[25]

At an earlier date, Tobit expresses love to one's neighbour in the negative form of the Golden Rule: "what you hate, do not do to any one."[26]

7. THE HOLY SPIRIT

The distinctive New Testament designation of the Spirit of God as the Holy Spirit has only a few Old Testament precedents. Around the New Testament period we find it in *Wisdom* (where God's Holy Spirit is practically synonymous with his gift of wisdom),[27] in *the Psalms of Solomon* (where the Davidic Messiah is empowered by the Holy Spirit),[28] in the *Martyrdom of Isaiah* (where Isaiah at his martyrdom speaks with the Holy Spirit until the moment of his death)[29] and in the *Apocalypse of Ezra* (where Ezra prays that the Holy Spirit may be sent to enable him to write down the lost scriptures).[30]

But the designation is nowhere so prolifically used before its Christian usage as in the Qumran texts. There "the Spirit of holiness" (and of truth and light) is the counterpart of the spirit of impurity (and of falsehood and darkness); these two between them have received all mankind as their lot.[31] The prophets of God in earlier days are called "the anointed ones of his Holy Spirit"[32]—those who have received a special anointing to impart the divine truth to their fellows. More generally, the Holy Spirit is the fount of knowledge: "I, as an instructor (*maskil*)", says the author of one of the *Hymns of Thanksgiving,* "have come to know thee, O God, by the spirit which thou hast set within me, and by thy Holy Spirit I have listened faithfully to thy wonderful secret counsel."[33] In the *Hymns* acknowledgement is also made of the guidance and help provided by the Holy Spirit: "I thank thee, O Lord, because thou hast upheld me by thy strength, and thou hast poured out thy Holy Spirit on me so that I shall not be moved."[34] Such experience is cause for gladness: "In steadfast truth hast thou upheld me and by thy Holy Spirit thou hast made me rejoice."[35]

Again, the Holy Spirit is the agent of inward purification: "By the Holy Spirit, given to the Community in his truth, a man will be cleansed from all his iniquities, and by the spirit of uprightness and humility his sin will be atoned for."[36] In particular, there is a prediction—unfortunately ambiguous —that at the ordained time of visitation "God will purify by his truth all the deeds of man, and will cleanse for himself one (some) of the sons of man, so as to destroy every evil spirit from the midst of his flesh and cleanse him by the Holy Spirit from all his wicked deeds; he will sprinkle the spirit of truth upon him like water of purification from every false abomination."[37] This is an amplification of the promise in Joel 2: 28 that when the time of wrath is past God will pour out his Spirit on all flesh. But it is possible to construe the passage so as to find a reference to a coming individual: "God will purify by his truth all the deeds of a man, and will cleanse him for himself more than the sons of man." This reading has been thought to present a striking affinity with what John the Baptist in the Fourth Gospel says about the mission of the Coming One.[38]

The Holy Spirit, moreover, dwells within the Qumran community as in a temple. The community has been established in these last days "for a foundation of the Holy Spirit, for eternal truth, to make atonement for the guilt of rebellion and the work of sin, and to procure divine favour for the land apart from (*or* more than) the flesh of burnt-offerings and the fat of sacrifice; the heave-offerings of the lips duly presented will be as a savour of righteousness and perfection of way as an acceptable free will offering."[39] Here we approach the New Testament conception of the age of spiritual worship superseding the order of sacrificial ritual.

But if the community is a habitation for the Holy Spirit, sin on the part of its members is a pollution of that Spirit, and they give a solemn undertaking to avoid all such pollution and not emulate the majority of Israel's religious leaders who "have polluted their holy spirit" by despising the commandments of God.[40] Here "their holy spirit" is scarcely identical with the Spirit of God; and in those other places in inter-testamental literature where the Spirit of God is called the Holy Spirit the term is not used personally as it is in the New Testament.

8. SIN AND ATONEMENT

The origin of sin is a subject for speculation: the devil,[41] fallen angels,[42] Eve,[43] Adam[44] are all named as responsible for it, although the (Syriac) *Apocalypse of Baruch* (*c.* A.D. 70) lays the blame squarely on each individual: "each of us has been the Adam of his own soul."[45]

Belief in the power of pious deeds, particularly almsgiving, to procure atonement for sin is widely attested. As Daniel counsels Nebuchadnezzar to break off his sins by practising righteousness, and his iniquities "by showing mercy to the oppressed,"[46] so Raphael assures Tobit and his son that "almsgiving delivers from death, and it will purge away every sin",[47] while Ben Sira affirms that "whoever honours his father atones for sins, and whoever glorifies his mother is like one who lays up treasure".[48] These means were universally available, whereas recourse to sacrifice was feasible only where the temple was reasonably accessible.

Ben Sira's reference to "laying up treasure" may suggest the treasury of merit, a concept which finds expression in this period. At the end of the period the *Apocalypse of Ezra* represents Ezra as having "a treasure of works laid up with the Most High" and reflects that, whereas "the righteous, who have many works laid up" with God, "shall receive their reward in consequence of their own deeds", those "who have no works of righteousness" must rely on the divine pity, manifested in consideration of "the endeavours of those who have kept the covenants amid afflictions".[49] The contemporary (Syriac) *Apocalypse of Baruch* similarly allows that the righteous die without fear because they have with God "a store of works preserved in treasuries".[50]

In line with this is the doctrine of the "piety of the fathers" —i.e. of the patriarchs—envisaged as so exceedingly meritorious that their descendants shared the credit of it.[51] While the explicit statements of this doctrine are later than our period, it is implied in the rebuke of John the Baptist: "do not presume to say to yourselves, 'We have Abraham as our father'."[52] In this context the 'binding of Isaac'—his patient submission to be sacrificed—was regarded as outstandingly propitiatory and efficacious on his descendants' behalf.[53]

The atoning value of suffering, not only for the sufferer's own sins but for those of others, is held to be specially great. This appears repeatedly in the Maccabaean martyrologies. The youngest of the seven brothers appeals to God "through me and my brothers to bring to an end the wrath of the Almighty which has justly fallen on our whole nation."[54] This thought is amplified in *Fourth Maccabees*. Eleazar, in his mortal torments, prays: "Be merciful to thy people, and let our punishment be a satisfaction on their behalf. Make my blood their purification and take my soul as a ransom for theirs."[55] Through him, together with the seven brothers and their mother, the writer says, "our land was purified, they having become as it were a ransom for our nation's sin; and through the blood of these righteous ones and the propitiation of their death, Divine Providence delivered Israel . . . through them the nation obtained peace."[56]

We may wonder how far such a conception was encouraged by the prophetic precedent of the vicarious suffering of the 'Servant of Yahweh'[57] His portrayal does seem to have influenced the outlook of the Qumran community, who in their devotion to the law of God and consequent endurance of privation and persecution may well have considered themselves called to the corporate fulfilment of what was written concerning him. They plainly expected that by their piety and suffering they would accumulate a store of merit sufficient to make atonement for their misguided fellow-Israelites and to obtain favour for the land, polluted as it was by ungodly leaders.[58]

9. JUSTIFICATION BY GRACE

Alongside this doctrine of merit there appears, at least in the Qumran literature, something which Reformation theology has regarded as incompatible with it—a doctrine of justification by grace, which in some important features anticipates the teaching of Paul. In one of the *Hymns of Thanksgiving* this confession is made:

I know that righteousness does not belong to mortal man, nor perfection of way to a son of man. To God Most High belong all the works of righteousness, and the way of mortal man cannot be established except by the spirit that God has fashioned for him.[59]

Similarly the *Hymn of the Initiants,* which comes at the end of the *Rule of the Community,* says:

I will call God "my righteousness", and the Most High "the establisher of my good".[60]

What this involves comes repeatedly to expression in the same hymn.

By God's righteousness my sin is blotted out . . . When I stumble in the iniquity of my flesh, my judgement [lies] with the righteousness of God, which will stand for ever . . . In his compassion he draws me near, and in his loving-kindnesses he brings forth my judgement. In the righteousness of his truth he judges me and in the abundance of his goodness he makes atonement for all my iniquities; in his righteousness he cleanses me from the impurity of mortal man and from the sin of the sons of men, that I may praise God for his righteousness and the Most High for his glory.[61]

Here we recognize the twofold sense of "the righteousness of God" which we find in Paul—not only his personal righteousness but also (in Luther's words) "that righteousness whereby, through grace and sheer mercy, he justifies us by faith."[62] According to the Qumran *Hymns of Thanksgiving,* man has no righteousness of his own—at least "not before God", as Paul says of Abraham.

For none is righteous in judgement with thee, and none is innocent when he contends with thee. One mortal man may be more righteous than another; one man may have more understanding than another . . . but none can vie in strength with thy mighty works and thy glory is [unsearchable].[64]

It is not difficult in the opening words of this passage to discern an application of Ps. 51: 4 and Ps. 143: 2 similar to that made in Rom. 3: 4, 20. Again:

As for me, I said in my rebellion, "I have been rejected from thy covenant". But when I remembered the strength of thy hand with the multitude of thy compassions I was fortified; I arose and my spirit was strengthened, standing firmly in the face of affliction, for I have leaned upon thy loving-kindnesses and the multitude of thy compassions. For thou makest atonement for iniquity and cleanest mankind by thy righteousness—not for man's sake [but for thy glory] thou hast done it.[65]

Although this righteousness is not explicitly said to be received 'by faith', it is clearly the speaker's faith that enabled him to appropriate the righteousness which God imparted to him in grace.

A somewhat different viewpoint is expressed in the Qumran commentary on Habakkuk, where the words "The righteous shall live by his faith" are treated thus:

Its interpretation concerns all the doers of the law in the house of Judah, whom God will deliver from the place of judgement because of their travail and their fidelity to the Teacher of Righteousness.[66]

This "fidelity to the Teacher of Righteousness" probably implies faith in his teaching and acceptance of his guidance. If, however, the Teacher himself is the author of the *Hymns of Thanksgiving* (as many believe), his own deliverance "from the place of judgement" could not depend on "fidelity to the Teacher of Righteousness". Since he acknowledged that his justification was due entirely to the mercy of God, faith in his teaching would logically involve a similar acknowledgement; but when we reflect how rarely Paul's teaching on this subject appears to have been properly appreciated in the post-apostolic Church, even among those who venerated his memory, we need not be surprised if many followers of the Teacher of Righteousness could not sustain his pure doctrine of justification by grace alone and began to ascribe some part in their justification to the merit accumulated by their endurance and fidelity. They did indeed aim at a standard which exceeded the righteousness of the scribes and Pharisees (whom they called "seekers after smooth things" or "givers of smooth interpretations");[67] and they may well have come to believe that their endurance and fidelity, which was calculated to procure atonement for the land, would incidentally win for themselves acceptance before God.

10. RESURRECTION AND IMMORTALITY

Only in a very few places in the later Old Testament do we find the belief in the resurrection of the dead (at least of the righteous dead) clearly expressed;[68] in the New Testament this belief is part of accepted Jewish orthodoxy, the Sadducees only (who in this as in other respects filled the role of 'old believers') being out of step.[69]

The scepticism which *Ecclesiastes* evinces with regard to any life after death[70] persists in Ben Sira, for whom the only immortality worth mentioning is posterity's remembrance of a good man's virtues, especially when these are reproduced in his descendants (this is the theme of the section on the Praise of the Elders, beginning "Let us now praise famous men . . .").[71] "Whether life is for ten or a hundred or a thousand years," says he, "there is no enquiry about it in Sheol."[72] A generation after Ben Sira, however, the persecution under Antiochus Epiphanes stimulated a great upsurge of belief in resurrection. When loyalty to God's commandments no longer meant length of days in the land but early and painful martyrdom, the world to come was invoked to redress the unjust balance of the present life. This emerges clearly in the martyrologies of *Second Maccabees,* where one pious Jew after another readily surrenders his body to torture and death, assured that the mutilated limbs will be restored in their integrity. "I got these from Heaven," says one of the seven brothers, holding out his hands to be cut off, ". . . and from him I hope to get them back again."[73] So he and his fellow-martyrs, as the writer to the Hebrews puts it, "were tortured, refusing to accept release [by apostasy], that they might rise again to a better life".[74] Not only the martyrs, but even some of Judas Maccabaeus's soldiers on whose bodies, after they had fallen in battle, pagan amulets were found, were believed to be destined for the resurrection of the just,

This, at least, is the inference drawn from the fact that Judas presented a sin-offering on their behalf, "for if he were not expecting that those who had fallen would rise again, it would have been superfluous and foolish to pray for the dead."[75] This outlook, which characterized the *hasidim* during these critical years, was inherited by the Pharisees and others who shared the hasidic heritage.

A view of immortality as something to be enjoyed immediately after death, and not postponed until a future epoch, as bodily resurrection was, is found towards the end of the inter-testamental period in *Wisdom* and *Fourth Maccabees*. According to the former book,

> the souls of the righteous are in the hand of God,
>   and no torment will ever touch them.
> In the eyes of the foolish they seemed to have died, . . .
>   but they are at peace.[76]

In *Fourth Maccabees*, unlike the material resurrection hope of *Second Maccabees*, emphasis is placed on the supremacy of divinely inspired reason over bodily passions, and it is the martyrs and others like them who, "wholeheartedly making reason their first thought, are alone able to master the weakness of the flesh, believing that unto God they die not, as our patriarchs Abraham, Isaac and Jacob died not, but that they live unto God".[77] We cannot overlook the affinity between these words and Jesus' reply to the Sadducees, as rendered by the Gentile evangelist Luke.[78] It is possible that here *Wisdom* and *Fourth Maccabees* exhibit the influence of Greek thought, which is no more deplorable than the influence of Iranian thought.

II. ANGELS AND DEMONS

The Pharisees' belief in resurrection, followed by judgement and the life of the age to come, was probably denounced by the Sadducees as a 'Persianizing' of the old-time religion, because it seemed to import features of Zoroastrian doctrine.[79] The Pharisaic belief in angelic and demonic hierarchies was similarly rejected by the Sadducees.[80] The "seven holy angels who present the prayers of the saints and enter into the presence of the glory of the Holy One"[81] and whose names are listed in *First Enoch*[82] may well be influenced by the 'immortal holy ones'[83] of Zoroastrianism, while the relation of Asmodaeus[84] and his fellow-demons to the *daevas* of Zoroastrianism is patent (Asmodaeus being *Aesma-daeva*, the "angry demon", one of the seven *daevas*). The part played by the angel Raphael as guide, philosopher and friend to young Tobias recalls the Iranian concept of the *fravasi* or spirit-counterpart—a concept familiar to New Testament readers from the story of Peter knocking at Mary's door, when those within say "It is his angel."[85]

The Deuteronomic doctrine of the allocation of the nations of earth among the 'sons of God' becomes more explicit in inter-testamental angelology;[86] moreover, the natural elements —air, fire, water and so forth—are controlled by their appropriate angels.[87]

12. MESSIANIC HOPE AND KINGDOM OF GOD

The lively expectation of a restoration of the royal house of David, cherished at the time of the return from exile, seems to have grown dim with the disappearance of Prince Zerubbabel from public life,[88] and so far as our literature is any guide it is found only sporadically between that time and the Roman conquest, when it burns high again. The 'Palm Sunday' oracle of Zech. 9: 9 f., where Jerusalem is bidden to rejoice at the approach of her king, "humble and riding on an ass", evidently has the Davidic Messiah in view. The promise that

> his dominion shall be from sea to sea,
> and from the River to the ends of the earth

is a clear echo of the prayer for the Davidic king in Ps. 72: 8.

The Hasmonaean rulers who established their own dynasty of priest-kings after winning independence from the Seleucids did not encourage aspirations after a monarchy of another line than theirs. But in some circles the hope of a Prince of the house of David was cherished, and one of the causes of

resentment against the Hasmonaeans in the *Psalms of Solomon*
(*c.* 50 B.C.) is that they "laid waste the throne of David".[89] In
these *Psalms* the Romans are recognized as the instruments of
divine judgement on the Hasmonaeans, but the Romans'
oppressive empire is to vanish in its turn; the psalmist and his
associates pin their hopes to the promised son of David.

> See, Lord, raise up for them their king, the son of David,
>> In a time which thou knowest, O God,
>> That he may reign over Israel thy servant,
> And gird him with strength to dash in pieces the unjust ruler. ...
>
> He will have the nations to serve him under his yoke,
>> And he will glorify the Lord with the praise of all the earth;
> He will purify Jerusalem in holiness, as it was from the beginning,
>> That the nations may come from the ends of the earth to see his
>> glory,
> Bearing gifts for her sons that were utterly weakened,
>> And to see the glory of the Lord with which God has glorified
>> her;
> A righteous king, taught by God, is he who rules over them,
>> And there shall be no unrighteousness in their midst all his days,
>> For all will be holy, and their king is the anointed Lord.[90]

The last words of this quotation, *christos kyrios* in Greek, are
identical with those in which the herald angel outside
Bethlehem announces the birth of "a Saviour, who is Christ the
Lord".[91] The group of pious Israelites, members of "the quiet
in the land", whom we meet in Luke's nativity narrative, may
not have been at all unlike the group among whom the *Psalms
of Solomon* were composed a few decades earlier.[92] The canticles
in Luke's narrative breathe the same eager expectation of
God's raising up "a horn of salvation ... in the house of his
servant David"[93]—a salvation incarnate in the prince of whom
Gabriel says:

> The Lord God will give him the throne of his father David:
> and he will reign over the house of Jacob for ever;
> and of his kingdom there will be no end.[94]

The Qumran community also cherished the hope of the

Davidic Messiah, in fulfilment of a wide range of ancient oracles. In Jacob's prophecy that the sceptre would not depart from Judah,[95] in Balaam's vision of the "star out of Jacob",[96] in Nathan's oracle on the establishment of David's dynasty,[97] in Amos's prediction of the raising up of David's fallen booth,[98] in Isaiah's description of the "shoot from the stump of Jesse",[99] the men of Qumran saw references to 'the rightful Messiah'[100] of the latter days. When the Qumran texts mention 'the Messiah' without qualification,[101] they mean the Davidic Messiah, envisaged as a warrior king. Sometimes, however, they designate him 'the Messiah of Israel' (the lay Messiah) to distinguish him from 'the Messiah of Aaron', the anointed priest of the latter days, who will be head of state in the new age and have precedence over the Davidic Messiah,[102] just as in Ezekiel's blueprint for the new commonwealth 'the prince' (given the name of David) is subordinate to the priesthood.[103]

Alongside the Messiahs of Israel and Aaron one phase of Qumran expectation looked for the promised prophet like Moses to arise at the end-time,[104] though the prophet is not called a Messiah. This phase of Qumran expectation is in line with the Samaritan doctrine of the 'Restorer'.[105] In the New Testament Jesus is acclaimed as this eschatological prophet[106] (in addition to being hailed as the son of David) and this was the aspect of his ministry that in later generations was chiefly emphasized among the Ebionites.[107]

The evidence of the *Testaments of the Twelve Patriarchs* is problematical because, apart from Hebrew and Aramaic fragments found in the Old Cairo synagogue (see p. 43 above) and at Qumran, they have come down to us in a Greek Christian recension.[108] In their original form they were probably in line with the Qumran texts, acknowledging that God had given the kingship to the tribe of Judah and the priesthood to the tribe of Levi, but emphasizing that "as the heaven is higher than the earth, so is the priesthood of God higher than the earthly kingdom".[109] When, however, we find the announcement that "a king shall arise out of Judah and shall establish a new priesthood ... for all Gentiles",[110] it is not difficult to recognize the hand of a Hellenistic Christian editor. Similarly, when another passage assigns the kingship as well as the priesthood to the tribe of Levi,[111] we may recognize a supporter of the Hasmonaean dynasty at work on the text.

In the *Similitudes of Enoch*[112] the Messiah, also called 'the Righteous One' and 'the Elect One',[113] is a being of heavenly origin, identified with "that son of man" who "was named in the presence of the Lord of spirits . . . before the sun and the signs were created, before the stars of heaven were made".[114] This 'son of man' is probably a corporate entity, the community of the righteous and elect, but individualized from time to time in some outstandingly righteous person, like Enoch in his day.[115] In the *Ezra Apocalypse* a 'man' who comes up from the sea and flies with the clouds of heaven to judge the ungodly and deliver creation is acknowledged by God as his Son[116] and described in terms which elsewhere in the same apocalypse are used of the Messiah.[117]

With the divergent concepts of an earthly and a heavenly Messiah go the divergent concepts of the kingdom of God to which his people may look forward—on the one hand, a kingdom on this earth (after it has been duly purified by judgement);[118] on the other hand, an entirely new order of heavenly character to be established after the present creation has been annihilated.[119] These two concepts are not always kept completely apart in inter-testamental literature: some writers attempt to make the best of both worlds by envisaging a kingdom of limited duration on this earth followed by the bliss of the eternal state.[120] Such a reconciliation of the two concepts has persisted in certain phases of Christian eschatology.

Whatever estimate may be placed on the religious value or theological authority of the inter-testamental literature, a study of it brings us much closer to the threshold of the Christian revelation than if we confined our knowledge of its background to the Old Testament books, excluding or even including the Apocrypha.

For further reading

PRIMARY WORKS

Most of the primary texts are available in English translation in the encyclopaedic *Apocrypha and Pseudepigrapha of the Old Testament*, 2 volumes, edited by R. H. Charles, Clarendon Press, Oxford, 1913, reprinted 1963, and in the conveniently small volumes of the S.P.C.K. "Translations of Early Documents"—Series I, Palestinian Jewish Texts (Pre-Rabbinic), 1917 ff; Series II, Hellenistic Jewish Texts, 1917 ff; Series III, Palestinian Jewish Texts (Rabbinic), 1919 ff. The non-biblical Qumran texts published to date have been translated by T. H. Gaster, *The Dead Sea Scriptures in English Translation*, Doubleday, New York, 1956; A. Dupont-Sommer, *The Essene Writings from Qumran*, Blackwell, Oxford, 1961; G. Vermes, *The Dead Sea Scrolls in English*, Pelican, Harmondsworth, 1962. The best edition of the works of Philo is that in the Loeb Classical Library, Harvard University Press, Cambridge, Mass., and Heinemann, London, 10 volumes, Greek text with English translation by F. H. Colson and G. H. Whitaker (1929–62), with two supplementary volumes by R. Marcus (1961).

A SELECTION OF OTHER WORKS IN ENGLISH

These are arranged in order from the less technical to the more technical.

H. Anderson, "The Intertestamental Period", in *The Bible and History*, ed. W. Barclay, Lutterworth, London, 1968, pp. 153–244.

T. W. Manson, *The Servant-Messiah*, Cambridge University Press, 1953.

E. R. Bevan, *Jerusalem under the High Priests*, Arnold, London, 1904.

B. M. Metzger, *An Introduction to the Apocrypha*, Oxford University Press, 1957.

D. S. Russell, *Between the Testaments*, S.C.M., London, 1960, and *The Jews from Alexander to Herod*, Clarendon Press, Oxford, 1967.

H. H. Rowley, *The Relevance of Apocalyptic*, 3rd ed., Lutterworth, London, 1963.

R. Bultmann, *Primitive Christianity in its Historical Setting*, Collins, London, 1960.

E. R. Goodenough, *An Introduction to Philo Judaeus*, Yale University Press, New Haven, 1940.

W. R. Farmer, *Maccabees, Zealots and Josephus*, Columbia University Press, New York, 1956.

F. F. Bruce, *Biblical Exegesis in the Qumran Texts*, Tyndale, London, 1960.

K. Stendahl (ed.), *The Scrolls and Christian Origins*, S.C.M., London, 1958.

A. R. C. Leaney, *The Rule of Qumran and its Meaning*, S.C.M., London, 1966.

D. S. Russell, *The Method and Message of Jewish Apocalyptic*, S.C.M., London, 1964.

M. D. Hooker, *The Son of Man in Mark*, S.P.C.K., London, 1967.

F. H. Borsch, *The Son of Man in Myth and History*, S.C.M., London, 1967.

R. Otto, *The Kingdom of God and the Son of Man*, 2nd ed., Lutterworth, London, 1943.

J. Klausner, *The Messianic Idea in Israel*, Macmillan, New York, 1955.

S. Mowinckel, *He that Cometh*, Blackwell, Oxford, 1956.

M. Black, *The Scrolls and Christian Origins*, Nelson, London, 1961.

5

THE STUDY OF CHURCH HISTORY

E. GORDON RUPP
Dixie Professor of Ecclesiastical History, University of Cambridge

5

The Study of Church History

From death and Dark Oblivion (near the same)
The Mistress of Man's life, grave History,
Raising the world to good or evil fame,
Doth vindicate it to eternity.

High Providence would so: that nor the good
Might be defrauded, nor the great secured,
But both may know their ways are understood
And their reward and punishment assured.

SIR WALTER RALEIGH, poignantly summoned from the manuscript of his unfinished *Universal History* to his execution in the Tower, poignantly epitomizes his generation, with its preoccupation with death and mortality, and therefore with history. He inherited the traditional Christian view of Providence which derived from the Bible, and which combined the great Old Testament perception of the transitoriness of our human existence with the Christian urgency which gives to each moment an eschatological meaning. It is a view which has lingered, even when the Christian faith itself has vanished from the conscious mind, and it was classically expressed by J. A. Froude:

One lesson, and one only, history may be said to repeat with distinctness . . . that the world is built somehow on moral foundations, that in the long run it is well with the good: in the long run, it is ill with the wicked. But this is no more than the old doctrine taught long ago by the Hebrew prophets.

Modern men do not take kindly to this old moralistic view of history as a game of "Snakes and Ladders". They prefer the smash and grab of sociological "Monopoly". It is an age, as Thomas Fuller would have said, which has a crick in its neck so that it is unable to look backwards, let alone to think of history as he thought of it as a beautiful and entrancing "velvet study". More congenial to us is the scepticism of Dylan Thomas's Samuel Bennett with his wild cry, "History is lies..." And many would echo the sentiments of a modern schoolboy who found it the most pointless and boring of subjects.

> History was horrible: it drove you up the wall. And we didn't know nothing about it.——Napoleon and some battle. We'd say "We aint got no interest in this". And he'd say, "Then you've got to find interest: it may come in useful for you ... don't you ever read the papers?"... Yes, he said that all that junk would help you read the papers.[1]

It is unfortunately true that, of all disciplines, history suffers most at the text book stage: when, dehydrated, it becomes too often a catalogue of dates, events and names, meaningless, boring and irrelevant. It is true that those who study history must bring something to it, which includes a minimum of intelligence and interest. Wilfred Rhodes once said to a young cricketer, "God Himself can't put cricket into you unless there's something there already." Yet it may be hoped that it would belong to the education of most people in the coming generation, that they should learn from historical study what we might call "the language of the century". At present there must be millions who pass through our schools who would not know what to do with a book more than fifty years old, who would be offended by its get-up and its print, and who regard it as incomprehensible antiquarianism seriously to study a book which they regard as "very old—it's 's's were spelled like 'f's". To begin to master the language of the centuries means at least to be aware that men of other centuries may speak to us, and that we can understand at least part of their conversation with one another.

There are two things requisite to historical study, besides intelligent interest. It requires imagination. Without it, to study the past is like exploring the catacombs without a torch: you will not get far, and you will soon be lost, and you will not care to repeat the experience. But if imagination is the right hand of the historian, scepticism is the other. Without it, imagination leads astray, into romanticism or journalism. "Who knows whether this is true?" murmured the young monk Martin Luther as they told him the manifold and improbable marvels of the churches of Rome, and the student of history takes as little as possible for granted, is ready to question himself at every turn, submits his tentative conclusions to the rough criticism of the learned world, and like his fellow historians is ready to re-open any case on the submission of fresh evidence. At the heart of his discipline must be intellectual integrity. And this is why when we speak of intelligence, of imagination, of scepticism we add the equally important phrase—"controlled by evidence". The historian must be dedicated to the pursuit of truth to follow it wherever it leads and at whatever cost. It is because of this that a great succession of eminent and distinguished scholars, and multitudes of men and women who make no great claims for themselves but have enjoyed the study of history, have been glad to give of their time, and some their lifetime, to its pursuit. This is why, in the end, no university dare be without its history departments, and why the study of the past, and of man's reflections upon it, is a genuine part of Christian civilization. To perform the historian's task demands, at the highest level, the sensitive skill which consultant surgeons must bring to serious operations. And when we have called in Gibbon, and Macaulay, Froude, Ranke, Acton and the great company of more recent historians to bear witness to the dignity of the historian's craft, we had better remember Sir Herbert Butterfield's reminder that, after all, the historian is just a man sitting at a desk. He had better play the fool, than the part of God.

It has been necessary to say something about historical study, because those who see no point in it will find even less in the consideration of the story of the Church—an institution which many believe to be irrelevant to the modern world, and to the coming age. And one must ask seriously, Can the study of Church History fruitfully continue if reduced to the study of "that without which our present society cannot be understood" by reason of its involvement in the history of Western culture? Will it not be plausibly argued that Church History is so much at the mercy of dogmatic and pietistic presuppositions that it had better be left to those who can study it objectively and from without, simply as one among many human and religious institutions, and as a sociological phenomenon?

It was an insight of Newman to insist that, where a subject belongs to the spectrum of truth, you cannot remove it without creating a vacuum, and into it other subjects will then move, never quite filling the vacant space. What he applied to the place of theology in a university we may apply to the study of Church History within a theological faculty. Take it away and religious sociology, the history of ideas, and comparative religion (each of them a thoroughly legitimate discipline in its own place) will try, unsuccessfully, to take its place.

The first thing which then happens is to drive a wedge between the history of the Church as an institution (the German *Institutionsgeschichte*) and that of its invisible, inward life *(Geistesgeschichte)*. But in the end, and at critical points, the clues vanish from the outward and objective study of an institution, not simply into the history of ideas, but into faith and devotion, from Popes and Bishops and the structured church into the minds and hearts of saints and theologians. And yet this quality of interiority is constant in Church History, and not least those characteristic and, one might say, idiosyncratic aspects which mark the Church off from the other sacral institutions of religious man, and which will not be crammed into the typological straitjackets which from the time of Troeltsch have been the bane of sociologists.

This becomes obvious when we press the question, What is the 'Church' which is the object of this historical study? Since in our time it is fashionable to question the validity of the institutional, structured church, there is a tendency to return to an older sectarian view of Church History, as it began with Gottfried Arnold's *Unparteiische Kirchen- und Ketzer Historie*

(1700), which so stressed the virtues of the rebels throughout history as to turn received interpretation inside out. But this is to dissolve the continuity of Church History into isolated pockets of spiritual religion, or pure philanthropy, an anti-Establishment history of the kind which minority movements, from the Pietists to the modern radicals, find congenial.

For the rest of this chapter we shall treat of Church History as a proper colour within the spectrum of Christian Theology. Keeping the rules of the historical game, which apply to all historical investigation, there are certain Christian pre-suppositions which give coherence and sense to the story as a whole. On this view the Church is the People of God, and its story stretches from the dim borderlands between myth and history, from tribes of wandering nomads in the Middle East, to the 400 or so present varieties of institutional Christianity, and an indefinable penumbra of Christian influence.

But this definition begs questions about the meaning of God and the significance of time. History happens forwards along the flow of time. It is recorded backwards, however, and the historian works by hindsight, through the modern historians and their interpretations, through documents to events and to people, in the attempt finally to discover springs of human action about which a great part of the evidence has disappeared, and where perhaps some of the main clues are no longer intelligible. But this is why dates are important to the historian, for they peg down the progress of events which cannot happen again and can never 'un-happen'. A recent learned work on the philosophy of history repeated thrice in one page the historical inaccuracy that Martin Luther appeared at the Diet of Worms in 1525, and not in 1521. Dates, it might be inferred, were trivial things, in comparison with interpretations and meanings. And yet the whole setting of the Church in Germany, and not least the career of Luther himself, was changed in those four years between 1521 and 1525 by reason of what happened to him in April 1521. The kaleidoscope was shaken and the old pattern gone for ever. Thus the historian looks backward, like some mountaineer who looks along the path down into the foothills and the valley until all is blurred in the misty distance.

The Christian has also to look at history another way. The "things concerning Jesus of Nazareth" are central to the whole—and less like a straight line going back than a rock flung into the middle of a lake, from which the ripples spread out in ever widening circles.

> "The ecclesiastical historian is made constantly aware", wrote Norman Sykes, "that the Christian church which is the subject of his study claims to have its origin and foundation in a series of events in the life of its founder, of unique significance for the entire process of history to which they give meaning and purpose"[2].

For this reason, strictly speaking, New Testament studies, criticism and historical investigation are part of Church History and fundamental to it. They are also an excellent example of historical study 'in depth'. The rules of textual criticism, for example as defined by the great Cambridge scholar Hort, could be applied to other complexes of historical documents. Here is a great concentration of international scholarship, using the methods and accepting the canons of historical scholarship. But these events concerning Jesus of Nazareth and the first rise of the Christian religion cannot be understood, either, without the investigation of their entire historical context, and above all the study of the history and religion of Israel. In a sense, Old Testament studies also are part of Church History, in so far as they deal with the story of the People of God. What the significance of Jewish history is for Christians involves theological questions to which different Christian answers have been given from the time of Paul and Augustine, down to the recent commission of the World Council of Churches which is directing its attention to the significance of Israel in the divine economy of redemption, in the light of events in World War II.

But if for present purposes we except New Testament and Old Testament studies from consideration as Church History we might remember that two famous pairs of scholars, Westcott and Hort in England, and Adolf Harnack and Karl Holl in

Germany, insisted that you must not drive a wedge between the New Testament and the Early Church. The last half-century has underlined the point: archaeology, the Dead Sea Scrolls, the discoveries of Gnostic treatises in Egypt, have shed a good deal of light, as well as a certain amount of darkness, on New Testament studies. For this reason the study of the Early Church is indispensable as an ancillary to Biblical studies. It is also of immense importance in its own right. Hardly less important for the development of the Christian religion than its Jewish origins, is the Hellenistic-Roman culture into which the Christian Church emerged.

Not that Christianity is simply to be explained in terms of what it derived, so to speak, from its heredity and its environment. All important is its own dimension, its own way of life. We have to trace how a Jewish sect beginning amid unpromising circumstances, became a great world religion. The story of the first three centuries is, as T. R. Glover said, the story of the gradual and victorious spread of Christianity because the early Christians "out-lived, out-thought, out-died" the world around them. And if that sounds exuberant, we might remember Adolf Harnack's sombre comment that no religion could have spread so far and so fast simply by relying on its finest impulses and appealing only to the noblest motives.

Sir Herbert Butterfield has said that the one Christian dogma which history confirms is that of Original Sin, and the comment has its bearing on Church History, including the Early Church and not least those happenings in the first centuries which drew the scorn and irony of Gibbon. In that period and in the Age of the Fathers which succeeded the persecutions, the Christians faced problems of understanding, articulating and communicating their faith. They had on the one hand to understand their Jewish inheritance in terms of the new dimension of Christian experience, and they had then to express it in words and in a way of life embedded in Graeco-Roman culture. Using languages of varying flexibility and richness, they sought to understand what all this meant for the Christian doctrine of God, and for their belief and understanding about the Person of Christ. The result was a great corporate research across centuries which must rank among the outstanding intellectual achievements of mankind. Their findings were far from being as definitive as they perhaps imagined: they were limited by the philosophic and theological tools available to them, and by a host of non-theological factors less easy to appraise. But they did face these theological problems as they emerged in history, so that the study of Christian doctrine, not least in its origins, can never simply be left to the systematic theologians, but must always keep in step with the study of Church History.

As with faith, so with worship, and so with structure. This is why the study of the first five centuries is a normative period of Church History, and why scholars turn back again and again to the study of the Early Church, and indeed why the whole Church comes again and again to circle in ascending spirals over the great questions and answers given in the centuries which lie between the New Testament and St Augustine. It is the one essential period of study in Church History. Beside it the Reformation is of secondary importance, and more recent periods, for all their attractive relevances to our own time, can if need be be 'got up' by students on their own.

If Church History syllabuses often seem to leapfrog from the Early Church to the Reformation, it is not from undervaluing the significance of mediaeval ecclesiastical history, but because of the size and complexity of this thousand years of European history. The complete involvement of the Christian religion in an entire culture has involved a great network of historical study, such as can only in most universities be compassed by an autonomous department of mediaeval history. Mediaeval studies have always attracted great scholars and some of the best students, even though they make demands of a daunting kind in the way of technical tools, languages, palaeography and the like.

As Western Europe collapsed in the fifth–sixth centuries, the Eastern half of the Roman Empire made an astonishing series of partial recoveries, and in our century Byzantine studies have become an important and fascinating field, not least in the history of culture, art and architecture. For many centuries Byzantium was the bastion of Christendom, in its defence against the Persians and against the successive waves of attack from Islam. "We have all of us sheltered under the walls of Constantinople" is a saying of Sir Eric Maclagan which reminds students of the West of their standing debt to the Eastern Empire. In the West there came, in the seventh and eighth centuries the second conversion of Europe, as the Church attempted the baptism into Christ of the 'gentes', the tribes pressing down from the forests and mountains of the north and east. Here British Christianity, Celtic and Roman, knew its finest hour. From its monasteries and nunneries came a devoted and heroic missionary movement, and a succession of great and saintly men and women, while around them there was renewed an impressive culture of which the Lindisfarne Gospels and the Book of Kells are impressive memorials. The Venerable Bede had the gifts and instincts of a true historian, and his beautiful and often moving *Ecclesiastical History of the English Nation* is on that short list of classics of historical study which all students should have read.

With the ninth century and with the court of Charlemagne we enter the mediaeval period, and the slow emergence of Christendom. On the one hand, the institutional church centred in the Papacy, at its best a model and example to the secular kingdoms and ahead of them in law and government. But at every level in feudal society, from the Pope and Emperor at the top of the pyramid to the lord of the manor and parish priest at the bottom, there was tension, conflict and in the end compromise, about the relative rights and duties of the spiritual and the temporal powers. If involvement in the secular order be the mark of maturity, then European man came of age in the eleventh century. Indeed so closely was the Christian religion involved in the surrounding culture that in all this thousand years there are few entirely secular and few entirely spiritual problems and none that can be studied at any length without involving the whole bundle of mediaeval life. This is but one side of mediaeval church history. Episcopal and parish organization, the development of canon law and papal administration have been centres of scholarly investigation and given rise to classical works of historical writing. The histories of the religious and mendicant orders, of the mystics and of spirituality, of heresies, of frustrated movements of renewal are almost equally full of problems for historical investigation. And the historian of culture, as a host of 'coffee table' picture books attest, has an embarrassment of riches as he seeks to describe the buildings and cathedrals, the glories of glass, mosaic and paintings, the universities and the great intellectual ferment which produced the massive systems of the great Schoolmen, which have been well described as 'Cathedrals of the Mind'.

The Protestant Reformation of the sixteenth century was a great, long-deferred ecclesiastical explosion which shook the world and the Church to its foundations. But it is becoming more and more apparent that there are important clues lying in the fifteenth century which in this respect is perhaps itself something of a 'tunnel' period where we need many more monographs, and much more research. As an earthquake might divide a river into separate streams each coursing its own tumultuous way and, as they go, making their own valleys, so with astonishing swiftness, new Christian patterns of faith and spirituality emerged, to go their own separate and divided ways into the modern world, taking form in the institutional confessions of Lutheranism, the Reformed churches, and the national churches in England and Scandinavia.

Despite much that was destructive, and the non-theological element which increased as the religious and theological protest became earthed in legal, political and in the end military ploys, there was an important creative ferment, and Luther's Bible and Catechism, Cranmer's Prayer Books, Calvin's *Institutes*, Hooker's *Laws of Ecclesiastical Polity* were productions of great merit, whose influence would endure for centuries, nourishing the souls of many millions. Reformation studies are still a moving and rewarding field, and Luther research alone attracts an international congress drawing on twenty-five nations, and involving hundreds of scholars. Most recently the editing and publishing of masses of documents concerning the Anabaptists has directed attention to the radical reformation, and has already led to a partial re-appraisal of traditional judgements.

Although Protestantism turned very quickly into its own world, the schism in the Church was a deep wound which was sorely felt. But apart from the Catholic reaction against what was felt to be heresy and error, and those parts of the so called 'Counter-Reformation' which were consciously directed against Protestantism, two further Catholic phases are to be noted. The first is what it is customary nowadays to call the 'Catholic Reformation', the renewal of the Catholic church which at least in Spain and Italy had begun before Luther's protest and which with persistent growth brought into being new religious orders, new forms of spirituality, new saints, and achieved a real measure of reform of the church in head and members, in life and discipline.

The one Christendom disintegrated into the many nations of modern Europe and henceforth the separateness of national cultures makes it difficult to comprehend the whole story of the one Church. As on a stage the leading characters in turn take their bow, and the spotlight is turned on them, so Spain, and then Holland, and then France dominate the European story in the seventeenth and eighteenth centuries. In England and America the religious and intellectual movements compre-hended within Puritanism became an important historical complex. Thenceforward American church history demands study in its own right, from the conquest and evangelization of Latin America by the Catholic church, and the expansion and revivals of Protestantism in North America.

The sixteenth century was still a Christian Europe, and the Reformers shared fundamental doctrines with their Catholic opponents. Overt unbelief, atheism, was an isolated and rare phenomenon. But the seventeenth century brought what Paul Hasard has called 'the crisis of European conscience', whereby as he says, France began the century by believing Christianity with

Bossuet and ended by disbelieving with Voltaire. The age of zeal, of Protestant Orthodoxy, of Jansenism and Puritanism, of Catholic triumphalism, the whole outlook of a century of religious wars, never without some religious and theological content, led to an inevitable reaction in the rational worldliness of the Enlightenment. In Germany and in America and England there were revivals of inward religion in the movements of Pietism and of the Evangelical Revival. The growth of the modern secular omnicompetent state brought new problems of the relation of spiritual and temporal power in Catholic countries, and in the movements of Josephinism and Febronianism. Much more desperate was the plight of the Church in France at the beginning of the French Revolution, face to face with a revolutionary ideology of human rights of which the Puritan Civil War and the War of Independence in America had shown premonitions. Thereafter the churches in Catholic countries were caught in the tensions of the liberal and national revolutions which swept Europe in 1815 and in 1848, and in the whole problem of reconciling Christian truth with the new learning of a dozen new scientific and historical disciplines which assaulted the minds of men in the first half of the nineteenth century. The whole of the nineteenth century with its diversity between nations, its common problems, its array of great men, its successes and failures in dealing with problems which still confront the Church, represents so interesting and even exciting a period, that one feels that this period, of all the periods of Church History, needs no argument, no persuasive, to induce students to pay attention to it and to concentrate their researches at this point. It is a period when the sociology of religion has much to give us, where it is possible to ask and to answer social and economic questions for which in many earlier periods the evidence fails.

But how narrow all this discussion of European Church History sounds to a reader living outside! Latourette's famous *History of the Expansion of Christianity* reminds us that the Church has spread into other lands and all continents, and not least during the remarkable expansion of missionary movements in the last three centuries. The Jesuits in China and India, the

Methodists in the West Indies and the Pacific, David Livingstone in Africa raise problems of the relation between religion
and culture which are far from being solved. In Africa and in
India, more attention is being paid to their own church history.

Contemporary history has become respectable in our life-time.
It need not degenerate into a superficial journalism. And indeed
the problems of our own age, and not least of faith, worship and
communication in the contemporary world, is of great importance for the ecclesiastical historian. His is not, or ought not to
be, an antiquarian dilettantism, but like every other Christian
his supreme concern is with the 'now', with the present,
existential, transient moment in which he is called to think
and speak and act. If the Christian Church is not to be like the
French Army, always ready for the last war, it will need church
historians who bring the lesson of the past to the study of the
present.

Without capitulating to the errors of patterned history,
pious, moralistic, ideological, while there are no 'lessons from
history' written in red, and while there are no laws of history,
there may be profitable clues. If we reject Bernard Shaw's
cynical remark that the only thing a man learns from
experience is that we learn nothing from experience, then we
may believe that as a man may learn from his mistakes, so the
People of God may learn from their experience, their experiences of folly, failure and mistake and their gratitude for the
action of divine grace. The People of God are a remembering
People; this is written in all their worship, and all their creeds
and confessions, and because this living *anamnesis* (recollection)
is at the heart of their existence, the church historians who are
their Remembrancers, have their important function. We
spoke on an earlier page about the language of the centuries
which all students of human history should learn. But for the
Christian this is of special importance, since all Christians of
all generations are contemporary with God in Christ, and so
with one another: they have this living experience of the one
God in common, at a deeper level than all the external and
bewildering differences of age, environment and culture. And a

Saul of Tarsus, a Pascal, a Dostoevski, may speak newly and disconcertingly to a later age, may intervene freshly to our modern ears, precisely at the points where they cut across our own presuppositions.

For Christians this communication between human beings across the centuries has added meaning. For them it is an important part of the doctrine of the Communion of Saints. The sharing of holy things is a sign and symbol of the unity of the Church in heaven and on earth, of that "glorious and celestial city of God's faithful people" which, as Augustine said, "is seated in the course of these declining times" but also "chiefly in that solid estate of eternity". The Church includes within its memory the lives of holy men and women, its heroes and its martyrs, and it treasures their memorial in hymns and liturgies, in the story of manifold forms of mission. And for Christians these things are all given coherence by their link with their Lord and Leader. The doings of the Church are part of the "Magnalia Christi". These things were written for our example, upon whom the ends of the world have come.

For further reading

In this chapter we have felt it timely to concentrate on the rationale of the study of Church History. Excellent bibliographies and manuals of historical research exist in England and in America. Attention may be drawn, in England, to the publications of the Historical Association, and especially to *The History of the Church : a Select Bibliography*, by Owen Chadwick (rev. ed., 1966). On both sides of the Atlantic there are journals devoted to Church History (in America *Church History* and in England *The Journal of Ecclesiastical History*) and learned historical societies which hold conferences and colloquies. A final word to the student would be to remind him that he who would write well must first read well, and that there can be no substitute for reading the works of the great historians, for whom the English language has been as much a musical instrument as a tool.

6

CREEDS AND CONFESSIONS OF FAITH

T. H. L. PARKER

Vicar of Oakington, Cambridge

6

Creeds and Confessions of Faith

SYMBOL, CREED, CONFESSION OF FAITH

THE WORD 'symbol' as a designation for official confessions of faith was in use by the middle of the third century. No earlier example in the Western Church is known than that in a letter of St Cyprian; in the East it first occurs a whole century later. Why creeds should have been called symbols, however, has been a matter of controversy from early days. Was it, as Rufinus suggested (*c.* 400), that creeds were used as passwords for testing the orthodoxy of strange preachers? Not unrelated to this, there is the theory first put forward in the later nineteenth century that the word was borrowed from the mystery religions, in which a formula was often used, both in rites of initiation and as means of identification. The Greek word for symbol *(sumbolon)* could bear these senses and the Latin word *(symbolum)* was used to refer to the secret formulae of the mystery religions. But *sumbolon* could also mean 'agreement' or 'covenant'. Was the word used, then, to bring out the idea that in baptism, the sacrament setting up or ratifying the covenant between God and man, the candidate affirmed his side of the covenant by assent to the creed? Or, more simply, is 'symbol' to be taken in its general sense of 'sign', so that the confession of faith in the Triune God is a sign pointing to him? Whatever the reason, *symbolum* was commonly used as a synonym for 'creed' from the fifth century onwards and retained its place during the Middle Ages and the Reformation.

'Creed' is easier to understand, being derived from the old English word *creda*, which in turn comes from the Latin *credo*,

"I believe", with which the 'Apostles' and 'Nicene' Creeds begin. It is used to denote these two and the 'Athanasian' Creed, but not, usually, the statements of the Reformation and post-Reformation churches, which are called 'confessions of faith'.

'Confessions of faith' presents no difficulties to anyone acquainted with the numerous passages in the New Testament which exhort believers to confess before men their faith in Jesus Christ. In the creeds this confession of faith is trinitarian in form, although the second section, the Christological, is by far the longest. In the confessions, 'faith' has come to mean belief in doctrine rather than trust in a person (cf. p. 318, n.10).

THE SCOPE OF SYMBOLICS

It is no use pretending that Symbolics, the orderly study of Christian creeds and confessions of faith, is anything but a highly complicated discipline. The difficulty is partly historical, in that some of the necessary evidence either does not exist or is ambiguous; partly accidental, in that ingenious and plausible theories have been advanced which have to be taken into account and which often can be disproved, if at all, only by recourse to *minutiae* of antiquarian learning and by close-knit argument. We may see seven branches of this discipline.

1. *The general origin of creeds.* We know what form the developed creeds took, because we possess many examples of them besides the two most familiar. But how did they develop into this form? Why did they so develop? Putting it in concrete historical terms this means: Can we find creeds in the New Testament, and if not, when and why did they originate?

2. *The form of creeds.* There are two problems here. First, the structure of the creeds as we know them is threefold. Was it ever thus? Second, our creeds are declaratory, we declare our faith; but there is another form, still in common use, in which the person is interrogated: "Dost thou believe in...?" and he replies affirmatively. This form is called interrogatory. Is one of these forms earlier and so original?

3. *The purpose of creeds.* Granted that the confession of Jesus

Christ is an inherent part of the Christian faith, it is still necessary to note on what occasions in the life of the Church and individual Christians confession was demanded, either by events or by church order. This general problem has been sharpened to a particular issue by the insistence of some scholars that baptism (and training for baptism) was the original occasion of a formal declaration of faith. Most would now wish to include several other occasions.

4. *Textual criticism.* The purpose of textual criticism is (a) to restore, if possible, the original text; (b) to learn why the text was changed. The textual criticism of the creeds is a matter chiefly of recovering variant readings from early writings, from the *acta* of church councils, and from liturgies. It is employed in the endeavour to settle questions of date, authorship, and origin.

5. *Date and authorship.* Strictly speaking, these are two separate problems, but, where it is possible to enquire into authorship, date is inevitably concerned also. We are now thinking of creeds which actually exist and are not merely hypothetical reconstructions. It will rarely be possible to assign creeds to particular authors; usually it is a question of establishing their provenance, i.e. the church or district in which they originate.

6. *The use of creeds.* This enquiry is not concerned with the original use of creeds, which is considered under the third heading, *The purpose of creeds.* It asks what use the developed creeds were put to in the churches, and therefore deals with the place of creeds throughout Church history up to the present day.

7. *The meaning of the creeds.* This is a subject which, because of its wide scope, will be omitted from the present chapter. Yet it is the goal of all the branches of credal study that we have mentioned. This special subject can be considered either as the history of doctrines or as dogmatics. The history of doctrines is concerned with discovering what the framers of a symbol intended, or perhaps what later users of it thought it meant. The writer of dogmatics, however, while not contradicting the original intention but rather being guided by it, will be free to

expound the creed with reference to later theological thought down to his own day (see p. 30).

The way in which these branches of the study apply also to the later confessions of faith we shall see in our final section.

NEW TESTAMENT CONFESSIONS OF FAITH

If we start the narration of the history of the creeds with the New Testament, it is with the awareness that within those pages there is nothing that remotely resembles the developed creeds. So much is obvious. But we may be even more radical in the face of attempts to discover rudimentary creeds or even 'credal formulae' in the New Testament. That such exist cannot be denied. The indiscriminate description of almost any Christological or Trinitarian statement as a credal formula, however, is doubtful exegesis. Moreover, a warning may be given against the confusion of different forms. Hymns or sermons may be confessions of faith, cast in a single, binitarian, or trinitarian form, but they are not thereby credal formulae. We shall be on surer ground if we look for statements that not only have a certain credal appearance but also are set in a context (e.g. baptism) in which some sort of confession of faith is demanded, or are introduced by such a verb as 'to confess' or 'to believe'. We are left with a sufficient number of examples to see that in the New Testament there is evidence for the existence, not of fully developed creeds, but of basic confessions of faith. Thus, the calls to "be baptized in the name of Jesus Christ" (Acts 2: 38; 8: 12; 10: 48) or "in the name of the Lord Jesus" (Acts 8: 16; 19: 5) suggest that in baptism a confession of faith in Jesus Christ or in the Lordship of Christ was demanded and given. Formulae introduced by 'confess' and 'believe' can relate to various circumstances. Peter confesses directly to Jesus: "Thou art the Christ" (Mark 8: 29), or "the Son of the living God" (Matt. 16: 16). The Christian on trial confesses his faith in Christ before his judge (I Cor. 12: 3). The candidate at baptism and, after baptism, throughout his life, confesses in public, whether to Church or world, that

"Jesus is the Son of God" (I John 4: 15). Confirmation of this appears in the confession of the Ethiopian eunuch, according to the Western reading. To Philip's indirect question: "If you believe with all your heart, you may [be baptized]" he replies: "I believe that Jesus Christ is the Son of God", or "I believe in the Christ, the Son of God" (Acts 8: 37).

Besides this single form expressing faith in Christ, we also find in the New Testament confessions of faith in God and Christ (i.e. the Father and the Son) and in the Trinity. The *locus classicus* here, of course, is the command to make disciples of all nations "baptizing them in the name of the Father and of the Son and of the Holy Spirit" (Matthew 28: 19). It is often held that the single form must be the original and the dual and trinitarian later developments. Against this widely held view J. N. D. Kelly properly insists that "The juxtaposition of the Father and the Lord Jesus Christ as parallel realities and the collocation of the Father, the Son and the Holy Spirit had become categories of Christian thinking long before the New Testament documents were written down."[1]

There is sufficient evidence that, when in the first century confessions of faith were demanded, they were customarily expressed in certain settled formulae. Thus the New Testament and the earliest Church passed on to succeeding generations not only the raw stuff out of which creeds could be fashioned ('the faith', 'the deposit', 'the word', 'the teaching', and so on) but also the rudimentary forms of creeds themselves. Nor was the raw stuff, the doctrine, itself a formless lump, for it was shaped everywhere as the Gospel about Jesus Christ, the Son of God, who had bestowed his Spirit on the Church. The classic creeds might have been worded differently, their clauses might have been arranged in a different order, but their general form was inevitable, for it was demanded by the teaching, expressed or implicit, of the New Testament.

THE DEVELOPMENT OF THE CREED

Although there is difference of opinion on the subject, it would appear most probable that the chief (though not the only) occasion for confession of faith lay in baptism and the preparation for baptism. At his baptism the candidate confessed his faith in Jesus Christ, either in the form of a straightforward declaration or in response to questions. The former would thus be a recital of the 'creed', the latter the affirmation to an interrogation in credal form. Which of the two forms is to be regarded as the earlier has been questioned. In the very early account of the baptism of the Ethiopian eunuch in Acts 8, the form is delaratory, in that the eunuch says: "I believe that Jesus Christ is the Son of God."[2] Nevertheless the form used in Rome in the mid-second century was interrogatory and all the evidence up to the fourth century is very strongly in favour of the interrogatory form being the one commonly used in baptism. It is probable that the declaratory form grew out of the interrogatory, though without at first completely displacing it. In the third and fourth centuries a custom of secrecy surrounded the creeds. The form of the creed, divulged to the catechumen as a secret a few weeks earlier, was handed back by him to the bishop in baptism as a declaration of faith: "I believe in . . ."

Many credal statements are to be found in the writings of the second and third century fathers, just as in the New Testament, although now they have a fuller theological content. In opposition to the heathen or to heretics they will say that "We believe in . . ." or that "The Church believes in . . .", and then will follow a single, dual or trinitarian confession of faith. Some of these confessions are certainly framed for the occasion by their author, and have no direct relationship with the catechetical and baptismal form current in his local church. Thus the warning we gave against reading every Trinitarian or Christological statement in the New Testament as credal is relevant here also. Some, however, possibly echo that form, even when they do not profess to do so. But what is significant is that writers quite naturally used the credal form. It was as if the Church not only expressed itself credally but also thought credally, so common was the 'creed' as early as the second century. In the third century the creeds as we know them began to take shape.

THE APOSTOLICUM

The name 'Apostles' Creed' is a very ancient one. It occurs first in 390, in a letter written probably by St Ambrose on behalf of the Synod of Milan. About now, too, is first heard the legend of the apostolic origin. Each of the twelve apostles, it was said, contributed a clause so that there might be handed down to successive generations an authoritative and formal declaration of the apostolic faith. By perhaps the eighth century circumstantial details had been added and it was known which clauses were to be ascribed to which apostles. This story, which had not been accepted by the Eastern Church, was so firmly held in the West that as late as the fifteenth century Lorenzo Valla in Italy and Reginald Peacock in England got into serious trouble for doubting it; the latter, indeed, lost his bishopric.

What is popularly called the *Apostles' Creed* is more precisely a form of the creed of the Roman Church (R, as it is commonly entitled for convenience). It is possible to identify R from the book *Commentarius in symbolum apostolorum* by Tyrannius Rufinus (*c.* 404), for here Rufinus compares his own baptismal creed (he was from Aquileia) with that of Rome. This creed, R, runs as follows:

> I believe in God the Father almighty;
> and in Christ Jesus his only son, our Lord, who was born of the Holy Spirit and the Virgin Mary, who was crucified under Pontius Pilate and was buried, the third day he rose from the dead, he ascended into the heavens, he sits at the right hand of the Father, whence he shall come to judge the living and the dead;
> and in the Holy Spirit, the holy church, the forgiveness of sins, the resurrection of the flesh.

But R was not a recent growth in Rufinus' day. In 340 Marcellus of Ancyra had, at the Synod of Rome, stated by inference that he accepted the Roman creed, which he quotes in a form almost identical with Rufinus'. But it would seem that R is still older than this. It has come down in diglot (two language) form, of which the Greek appears to be, if anything, rather the earlier. The language situation that best fits the evidence is the period when Greek and not Latin was still commonly used in the Roman Church. Latin was supplanting Greek in the first half of the third century; when it was fairly in control there would be no point in composing a Greek creed. R ought perhaps therefore to be dated fairly early in the third century. Harnack would put it "at least as early as the year 200".[3] If this is so, we are within hailing distance of the early credal statements that were discussed above; and indeed, attempts to establish earlier forms of R in the second century have been made. Such attempts must always be considered tentative and hypothetical, though we are on firmer ground if we conjecture that during the second half of the second century or the early years of the third, R as a declaratory creed evolved out of a similarly worded interrogatory creed.

If the origins of R are obscure, however, it is far easier to trace its subsequent development, even though the facts are somewhat unexpected. In the first place, the Roman Church itself seems to have continued to preserve R in the form that we have seen it. But Rome was not the only church that used R: indeed, it is not improbable that in that city R was superseded by the Constantinopolitan creed. Very similar creeds to R are to be found throughout the West—in Italy, in Gaul, in North Africa, in Spain. By the seventh century R had been developed into the 'Apostles' Creed' as we know it today.

But it will have been noticed that R differs somewhat from our creed. The form in which we have it is usually called the received text, *textus receptus*, and hence T. It runs:

> I believe in God the Father almighty, creator of heaven and earth;
> And in Jesus Christ, his only Son, our Lord, who was conceived of the Holy Spirit, born from the Virgin Mary, suffered under Pontius Pilate, was crucified, dead and buried, he descended into hell, the third day he rose from the dead, he ascended into the heavens, he sits at the right hand of God the Father Almighty, thence he will come to judge the living and the dead;
> I believe in the Holy Spirit, the holy catholic church, the communion of saints, the forgiveness of sins, the resurrection of the flesh, and the life eternal.

About the year 500 Caesarius, bishop of Arles in the south-east of France, gave a creed which differs from T only in substituting for "his only son, our Lord" the words "his only begotten Son eternal" and in some verbal changes. Caesarius' creed is to be taken as a slightly different form of T. In the eighth century several creeds closely approximating to T are known. Scholars are not agreed on the birthplace of T, although it is now generally accepted that this was not Rome. The evidence points to southern France.[4]

THE NICAENO-CONSTANTINOPOLITAN CREED

We have traced the growth of what was probably an interrogatory creed into R and finally into T. The similar process must now be followed by which emerged the one ecumenical creed, that is, the one creed accepted by both the Eastern and Western Churches. Instead, however, of having one local creed as a firm starting point, we are presented with several of quite early date in the great centres of the Eastern Church—Jerusalem, Antioch, Alexandria, Caesarea and so on. They have the same general trinitarian form as the Western creeds, and the clauses attached to the third section, on the Holy Spirit, are roughly the same. But they show a family likeness which distinguishes them from the Western creeds. There is fuller and more sophisticated theological content given to all three parts. The Father is the maker, not only of heaven and earth, but "of all things visible and invisible". The deity of the Son is confessed more fully and carefully. The relationship of the Spirit to the other Persons of the Trinity is declared, as well as his activity.

When the occasion came, therefore, for the Eastern Church to accept a common confession of faith, the form it was going to take would follow the general pattern of existing Eastern creeds even if it did not, as seems likely, utilize one or more of them to serve as a basis. The occasion was, of course, the Arian controversy and the dogmatic decisions of the Councils of Nicea (325), Constantinople (381) and Chalcedon (451).

A knowledge of the theological issues involved and of the general course of the history of the controversy must here be assumed; but we may refresh our minds about the councils themselves. The emperor Constantine had called upon the bishops of East and West to meet together to settle the increasingly violent quarrel on the deity of Jesus Christ. In the event only some three hundred bishops turned up at Nicea; but they were representative of the Church as a whole, so that the council is rightly regarded as ecumenical. The outcome was that Arianism was completely defeated and discredited. But the orthodox fathers experienced unbelievable difficulty in framing Christological statements that could not be reinterpreted by the Arians. They succeeded, in fact, only by making use of a term non-Scriptural and already tarnished by Sabellianism, *homoousios*—Jesus Christ is "*of one substance with* the Father." The creed that they drew up was in Greek but it was the confession of the whole Church, Western and Eastern. It ran as follows:

> We believe in one God, the Father All-ruling, the maker of all things both visible and invisible:
> And in one Lord Jesus Christ, the Son of God, begotten of the Father, only begotten, and that of the substance [ousias] of the Father, God from God, Light from Light, true God from true God, begotten not made, of one substance [homo-ousion] with the Father, through whom all things became, things in heaven and things on earth, who on account of us men and on account of our salvation came down and became flesh, becoming man, suffered, and rose on the third day, went up into the heavens, and will come to judge the living and the dead:
> And in the Holy Spirit.

To their creed were added denials of specific Arian positions, which served to define and elucidate its Christological statements.

Before we continue with the subsequent history of N (as this creed is designated), we must ask about its relationship to its Eastern predecessors. The general likeness has already been noticed, but they differed in important points of detail. Of those known to us the one that resembles N most nearly is the creed of Caesarea. Now this was the creed that Eusebius, bishop of Caesarea and the famous church historian, presented at the Council of Nicea as the baptismal creed of his church.[5]

It differs from N, apart from small verbal differences, in the main Christological statements. Some scholars have regarded Eusebius' creed as the prototype that was fashioned at Nicea into N. Harnack could say at the time when he still held this opinion: "So much is certain, that Eusebius was fundamentally correct in saying that the symbol which he submitted ... formed the basis for the new creed."[6] Other scholars, notably Hans Lietzmann, looked to something resembling a creed that can be put together from the Catechetical Lectures of Cyril of Jerusalem and that may be taken as representing the creed of Jerusalem. J. N. D. Kelly very sensibly concludes that there is insufficient evidence for precise identification: "We are left with the meagre conclusion that N consists of some local baptismal creed, of Syro-Palestinian provenance, into which the Nicene keywords were somewhat awkwardly interpolated. To go beyond this and attempt to identify the underlying formula would be an unprofitable exercise."[7]

The Council of Nicea had declared the faith of the Church. But the Church was very far from unanimity in accepting it, and even N itself seems to have been pigeon-holed for some fifteen or twenty years. The controversy continued and the victory for a time went to the semi-Arians. It would be claiming too much to represent, as A. E. Burn did,[8] the creed of the Dedication Council of 341, the so-called Second Creed of Antioch, as a movement towards semi-Arianism. Rather it seems to have been composed as if Nicea had never happened. Hence, although its Christological clauses are at least compatible with catholicity, it is more notable for what it omits— the Nicene *homo-ousios*.

Over the next forty years the moderate Arians consolidated their position in the Church, and even the thorough-going Arians had their victory, although this turned out to be Pyrrhic. It is not until the mid-sixties that N begins to return to favour among the 'moderates' and to be taken into account in framing confessions of faith. Another dozen years were to elapse before the appointment of a co-emperor of the catholic persuasion opened the way for the complete rehabilitation of the Christology of N at the Council of Constantinople in 381.

The Constantinopolitan Creed (*Constantinopolitanum*, C) which emerged from this council is known as it was quoted at the Council of Chalcedon (451), for the *Acta* of Constantinople no longer exist. It reads:

> We believe in one God, the Father all-ruling, maker of heaven and earth, of all things visible and invisible:
>
> And in one Lord Jesus Christ, the only-begotten Son of God, begotten from the Father before all the ages, light from light, true God from true God, begotten not made, of one substance [homo-ousion] with the Father, through whom all things became, who because of us men and our salvation came down from the heavens, and became flesh from the Holy Spirit and Mary the Virgin, and became man, was crucified also on our behalf under Pontius Pilate, and suffered and was buried, and rose on the third day according to the Scriptures, and went up into the heavens, and is seated on the right hand of the Father, and will come again with glory to judge living and dead, of whose kingdom there will be no end:
>
> And in the Holy Spirit, the Lord and the Life-giver, who proceeds from the Father, who is both worshipped and glorified in company with the Father and the Son, who spoke through the prophets: in one holy catholic and apostolic church. We confess one baptism unto the remission of sins: we await the resurrection of the dead and the life of the age to come. Amen.

It will be seen that C differs from N in the addition of "of heaven and earth" in the first part, in a somewhat different Christological section, and in an expanded section on the Holy Spirit, with the inclusion of clauses on the church, baptism and resurrection.

But we must now query what we said above about the origin of C. The traditional view is that it originated as the statement of the Council of Constantinople, and that it was simply an adaptation and enlargement of N by the fathers of that council designed to meet a changed doctrinal situation. The Council of Chalcedon accepted C as Constantinopolitan and at least some of those present regarded it as an enlargement of N. But in 1876 F. J. A Hort[9] emphasized the differences between the two creeds and propounded the thesis that there was no direct relationship between the two, that C was adapted from the Creed of Jerusalem (this theory dates from the seventeenth century), that, in fact, it was in existence before the Council of Constantinople, and that the reviser of the Creed of Jerusalem and thus the framer of C was probably Cyril of Jerusalem. Hort's theory was accepted by some of the best-known students of the creeds, like Harnack, Kattenbusch and A. E. Burn. On the other hand, critics have not been wanting, from Badcock and E. Schwartz to J. N. D. Kelly, to indicate shortcomings in the theory. The subject is one of the most involved in all Symbolics, and the reader must be referred to the bibliography.

Leaving aside this problem, however, it is clear that from the middle of the fifth century C came to be regarded as equally authoritative with N as the statement of the catholic faith and at last supplanted it and became the ecumenical creed of Christendom.

THE CHURCH'S USE OF THE CREEDS

The 'Athanasian' Creed is best dealt with separately; and before we come to it we must see what use was made of the other two in the subsequent life of the Church. We have seen that both sprang from creeds used in catechizing and baptism, and indeed that baptism was one of the major occasions, if not the major occasion, for the rise of creeds in the early Church. But we have also seen that in the period of the great controversies the Eastern creeds were used both as tests and as statements of catholicity. This is a change of emphasis rather than a complete change of character. Their use in baptism in an interrogatory form was clearly intended as a test of faith, and in a declaratory form as a statement of faith. But now they become standards of orthodoxy, demanded of those already baptized and whose orthodoxy is suspect, or they are asserted as the orthodox doctrinal position. This emphasis was to remain with them to some extent, and was to be such a marked feature of the confessions of faith in and after the Reformation.

Yet, having said this, we must at once go on to point out that the two great creeds continued their life within the liturgy of the Church. The Apostles' Creed was, as we saw earlier, a form of the Roman baptismal creed which originated, perhaps, in south-west France. That it gradually won its place as the sole baptismal creed of the Western church was largely due to the policy of Charlemagne in imposing the liturgies and customs of the Roman church on other churches within his empire. Once established, in the latter part of Charlemagne's reign (768–814), it held its position during the Middle Ages, through the upheaval of the Reformation, and down into modern times. At this point it is convenient to mention its role as the basis of Christian teaching in the mediaeval and post-mediaeval church. This was a continuation of the early church practice, but now that infant baptism was the custom, the instruction came after baptism instead of before. The catechisms, which became such marked features of mediaeval and Reformation church life, were constructed around the framework of the Apostles' Creed and the Lord's Prayer, with the Ten Commandments coming in later. Indeed, those Anglican clergy who still use the 1662 form will enjoin on the godparents that "ye shall provide that he may learn the Creed, the Lord's Prayer, and the Ten Commandments." This creed also found a place in the daily offices, certainly as early as the seventh century in compline, less certainly as early as that in mattins and prime.

The Nicaeno-Constantinopolitan Creed, accepted at Chalcedon, is too easily stamped as "conciliar" and as a criterion of orthodoxy. It led also a less exciting life as the baptismal creed of Constantinople, perhaps even before Chalcedon, certainly from the second half of the fifth century. We may suppose that it was its endorsement by the general council that won C its position as the baptismal creed of the orthodox Eastern churches. (For a time after the sixth century, indeed, even some Western churches, among them notably Rome, seem to have used C for catechetical instruction and therefore, one must suppose, in the baptismal rite also.)

Just as the *Apostolicum* had become part of the Western daily offices, C was incorporated into the eucharist, first in the East, much later in the West. It was, according to the tradition, at

Antioch that this first occurred, and the innovation was intended by the Monophysite patriarch of that city as a symbolic acceptance of Nicea and rejection of Chalcedon, regarded as going too far. At any rate what began as a piece of sophisticated ecclesiastical charade caught on and the practice spread rapidly among the Orthodox churches.

In the West it was Spain that seems first to have followed the East. The anti-Arian (third) Council of Toledo in 589 passed a canon: "before the Lord's Prayer is said, the creed (of Constantinople) shall be chanted aloud by the people." The custom is found in the eighth century in the court of Charlemagne in Aachen, in Ireland and perhaps in Northumbria. But not, it would seem, at Rome until so late as 1014, when the Emperor Henry II persuaded Pope Benedict VIII to follow suit.

THE QUICUMQUE VULT

This symbol was, of course, traditionally associated with St. Athanasius, the Greek father of the fourth century. But even in the sixteenth century some doubts were felt, and by a hundred years later questionings about its authorship were being given free range. It is clear that this 'creed' was written in Latin and not Greek and that it should be ascribed at the very earliest to the late fourth century. Its only relationship with Athanasius can be that it represents the theology of the uncompromising champion of Nicea who stood *contra mundum*. But with that we have not here to deal. The name *Quicumque* (or *Quicunque*) *vult* stems from the ancient practice of calling documents by their opening words; in this case, *Quicumque vult salvus esse,* "Whosoever wishes to be saved".

The two chief problems concerning the *Quicumque* are its form and its date. In form, it is clear that this 'creed' differs completely from the *Apostolicum* and our 'Nicene'. Here is no confession of faith, beginning with "I [We] believe", but a statement of faith, a definition of catholic doctrine. Indeed it is better not to treat it as a creed at all, "but only as a theological explanation of the faith of the Trinity and Incarnation which is found in the [Apostles' Creed]".[10] It was used, therefore, as a dogmatic aid to teaching. From at least the seventh century clergy were commanded to teach and expound it to their people. The fact that it is written in metre and therefore was intended to be chanted or sung also made it easier to learn by heart. It is to be found as a canticle forming part of Psalters in the eighth and ninth centuries, and it held the place it had won in the liturgies of the Western churches.

The dating of the *Quicumque* rests, partly on the earliest mention of it, partly on the theological situation that it seems to speak to. The so-called "Two-document theory", apparently first suggested by B. F. Westcott, provides no help and proved to be a blind alley. The difficulty in discovering the earliest mention of this symbol lies in the dating of other documents and their manuscripts. Thus Dom G. Morin, in two essays in the *Journal of Theological Studies*,[11] refused any earlier reference than that made in the Canon of the Fourth Council of Toledo in 633. But A. E. Burn[12] would find it quoted, not only in a certain sermon that he ascribed (as did Dom Morin at one time) to Caesarius of Arles in the earlier part of the sixth century, but also possibly in writings of the fifth century. Badcock[13] indeed ignores Dom Morin's criticisms and boldly accepts the validity of these very early writings.

The internal evidence for dating this creed is also difficult to assess. That its statements are aimed at specific heresies is clear. But precisely what are those heresies? Are they, as, for example, Badcock thought,[14] Sabellianism, Arianism, Apollinarianism and Macedonianism? If so, the creed may be dated later than the Council of Constantinople, but (because of the supposed fifth century references) not much later. In fact, Badcock places it between 382 and 384 and plumps for St. Ambrose as the author. We find another view altogether in the greatest of all works on any of the creeds, Daniel Waterland's *Critical History*. The external evidence at his disposal was necessarily imperfect both in extent and also in being sometimes incorrectly dated, but his handling of the internal evidence (i.e. the evidence from the document itself) is worthy to rank with the most masterly essays in literary criticism. For Waterland the author was Hilary of Arles, the date before the rise of Nestorian-

ism and Eutychianism and after St. Augustine's *de Trinitate*—
in effect, between 420 and 430.[15] Dom Morin's two essays
already mentioned seem almost to have been written to show
how difficult the subject is; the identity of the author is an
insoluble mystery. But it is possible to put an approximate
date to the *Quicumque*—the second quarter of the sixth century.[16]
This date J. N. D. Kelly would make more precise, towards
540. He would not share Dom Morin's pessimism on the
authorship, but would regard the creed, not indeed as the
work of Caesarius of Arles, but as coming from his circle, and
composed "possibly at his instigation."[17]

PROTESTANT CONFESSIONS OF FAITH

Whether the Romanists were right in calling the teaching of
the Reformers a novelty, or whether the Reformers were right
in their claims to be the legitimate heirs of the Scriptures and
the early Church, does not concern us. We shall satisfy the
shades of both sides if we agree that Reformation theology was
something that had not been taught consistently for some
hundreds of years. And that being so, it was incumbent upon
the churches of the Reformation, when they had passed from
their early formlessness into coherent corporate existence, to
declare their beliefs. Did they stand with the early Church on
the cardinal doctrines of the Trinity? Then they must say so.
Did they disagree with the penitential system of the mediaeval
Church? Then they must explain in what respects and why
they disagreed. Did they differ from other Reformation
churches on the doctrine of the eucharist? This, too, must be
stated and justified.

All the churches of the Reformation issued statements of
their position. Groups which broke off from these churches
sooner or later followed their example. A large number of
confessions was therefore put out, far more than we can deal
with adequately in this chapter.

But before we proceed we must define the term 'confession of
faith'. What documents are to be included in this category?
First, the title should be reserved to public doctrinal statements

issued by churches, and not used of writings by private individuals. Secondly, the document concerned should be intended as a confession of faith. By this rule we would not wish to regard Luther's two Catechisms as confessions of faith because they were included in the Lutheran *Book of Concord,* or the Catechism in the *Book of Common Prayer* because it was an authoritative formula of Anglican doctrine. Here we must distinguish between a document's original purpose and its subsequent convenient employment. By the same rule, however, we should have to admit other documents which are not usually regarded as confessions. One outstanding example is Part II of *An Apologie of the Church of England* (1562 and 1564), popularly called *Jewel's Apology*.[18] This was undoubtedly intended by the leaders of the Church of England to be a statement of the faith of that church. It is prefaced by the words: "This therefore is our belief", and each section begins in the manner of the creeds with the words "We believe". Therefore, thirdly, the form of the document is not important. Confessions of faith may be cast as straightforward creeds, or as long doctrinal statements, or as catechisms, or as sets of articles. The definitive consideration is intention, not form.

The Lutheran confessions are conveniently assembled in one work, *The Book of Concord.* This comprises the three ancient creeds, the Augsburg Confession and its Apology, Luther's Articles of Smalcald, his two Catechisms, and the Formula of Concord.

The first major Lutheran confession was the Augsburg Confession of 1530 *(Confessio Augustana).* The Emperor Charles V had summoned the rulers of the states which comprised the Empire to a conference, or diet, in an attempt to procure religious peace. It must be remembered that nearly thirteen years had passed since Luther's attack on the Roman system of indulgences in his Ninety-five Theses. There was already a well-defined body of Lutheranism standing over against Rome, as well as over against Zwinglianism. But the split from Rome was not yet regarded as completely irrevocable. At the Diet of Augsburg the Lutherans, largely through their chief theological adviser, Philip Melanchthon, presented their confession of faith. Melanchthon had based it on earlier statements, the Schwabach Articles of 1529 and the Torgau Articles of March, 1530. It was a moderate document, intended eirenically, but it failed to satisfy the Romanists at the Diet, who drew up their Confutation. This, although in its turn also moderate in tone, was far from accommodating the Lutherans, who replied through Melanchthon with an official explanation, the Apology of the Augsburg Confession. There are two versions of the *Augustana,* called *Invariata* and *Variata.* The former is the original confession presented at Augsburg, which was later accepted as an official Lutheran formulary. The latter is a variant, also by Melanchthon, put forward as a basis for agreement between Lutherans and Romanists at the Council of Ratisbon in 1540, where it was accepted by Calvin but not by the Romanists. Many Reformed churches in Germany subscribed to the *Augustana Variata,* which thus became an instrument of unity between Lutheran and Reformed. Within the Lutheran church, on the other hand, it was a cause of dissension as crypto-Calvinism.

The occasion of the Smalcald Articles of 1537 was the attempt by Pope Paul III to convene a general council at which the Reformers would be represented. Negotiations were opened with Luther through a Papal nuncio, and he was urged by his friends to prepare a set of articles for the council. At the same time there was taking place in Smalcald the deliberations leading to the formation of a political league of Protestant states in Germany. The articles which Luther had composed were presented to the Lutheran reformers met at Smalcald and thus received their subsequent name. They were, however, quite unfitted for the ecumenical purpose that evoked them, being rather a bold declaration emphasizing the differences between Rome and Lutheranism and a strong rejection of the Papacy.

A generation later, in an effort to end fearful theological quarrels which had developed within Lutheranism, the Elector of Saxony formed a committee of six theologians. They met in 1577 and drew up a document consisting of twelve closely argued and lengthy articles, the *Formula of Concord.* This, when it was published in 1580 met a varied reception. Sweden accepted it, but the King of Denmark threw it in the fire. Most of the German churches subscribed to it, but the number who did not was sufficient to stir up renewed controversy. Nevertheless in course of time it won its way so far as to be regarded for a time as divinely inspired.

Perhaps more important than the Formula, however, was the *Book of Concord (Concordia)*, published at the same time. As already stated, it contained the official Lutheran formularies of faith. The significance of this is that Lutheranism possessed from the end of the sixteenth century a completed body of dogma. It was not later augmented, although some of its documents lost their authority in course of time. The Lutheran position in regard to the Book of Concord might be compared with the Roman Catholic in regard to the decrees and canons of the Council of Trent. In both we see a world-wide church subscribing to a settled authoritative body of dogma.

This was not the case with the Reformed churches. They neither subscribed to one central confession nor did they feel so bound to existing confessions that they refrained from promulgating fresh ones. In the first place, the Reformed confessions were generally national; Geneva, Heidelberg, France (*Confessio fidei Gallicana*, 1559), the Netherlands (*Confessio Belgica*, 1561), Scotland (1560), all put forward their own confessions. If, later on, one or another gained more than local allegiance, it was due to its intrinsic excellence as an expression of Reformed belief. One of the most interesting studies in this field is to view the rise, dominance, and decline of the major Reformed confessions—the Genevan Catechism, the Heidelberg Catechism, the Westminster Confession.

Calvin's *Catechism of Geneva* (1545) was originally written in French during the time of his first stay in that city (1536–38). It was then intended simply for "the instruction of children in the Christian religion", as the sub-title puts it. Some seven years later, however, he issued a new catechism in Latin and French. The French version was still intended for teaching children, and was used for that purpose in Geneva, but the Latin was meant as a confession of faith among the churches.

In his introduction Calvin shows that he is very well aware of the whole early Church nexus of baptism, belief, unity, and declares that his catechism is "as it were, a solemn *symbolum* of the Christian communion".[19]

The *Heidelberg Catechism* of 1563 springs directly from the eucharistic controversy between Lutheran and Reformed there. The Reformation in Heidelberg, the capital of the Palatinate, was Melanchthonian in character. That is to say, it was firmly but not rabidly Lutheran, held the Augsburg Confession as its doctrinal basis, but was tolerant of Calvinism. After 1559, under a new ruler, the Elector Frederick III, the Palatinate left the Lutheran side and allied itself with the Reformed churches. One of the professors in Heidelberg, Tilemann Heshusius, a Lutheran, excommunicated a deacon for holding 'Zwinglian' views on the eucharist. To quieten the resultant controversy, Frederick appointed two young men aged twenty-eight and twenty-six to draw up a confession of faith for the use of schools in his dominions. They were Zacharias Ursinus and Casper Olevianus. Ursinus had been a pupil of Melanchthon and was also a friend of Bullinger and Calvin. Olevianus, an alumnus of the universities of Paris, Orleans and Bourges, had also studied at Geneva and Zürich. They were therefore both 'Reformed', and the confession in catechism form which they collaborated to produce was based partly on the catechisms of Calvin and Bullinger. Besides serving the Palatinate, the Heidelberg Catechism was also adopted as a confession by many other Reformed churches—in Germany, Switzerland, Hungary, and Poland, for example.

The other Reformed confession which claimed more than a local allegiance was the *Westminster Confession of Faith* (1647). The struggle between the Crown and Parliament involved at its centre a corresponding struggle between the established Church of England and the Puritans, who regarded it as, at best, an imperfectly reformed church. After the Civil War had started the Long Parliament convened an assembly to meet at Westminster and to reform the doctrine, worship and organization of the Church of England. The first task of the Westminster Assembly was to revise the Thirty-nine Articles. This was laid aside after two and a half months, however, when the Assembly proceeded by order of Parliament to draw up a confession of its own, an undertaking which occupied it between 1644 and 1646. The Westminster Confession of Faith which they produced was authorized by Parliament, but was at the Restoration of the Monarchy revoked in England in favour of the Thirty-nine Articles, although it became the standard of faith in Scotland and among some American Presbyterians.

Our account of the Church of England's confessions of faith must begin with the official statements issued under Henry VIII, the Ten Articles of 1536, (with its companion *The Institution of a Christian Man* (1537), called "The Bishops' Book") and the revision of this, "the King's Book", or *A Necessary Doctrine and Erudition for any Christian Man* (1543), the Thirteen Articles of 1538 and the Six Articles of 1539. The last named could hardly be classed as a confession of faith, though its doctrinal intentions were not in any doubt. It should rather be regarded merely as a violent governmental corrective to Reformed ideas and practices. The Ten Articles, the *Institution*, and *A Necessary Doctrine* did not directly lead on to the statements of Edward's and Elizabeth's reigns, but represent specifically the state of Anglican doctrine under Henry. The Thirteen Articles, however, do constitute part of the main development. They formed the result of the discussions on the Augsburg Confession in 1538 between the English, led by Cranmer, and a Lutheran delegation. They were not authorized, or even published, but some of the articles were used again fifteen years later.

The Forty-two Articles of 1553 were composed by Cranmer at the bidding of the King and the Privy Council in 1551. Cranmer had them revised by other bishops, by members of the Council, and by certain other scholars in the following year. Whether they were ever authorized by Convocation is more than doubtful. In any case, before subscription to them could be demanded, the King's death and the accession of his Roman Catholic sister Mary made them a dead letter.

Or, rather, a temporary dead letter. In 1562 Matthew Parker, now Archbishop of Canterbury, revised the Latin

edition with the help of other bishops, and in 1563 the Convocation of Canterbury considered them and, after striking out
three, subscribed to them. The number was further diminished
by one before they received the Queen's assent. Thus in 1563
were published the Thirty-eight Articles. In 1571 the English
version was again revised, chiefly by John Jewel, and the
offending article was restored. At last in 1571 were published
the Thirty-nine Articles of Religion. The Articles derive from
the Lutheran family of confessions, since the Thirteen and the
Forty-two drew on the *Confession of Augsburg*, and were revised
in the light of the *Confession of Würtemburg*, composed by Johann
Brenz and presented at the Council of Trent in 1552. Yet it
would be incorrect to regard the Thirty-nine Articles as
Lutheran. Not only was Brenz one of the theologians who
mediated between the Lutherans and the Calvinists, but the
changes introduced by Cranmer, Parker, and to a lesser extent
Jewel, gave the Articles an individuality which distinguishes
them from both the Lutheran and the Reformed type.

The usual title for Protestant confessions was just "Confession
of Faith". The rare exceptions designated the form of the
confession—e.g. "Heidelberg *Catechism*", "*Articles* of Religion".
The term "symbol", which commonly referred to one of the
three ancient creeds, is nevertheless at least twice used of a
Protestant confession. The first is when the *Formula of Concord*
treats of the norm by which all dogmas are to be judged. The
primary and unique norm is Holy Scripture. After Scripture
come the "witnesses", in the primitive Church the symbols,
"that is, brief and explicit confessions embracing the unanimous consensus of the Catholic Christian faith and the
confession of the orthodox and true Church (such as are the
Apostles', Nicene and Athanasian Symbols)".[20] To these
the Formula gives assent. But there is another symbol, "the
symbol of our own age, the first and unchanged Augsburg
Confession". The second goes further, in that it applies the
term *symbol* to itself. This is Calvin's preface to the 1545
Genevan Catechism, which, he says, sets out to be "as it were a
solemn symbol of the Christian communion."[21]

Sometimes, therefore, the later confessions were placed in the same category as the creeds. They were intended in their age to fulfil at least a part of the office of the creeds in days gone by. Both the *Formula of Concord* and Calvin's *Catechism of Geneva* expressly claim this. The creeds, says the Formula, were composed against false teachers and heretics: "And as concerns the schisms in matters of faith which have come to pass in our times, we judge the unanimous consent and declaration of our Christian faith, especially against the Papacy and its idolatrous rites and superstitions, and against other sects, to be the symbol of our own age", the *Augustana*.[22] The Geneva Catechism not only sees the need for combating heresy "in the dreadful devastation of the Christian world", but also insists on the need for statements of sound doctrine in order to maintain "the unity of the faith", "agreement in the teaching of godliness", "consensus of belief".[23] The ideal would be a single catechism used by all the churches, but this is impracticable. Therefore the churches must aim at teaching the same doctrine in a variety of forms. Calvin is clearly calling for a body of doctrine to be declared by the Protestant churches, and he uses the same language for this body of doctrine as for the creed—it is "the sum of the faith", "the solemn profession of the faith", "the solemn symbol of the Christian communion".[24]

Yet the Reformers are not intending to supplant the creeds by their confessions. Of the two works we have mentioned, the *Formula of Concord* expressly embraces the creeds, and the *Catechism of Geneva* devotes the whole of its first part to an exposition of the Apostles' Creed. Nearly all the confessions, indeed, declare their assent to the creeds. It is quite clear that they acknowledge in the creeds a certain teaching authority higher than their own and which they do not feel at liberty to repudiate. It would be difficult to define in what this authority consists. The creeds are not the rule of faith in the way that Scripture is. But they must be heard reverently as the voice of the Church, and above all, they may be validly criticized only by Scripture.

The problem of the difference between the three creeds and the Protestant confessions of faith is also very hard. Some apparent differences break down when they are examined more closely. Thus Kattenbusch, in his article *Symbol* in Hauck's *Realencyklopädie*,[25] finds it significant that the creeds begin with "*I* believe", the confessions usually with "*We* believe". This, he says, is the difference between the genuine personal confession which faith must always be and a group confession. But some early creeds begin with "We believe"; and in any case the Reformation can hardly be accused of minimizing the personal nature of faith. It is not infrequently accused of doing precisely the opposite.

Kattenbusch is on surer ground when he points to the relationship of the creeds and the confessions to the Church's liturgy.[26] As we have said, the creeds, even if they did not originate solely in the rite of baptism, existed from a very early date within the context of baptism and then, rather later, of the eucharist, and in course of time of the daily offices. And this liturgical relationship held, not only of the two creeds proper, but also of the exposition on the creed, the *Quicunque vult*. The confessions of faith, however, were not intended to fulfil a liturgical purpose, but were purely statements of doctrine. Of course, there were exceptions; the catechisms continued to play a dual role. But in general there is a genuine difference here. It is a difference, however, which springs not from a weakness but from a different intention. Those churches, and they were the majority, which continued to use a confession of faith in their liturgy used the creeds and not a confession of their own making. They were content to follow the lead of the primitive Church.

The confessions of faith are allied rather to the creeds used as standards of catholicity. They came into being because theological situations arose on which the creeds had nothing directly to say—the relationship of faith and merits in justification, the nature of the presence of Christ in the eucharist, the authority of Scripture, and so on. In this respect, the confessions of faith may be regarded as both a re-affirmation of the doctrines of the creeds and a widening of their scope.

For further reading

1. SYMBOLICS

(a) F. Kattenbusch, Article, *Symbolics* in *The New Schaff-Herzog Encyclopedia of Religious Knowledge,* ed. by S. M. Jackson, 1911, Vol. XI, pp. 199–203.

(b) W. Niesel, *Reformed Symbolics. A Comparison of Catholicism, Orthodoxy, and Protestantism,* tr. by D. Lewis, Oliver & Boyd, Edinburgh, 1962.

2. THE ORIGIN OF CREEDS

O. Cullmann, *The Earliest Christian Confessions,* tr. by J. K. S. Reid, Lutterworth, London, 1949.

3. THE CREEDS

J. N. D. Kelly, *Early Christian Creeds,* 2nd ed., Longmans Green & Co., London, 1960.

P. Schaff, *A History of the Creeds of Christendom,* pp. 1–202, Hodder & Stoughton, London, 1877.

4. TEXTS OF THE CREEDS

P. Schaff, *The Creeds of the Greek and Latin Churches,* Hodder & Stoughton, London, 1877.

H. Denzinger, *The Sources of Catholic Dogma,* tr. by R. J. Deferrari from the Thirtieth Edition of Henry Denzinger's *Enchiridion Symbolorum,* B. Herder Book Co., St. Louis & London, 1957.

5. ON INDIVIDUAL CREEDS

A. v. Harnack, *The Apostles' Creed,* tr. by S. Means, rev. and ed. by T. B. Saunders, London, 1901.

J. N. D. Kelly, *The Athanasian Creed*, A. & C. Black, London, 1964.

F. Loofs, Article *Athanasian Creed* in *New Schaff-Herzog*, 1908, vol. I, pp. 338–42.

Daniel Waterland, *A Critical History of the Athanasian Creed: representing the opinions of Ancients and Moderns concerning it* in *The Works of the Rev. Daniel Waterland, D.D.*, 3rd ed., Oxford, 1856. Vol. III, pp. 97–272.

A. v. Harnack, Article *Constantinopolitan Creed* in *New Schaff-Herzog*, 1909, vol. III, pp. 256–60.

F. J. A. Hort, *Two Dissertations*, Part 2: *On the 'Constantinopolitan' Creed and other Eastern Creeds of the Fourth Century*, Macmillan, Cambridge & London, 1876.

6. CONFESSIONS OF FAITH

P. Schaff, *A History of the Creeds of Christendom*, pp. 203–919. See also Kattenbusch, *Symbolics*, and Introductions to works in the next section.

7. TEXTS OF THE CONFESSIONS

A. C. Cochrane, *Reformed Confessions of the 16th Century*, ed., with historical introductions, S.C.M., London, 1966.

Concordia or Book of Concord. The Symbols of the Evangelical Lutheran Church, St. Louis, 1957.

P. Schaff, *The Creeds of the Evangelical Protestant Churches*, Hodder & Stoughton, London, 1877.

7

THE STUDY OF CHRISTIAN DOCTRINE

M. F. WILES

Regius Professor of Divinity, University of Oxford

7

The Study of Christian Doctrine

I T IS a notorious fact that Christians differ deeply from one
another in matters of doctrine. Behind all such differences
about the substance of Christian doctrine lie more basic
differences about the nature of doctrine as a subject for theological study and about the proper method of dealing with it.
It is with the attempt to clarify these basic issues that this
chapter will be concerned.

As a working definition from which to begin we may speak of
Christian doctrine as what the Christian message adds up to, or
as the attempt to give formal expression to the truth of the
Christian gospel. Christian faith is certainly more than the
acceptance of a set of propositional statements as true. It
involves personal trust and commitment to a way of life (see
p. 23). But this trust or commitment has intellectual implications. 'Belief-in' is not unrelated to 'belief-that'. Christian
doctrine is concerned with the elucidation of those 'beliefs-that'
which spell out the inner substance of Christian commitment.
It is the attempt to give explicit statement to the truths
that are involved in the affirmation and practice of Christian
faith.

This definition is intentionally loose. It can be interpreted
with varying degrees of strictness. Some truths are more directly
involved in the affirmation and practice of Christian faith than
others. The following are some of the ways in which our
definition might be filled out. Doctrine could be regarded as
comprising: (i) those truths to which any member of a church is
absolutely committed; (ii) those truths to which any authorized
teacher of a church is absolutely committed (this might be

identical with (i), but it might be more extensive); (iii) the central core of beliefs as taught and practised by a church; (iv) the most full and coherent expression in systematic form that can be given to all that is implicit in Christian faith as understood and lived in the contemporary world. I would not wish to exclude any of these from the sphere of what is properly understood by Christian doctrine. If we take one of the narrower definitions, the special position given to the particular truths will require justification, and that can only be done in the light of their relation to a wider scheme of knowledge. If we take the widest definition, it will still be important to make clear the relative importance and centrality of certain propositions within the whole corpus of belief. The kind of distinctions which I am indicating here have often been made in varying ways with the aid of such distinguishing labels as 'dogmatic theology', 'doctrinal theology' and 'systematic theology' (cf. p. 30 above). Such distinctions are perfectly legitimate if they are not too sharply drawn. They appear in an extreme form in the Roman Catholic distinction between dogmas (to be believed by all Christians as divinely revealed truths guaranteed by the infallible teaching authority of the Church—see note 15 on p. 319) and theology (the human attempt to systematize or explain such truths). The sharpness of the distinction here is dependent upon a conception of the Church as having (under certain specific conditions) infallible teaching authority. Where that view is not held the distinctions are likely to be less clear-cut, and in general it seems more important to stress the interrelatedness of these different forms of doctrinal activity and the impossibility of pursuing any one of them satisfactorily in even relative isolation from the others.

This whole doctrinal enterprise has been one of the principal grounds of division between the churches in Christian history. Christian bodies who have used the same Scriptures have found in them diametrically opposed meanings; Christian groups who have preserved the same sacramental practices have expressed what they believed to be happening in those practices in strikingly different ways. Even where the immediate grounds of division belonged more to political or practical causes than to intellectual or doctrinal ones, differing forms of doctrinal expression have normally developed as a result of institutional separation. It has already proved necessary in the previous paragraph, when trying to spell out more fully what was involved in my initial definition of Christian doctrine, to speak of that which may be required, taught or practised by 'a church'. Thus it has come to appear that there is no such empirical reality as Christian doctrine; rather there are a variety of church doctrines. There is Roman Catholic doctrine, Lutheran doctrine, Anglican doctrine and so on. These actually exist, and are therefore possible (and so proper) subjects of study. But Christian doctrine, it would appear, is a non-existent entity—unless it be arbitrarily identified with some one of the varied and competing forms of church doctrine. Since it does not exist and there is no agreed procedure for discovering what it would be if it did, it cannot be, it has been argued, an object of serious and rational study.

Yet not all Christians have been content with this situation; not all have been happy to regard the study of doctrine as something that is only possible within strictly confessional bounds. The most obvious avenue of escape had seemed to be to go back behind the break up of the Church into differing confessions and denominations. The ecumenical creeds (the Apostles' Creed, the Nicene Creed and the Athanasian Creed) and the findings of—at least—the first four general councils (Nicaea, Constantinople, Ephesus and Chalcedon) seemed to provide material that could properly be treated as the true substance of Christian doctrine. This approach has had particular appeal within Anglicanism with its traditional stress on the role of the Fathers, but its proponents could reasonably claim that it did represent something more than a limited confessional approach. Thus in the University of Oxford since 1904 the paper entitled Dogmatic Theology has in fact been the history of Christian Doctrine to 461 A.D.[1]

This approach has led to a tendency in English university circles to identify the study of Christian doctrine with the study of the history of early Christian doctrine in general and with the study of the theology of the ecumenical creeds and the general councils in particular. That such study is an essential preliminary to the study of Christian doctrine no one would wish to deny; but to claim that it constitutes the whole proper substance of such a study is a very different matter. The historical approach to that early doctrine, which has so dominated the English scene in doctrinal studies, has itself done much to reinforce the difficulties involved in locating the subject-matter of the study of doctrine exclusively in the early centuries. The difficulties involved are of two main kinds.

In the first place, historical study of early doctrine, like historical study of the Bible, places its subject-matter firmly within the context of the history of its own times. It has always been recognized that the concepts used in the early doctrinal formularies, such as 'substance', 'person' and 'nature', have a specialized meaning and cannot be assumed to carry there the precise connotation that those words would convey in contemporary English. But it has also to be emphasized that the meanings of those words can only be expressed with precision in terms of the thought-forms of their own day. If therefore they are to be treated as normative for Christian doctrine today, the student of doctrine will have to engage in a process of interpretation of a far more comprehensive kind than has normally been acknowledged. The problem is not one of finding modern equivalents for a few outdated terms; it is the far more hazardous one of asking how (if at all) the fundamental intention of the early doctrinal statements can find equivalent expression today.

But it is the second difficulty that is the more serious. Historical study not only attempts to understand the early doctrinal affirmations in terms of their own cultural and religious settings; it also enquires how they were arrived at, by what processes (political and intellectual) some particular statements came to be accepted and others to be rejected. This investigation has led some Christians at least to the view that the methods used in the determination of those doctrines are not at every point methods with which we can identify ourselves today, and also that, even within the terms of their own avowed intentions and methods, not every decision was such as would seem to be wholly justified. For anyone convinced of such conclusions, it is no longer possible to regard even the formal pronouncements of the undivided Church as normative in any strong or binding sense. For him they do not necessarily express 'what the Christian message adds up to'—even if he were satisfied that they could be and had been translated successfully into meaningful contemporary equivalents. If that were only the judgement of a few individual scholars, it would be possible to say simply that it was they who had abandoned Christian doctrine; if (as seems to be the case) it is, in varying degrees, the judgement of a wide range of Christian scholars, then it is clear that it is the understanding of Christian doctrine as being constituted by the affirmations of the creeds and the general councils which will have to be abandoned.

The study of Christian doctrine, then, is something more than the accumulation of all the varied beliefs that differing Christian bodies do in fact teach (see p. 30 above). We have also given reasons for saying that it is more than the interpretation of certain universally accepted formulae from the era of the undivided Church. The study of Christian doctrine is concerned to do more than simply to give an account of what the various churches do teach or of what the undivided Church has in the past affirmed. It is not purely phenomenological nor purely historical in character.[2] It is concerned to show the grounds of Christian teaching and to present it as something with a claim to be true. It is more therefore than a purely descriptive science. It has also to give reasons for the acceptance of what is being set forth as Christian doctrine; it is concerned not only with what is taught or has been taught but with what ought to be taught.

This brings us back to the basic difficulty which has led to its treatment in the past as a subject only open to study in a strictly confessional setting. Christians have not simply gone their separate doctrinal ways in the past without taking cognizance of one another; nor have they always tried to overcome opposing forms of doctrine by force of arms or rhetoric. They have reasoned with one another, and have recognized that the ground of their differences has often been a different understanding of the sources of Christian doctrine and of the methods by which it should be derived from those sources. Most obviously Protestants have tended to claim the Bible as the sole source of doctrine; Roman Catholics have stressed the importance of tradition as well as Scripture as necessary sources. Where there are such opposed views about the proper sources for the pursuit of a subject of study, the possibility of its pursuit as a single, coherent discipline is bound to remain precarious. It is important therefore to try to assess whether the disagreement about the sources of doctrine is as serious today as it was at the time, for example, of the Reformation and whether it is such as to undermine the possibility of the study of Christian doctrine as a common Christian enterprise.

It is clear that there are still serious differences on this issue, but also that they are not the same in character as those which have dominated the life of the churches in the past. The development of the critical study of the Scriptures has not simplified the problem but it has certainly shifted its contours. Roman Catholic scholars have very largely abandoned the conception of tradition and Scripture as two separate and distinct sources of doctrine; while few Protestants would deny that tradition, in the sense of the continuing stream of the Church's life, must have a part to play in her understanding and application of scriptural teaching. Thus although we are very far indeed from having any agreed understanding of what should be the sources of doctrine, the present position is sufficiently open to give some encouragement to those who would hope to see a common approach of all Christians to the study of doctrine (cf. pp. 307 ff. below).

Before we go on to consider some of the ways in which doctrinal study is being pursued today and the lines which a common study might follow, a further preliminary question needs to be asked. We have been speaking of Christian doctrine as 'what the Christian message adds up to' or as 'the statement of those truths that are involved in the affirmation and practice of Christian faith'. But the truths that are involved in a living commitment can normally be expressed in a variety of ways. The particular way in which we may choose to express them at any given time will depend on the particular purpose with which that expression is being made. We need therefore to ask not only what are the proper sources of doctrine, but also: What is its aim, what is Christian doctrine for?

To take a political analogy: someone undertaking to produce a statement of socialist 'doctrine' might do so for any one (or more) of a number of different reasons. His aim might be: (i) to provide a sense of continuity with the pioneering heroes of the past who made the first challenge to the capitalist system; (ii) to provide a clear and consistent platform for his party to proclaim in electioneering; (iii) to clarify his own mind about the implications of socialism in a changing environment with a view to seeing what new developments may be called for; (iv) to answer specific questions about socialism being asked by other people, whether members of the party or not. His statement will differ according to where his main aim lies, without necessarily being any more or less true in the differing cases. If his main aim is either of the first two, his statement is likely to be of a traditionalist character, stressing the familiar and distinctive features of socialism in a well-acknowledged manner. In cases (iii) or (iv), his statement is likely to be more flexible, more attentive to challenges of the contemporary environment.

A similar variety of aims may enter into the formulation of doctrine. In some cases the primary purpose may be to give expression to the continuity of the life of the Church; in others it may be designed rather to serve the cause of proclamation; yet again it may have a more exploratory or apologetic purpose. These various aims are not mutually exclusive, but which motive is predominant is an important factor in determining the character of doctrinal statements. Differences in doctrine may often therefore arise from different aims, as well as from the use of different sources or the differing use of the same sources.

The close interrelation of these two issues of the sources of doctrine and the aims of doctrinal formulation is well illustrated by a comparison of the two outstanding figures in recent Protestant theology, Karl Barth and Paul Tillich. Each begins his major doctrinal work with the insistence that "theology is a function of the Church".[3] But it is a different function which each has in the forefront of his mind. With Karl Barth it is the Church's task of proclamation; with Paul Tillich it is the task of answering the questions implicit in the contemporary situation. Barth is thereby led to define dogmatics as the "scientific test to which the Christian Church puts herself regarding the language about God which is peculiar to her";[4] whereas Tillich speaks of the 'method of correlation' which "explains the contents of the Christian faith through existential questions and theological answers in mutual interdependence".[5] A similar contrast is to be seen also in terms of sources. For Karl Barth the basis of dogmatics is the Word of God; the Word of God is emphatically not to be identified simply and directly with the words of Scripture, yet its relation with Scripture is so close that Barth can write "It (i.e. dogmatics) must endeavour ... to give heed to Scripture and therefore to allow itself to be set no problems from any source save Scripture."[6] Tillich, on the other hand, can speak explicitly of the "sources of systematic theology" as being of an "almost unlimited richness. Bible, church history, history of religion and culture."[7] The contrast is certainly striking, yet it can be overdrawn. Tillich is quite clear that in the method of correlation the answers are not derived from the questions; the content of the answers is drawn from the Christian tradition.[8] And when Barth speaks of the Church 'criticizing and revising her language about God',[9] she cannot surely help but do so in practice on the basis of the cultural situation in which she finds herself. Thus, for all their very real differences, both are in fact involved in bringing together the Christian revelation as recorded in Scripture and received in the life of the Church on the one hand and the thought world in which they are living on the other.

Tillich would have been more prepared to accept such a description of what he was doing than would Barth. But it is important to recognize that it is truer of Barth than he would be willing to admit. Barth is quite clear that the task of dogmatics is not to be identified with that of exegesis. Theology, in his view, is not to be "content with the repetition of biblical texts, for it seeks to make statements about truth revealed in the inner text and therefore must seek a conformity to the truth at a deeper level beyond formal conformity to the external text". Its specific task is "to penetrate to the solid truth upon which biblical statements rest", "to enquire into what we ourselves have to say on the basis of the biblical revelation, and to articulate its relation to the object in such a way, that our knowledge may be established as true".[10] In practice it is extremely doubtful whether doctrine can be determined as directly as Barth implies by the nature of its object, conceived as the inner text, the solid truth upon which biblical statements rest. It seems clear that other criteria do enter into determining what is actually seen and proclaimed on that basis. This can be illustrated by a consideration of the fundamental character of Barth's own theology. For Barth the central theme of the Bible, the heart of its inner text, is the self-revelation of God to man—to man whose basic condition is a lack of the knowledge of God and of any way to that knowledge. In Barth's view this is the impact which Scripture must have on the truly obedient listener, who brings to it nothing but a readiness to hear. The Swedish theologian, Gustaf Wingren, argues that what Barth sees here is not determined exclusively by the character of the biblical text but by the condition of modern man, for whom the basic problem appears as the problem of agnosticism. "Barth's question", writes Wingren, "is the question of the twentieth century", and because he addresses himself to that question it is "clear that by doing so no contact is made with what is central in the Bible". If the inner text itself were really the sole determinant of what Barth were seeing, he should more properly have seen what Luther saw—a central theme of the justification of man the sinner.[11]

Thus for Karl Barth himself doctrinal theology is to be distinguished from exegesis of Scripture by its concern with the inner as contrasted with the external text. Moreover we have argued that in practice other human factors beyond the text of Scripture and what is to be seen there do inevitably enter into determining the substance of Barth's theology. A similar picture emerges if we consider the method pursued by Rudolf Bultmann and those who, like Gerhard Ebeling, have followed him in his stress on the problem of interpretation. Ebeling can speak of Scripture as '*the* absolute source of present proclamation and therefore the authoritative text of theology'. Yet while maintaining a principle of *sola scriptura* he is fully aware of the drastic process of interpretation that is involved in deriving theological truth from it. He can even assert paradoxically that "because of the '*sola scriptura*', rightly understood, the systematic theologian must address himself to every text that is relevant to the coming of God's Word to the world: not only the texts of the church tradition, but also and particularly the texts which voice the world's opposition to God."[12] A hermeneutical process so far-reaching in its implications ought surely to be acknowledged as itself a contributory source to the resultant doctrinal theology, and not just as a method of using the biblical source.

Roman Catholic doctrinal theology has a similar kind of orientation towards the apostolic age, on the basis of its conviction that public revelation ceased with the death of the last apostle. For it therefore all subsequent theology has to be understood as in some sense an elucidation of what was already implicit in the faith of the apostles. On the face of it later doctrine often appears to be very far indeed from that taught and believed by the apostles. This is particularly true of the recent Mariological dogmas, and their definition has given rise to a vast literature on the subject of the development of doctrine.[13] It would certainly appear that any account of that development which is going to do justice to the evidence will have to allow for a more genuine element of novelty in doctrinal formulation than has been generally admitted in the past. Here too, therefore, in development as in demythologization (see p. 55 above), it is clear that there is more to the task of giving adequate expression to doctrinal convictions than the translation of past beliefs into a contemporary language.

It is vital therefore for the doctrinal theologian to recognize that his task is not simply one of the reinterpretation of past texts. It has a genuinely creative character about it. This fact cannot seriously be questioned. The creative character of Barth's insight into the inner text, or Bultmann's existentialist interpretation of the New Testament, is unmistakable. Reluctance to acknowledge this creative quality openly is largely due to the fear that it will undermine the objectivity or truthvalue of its subject matter. It is certainly a right and proper thing that anyone concerned with the task of expounding Christian doctrine should feel this kind of concern about objectivity. Yet in this particular form the fear is a false one, arising from an oversimplified view of the relation between human language and the truths which it is designed to express (for a discussion of this, see Chapter 9, esp. pp. 198f. and 206f.). We do not have to choose between an understanding of doctrinal statements as either arbitrarily subjective on the one hand, or so precisely corresponding to some external reality that there is only one proper or adequate way in which they can be expressed on the other. Emphasis needs to be placed on the complex nature of all doctrinal statements. This complexity can only be briefly indicated here. Theology is concerned with that which is ultimate and transcendent. It can only therefore speak of its subject matter indirectly by means of analogy or symbols.[14] But it is not concerned exclusively with the ultimate; it is concerned with particular historical events, such as the crucifixion of Jesus of Nazareth, as real historical happenings with an eternal significance. Moreover the truths which it seeks to enunciate are not of a kind that can be kept at arm's length from man's concern; they are of an intensely personal or existential nature. Furthermore they are not related to man only in his individuality or solitude; they are intimately concerned with man in his relationships within society. The student of doctrine has therefore to pay attention to what the philosopher and the historian, the psychologist and the sociologist are saying. Just as the psychologist must take note of what the physiologist tells him but still has his own proper role to play, so the dogmatician must take account of the work of these various related disciplines but has still his own peculiar task to fulfil (see p. 22f.).

What then is the nature of the doctrinal scholar's specific task? Like all creative skills it is enormously difficult to describe. The subject matter which he is concerned to interpret is the way of God with man. As a Christian scholar he is convinced that the events to which the Bible bears witness and the biblical interpretation of those events are of central importance in giving him access to his subject matter. But they are neither exclusive nor unchallengeable. The subsequent life of the Church and man's ever increasing knowledge and experience of the world in which he lives are also relevant data for him. Neither the Christian tradition nor contemporary understanding of the world can be treated as fixed starting points. Each has to be assessed critically in the light of the other. On the basis of such a dialectical process, the Christian scholar has to declare what he, from within the living fellowship of the Church, believes to be the truth about God and his activity towards men. There is no straightforward way of confirming the truth of his assertions. But the same is true also of assertions in the field of ethics or of history. What is to be found in such fields is rather a relative measure of agreement about the procedure for assessing evidence and drawing conclusions. It is this in fact which can give us confidence, despite the absence of any more precise or formal method of verifying our convictions, that the subject matter of those branches of study has a real basis outside ourselves and that they are more than the mere expression of individual predilections. We ought not to expect more in the case of Christian doctrine.

If original work in Christian doctrine must have this kind of creative character about it, how may the study of the subject be best approached? Syllabuses for the study of the Philosophy of Religion are frequently divided into two halves, entitled 'texts' and 'problems'. Basically their concern is the same, namely what ought we to say about the fundamental philosophical problems posed by religion, such as evil, miracles or immortality? But they approach the issue in different ways. In the one case they do so by way of a critical study of some of the great thinkers of the past; in the other the attack is made more directly on the various problems as they impinge on us today. Doctrine also can best be studied in these two ways. In the first place it can be approached through a critical study of some of the great doctrinal thinkers of the past. It is a significant fact that both Barth and Tillich have bequeathed to us valuable treatments of nineteenth-century theology of just this kind,[15] as well as other writings on the history of Christian thought which throw light not merely on the historical periods concerned but on their own doctrinal method.[16] Secondly the study of doctrine can be approached more directly through the discussion of particular doctrines, such as Christology, atonement, etc. An approach of this kind will draw widely upon Scripture, Christian history and contemporary experience. None of these will be treated as absolute or binding in itself. Each will be assessed critically in the attempt to find the most adequate expression of those realities to which Christian witness as a whole throughout its history points us today.[17]

For further reading

This list is designed to include a few of (i) the most important comprehensive works of doctrine, and (ii) recent discussions of doctrinal method published in English in recent years.

I

The three outstanding major contributions are:

K. Barth, *Church Dogmatics*, Vols. 1–4, T. & T. Clark, Edinburgh, 1936–61.

P. Tillich, *Systematic Theology*, Vols. 1–3, Nisbet, London, 1953–64.

K. Rahner, *Theological Investigations* Vols. 1–4, Helicon, Baltimore Press; and Darton, Longman & Todd, London, 1961–68.

In each case the first volume contains an important discussion of doctrinal method.

Many important contributions are concerned with particular doctrines and are too numerous to list here. Good general treatments are:

O. C. Quick, *Doctrines of the Creed*, Nisbet, London, 1938.

J. Burnaby, *The Belief of Christendom*, S.P.C.K., London, 1959.

J. Macquarrie, *The Principles of Christian Theology*, S.C.M., London, 1966.

Valuable discussion of the method of doctrinal study will be found in:

ed. J. Coulson, *Theology and the University* (Section III by Charles Davis, J. K. S. Reid, David Jenkins, A. Richardson and H. F. Davis), Darton, Longman and Todd, London; Helicon Press, Baltimore, 1965.

T. F. Torrance, *Theology in Reconstruction* (Ch. 3: The Problem of Theological Statement Today), S.C.M., London, 1965.

ed. F. G. Healey, *Prospect for Theology* (Chs. 3, 4 and 5 by G. F. Woods, N. Smart and P. Lehmann), Nisbet, London, 1966.

E. Schlink, *The Coming Christ and the Coming Church* (Part I Considerations of Method), Oliver and Boyd, Edinburgh and London, 1967.

8

SCIENTIFIC STUDIES OF RELIGION

NINIAN SMART

Professor of Religious Studies, University of Lancaster

8

Scientific Studies of Religion

THE HISTORY of religions and comparative study of religion, the sociology and psychology of religion— such studies are sometimes called 'scientific'; and this is a way of showing what they are *not* attempting to do. Roughly one can describe the object of Christian theology as being to explore, present and apply the Christian faith (see note 10 on p. 318) in successively changing cultural and intellectual situations. The 'scientific' study of religion is, on the other hand, not concerned with presenting or applying a particular faith, though it is relevant to such a task. Naturally, much of what comes under the head of the scientific study of religion is used in an ancillary way by those who are doing Christian theology, but I shall confine attention in this chapter to those aspects which are less closely tied up with theology as traditionally understood. I shall, however, indicate ways in which these studies and Christian theology are liable to interact.

In order to exhibit something of the logic of the study of religion, it is necessary to make some remarks about the different types of approaches and fields which it embraces. These remarks unavoidably over-simplify; but they may provide a map of the subject. It is useful to begin with the problem of what can be intended by the commonly-used phrase 'the comparative study of religion'. Very often this is used loosely to refer to the study of religions other than Christianity. This is illogical for two reasons. First, Christianity is itself a religion, and the study of religions naturally includes the study of Christianity. Second, one may study a religion or religions without having any intention to compare. We shall later see what the point of making comparisons is; but it is not a *necessary* feature of studying a faith, for one might simply be exploring the history of that faith.

It so happens that the title 'comparative study of religion' has been open to criticism in that sometimes those who have made comparisons have been inclined to draw unfavourable ones, sometimes because they start from a position in one faith and see others as defective in the light of that faith. Of course, it is legitimate for a person or a group to evolve a theology of other religions—expressing (say) a Christian perspective on, and interpretation of, other religions. But such an exercise falls more clearly under the head of theology (see pp. 21 and 31 above) than of the scientific study of religion.

For such reasons, it has become more common among scholars to speak of the 'history of religions'. For instance, the international organization for co-ordinating work in the field is called the International Association for the History of Religions. But even this title needs some elucidation. Consider a situation where one person is studying the history of Zoroastrianism, another the history of Buddhism, another the history of Shinto, another the history of Christianity, and so on. These could be so many separate studies (except in so far as the stream of events in one tradition flows into and out of another: for example, Zoroastrianism had some influences, via Judaism, on early Christianity). Is there any special need to group these separate studies under one head as 'history of religions'? It might turn out that phenomena in one tradition can throw light on those of an independent tradition (cf. pp. 31 and 300 f.), and that methodological tools employed in one history can be applied in another. But this would be, roughly, because each history would be dealing with the same sort of aspect of human existence, namely the religious aspect. There would be a parallel here with economic or political history. Economic history abstracts from total history an aspect of human existence, namely the economic behaviour of men. So likewise it can be argued that histories of religions abstract the religious aspect of the traditions concerned.

Necessarily there are problems here about the definition of

religion, which I shall leave on one side for the moment. Let us summarize briefly some conclusions that might so far be drawn from the foregoing. (1) There are various social traditions, very often largely separate histories. (2) There are various histories which can be studied, therefore; and it is possible to study them from the point of view of abstracting one aspect of human existence, namely the religious aspect. (3) There remains the question of the point of making cross-cultural comparisons of features of these histories.

Here it is possible to point to a positive sense in which the study of religions may be 'scientific', as distinguished from the negative sense mentioned earlier, namely that such a study is *not* theological in intent. At one level of scientific enquiry, not admittedly a very high one, there is the task of classification, of typology. Thus an important part has been played, in the early stages of the evolution of botany as a science, by the systematization of the data—by classifying plants according to genera and species, etc. (Similar remarks apply to zoology, ornithology, philology and so on.) It is not therefore unreasonable to expect that it is possible to construct a typology of religious experience, belief, ritual, etc. Such a typology is central to modern phenomenology of religion (see below). It is part of what was meant by the comparative study of religion, for the whole essence of a typology is to arrive at cross-cultural classifications, inevitably and truistically entailing comparisons. Of course there is a limit to such typology, for a given religious tradition is bound to have unique features. Nevertheless, there is no reason why one should not classify, say, Eckhart (*c.* 1260–1327) and Buddhaghosa (fifth century A.D.) together as mystics, or sketch out a typology of initiation rites, etc.

The phrase 'phenomenology of religion' as used in the modern context has connections with the work of Edmund Husserl (1859–1938), who advocated a descriptive method of discovering the fundamental structures of human consciousness—a programme which he saw as central to philosophical enquiry. However, the title is not now generally used to indicate any particular attachment to a philosophical school; and the main emphasis is on the *descriptive* character of religious

175

typology. On the other hand, speculative elements sometimes enter into phenomenological enquiries, in as much as the typological material moves scholars to speculate about the origins of religion, the functions of certain myths, and so on. Thus speculative elements occur in the work of the foremost phenomenologists of this century, e.g. Rudolf Otto, Gerardus van der Leeuw, Raffaele Pettazzoni and Mircea Eliade (most notably, perhaps in the writings of the last-mentioned). This brings us to another level in which the study of religion may be 'scientific'.

A crucial property of scientific endeavour is the search for explanations. Crudely, an explanation is provided by a *theory*. So the formation of theories to explain data is crucial. Naturally a theory may turn out to be false; but this does not imply that it is not scientific. Darwin's evolutionary hypothesis might, say, turn out to be radically wrong; but this would not detract from its status as a scientific theory. It is in this way that theories, for instance, about the origin of religion can be said to be scientific, even if none of them can as yet be shown to be correct and most of them are virtually certain to be false. Thus as well as descriptive typology (phenomenology of religion in its 'pure' sense), there is the search for theories to explain types of religious behaviour, beliefs, etc. One might distinguish such theories from historical explanations in that the latter are primarily orientated towards the particular sequence, the 'narrative', through which the particular developments of a particular tradition occur. For instance, the attempt to raise money for the building of St. Peter's is an important element in the historical explanation of the events of the Reformation; on the other hand it might be possible to give a typological explanation of Luther's religious experience.

It would be natural here to ask: If a theory purports to explain the genesis of religion, or of a particular feature of religions, in terms of *what* does it so explain? Are not some explanations *reductionist*—that is, do they not explain religious phenomena in terms, say, of psychological phenomena (e.g. in the work of Freud)? Before we can look at this problem, it is necessary to essay something towards a definition of religion, or at least a characterization of it as it typically manifests itself. Without entering into recent discussions of definitional issues, I would here propose some features often or always present in religious systems.

Typically, a religion has a belief-aspect and a practice-aspect. The belief-aspect often comprises doctrines (notably where a religion has developed a written literary heritage, etc.); myths (in a wide and neutral sense—neutral because the use of the term as a technical one does not imply that a myth need be false or fictional); and norms of conduct. The practice-aspect comprises rituals (again in a wide sense, and including such activities as worship, prayer, sacramental occasions, etc.); experience (dramatically, the experience of prophets and mystics; but more generally the numinous and other experiences of the faithful); social institutions (such as a church, a framework of initiatory customs, and so on). Naturally the meaning of the practice-aspect has to be found in the belief-aspect and the meaning of the belief-aspect in the practice-aspect (cf. p. 28). For example, belief in a God implies belief in a focus of worship, so that worship here gives meaning to doctrine; while the content of worship has in turn to be defined doctrinally or mythically. In terms of this characterization of religion, one can see overlaps between religion strictly so called and ideologies. Thus Maoism, as currently evolved in China, contains doctrinal, mythic, ethical, ritual and institutional elements—though these as it happens are not focused on a transcendent being or state (a feature of the more prominent religions of history). It is useful therefore to characterize some ideological systems as 'quasi-religions', in order to indicate that religions have a large penumbra in which the student of religion can legitimately take an interest.

The above profile of religion indicates ways in which varying branches of enquiry can be brought to bear on religion. In so far as religion is institutionalized socially, and in so far as this institutionalization is connected up with the other dimensions of religion, there is the possibility of doing 'the sociology of religion'. In so far as religious experience and its related beliefs is present, there is the possibility of doing 'the psychology of religion'. Again, the nature and functions of myth are in part illuminated by anthropology. (Matters of the *truth* of doctrine and myth are crucial to theology and philosophy—see p. 22; but the main emphasis of the present article is not on this area of enquiry.)

It is possible now to say something, admittedly crude, about kinds of theory in regard to religion. There are those which are, so to say, intra-religious (explaining one feature of religion in terms of another)—for example, trying to show systematic connections between types of religious experience and types of doctrine; and there are those which are extra-religious (explaining a feature of religion through recourse to some feature or features of human existence which is not specifically religious)— for example, Freud's theory of the genesis of the Father-figure in religion. There are also mixed theories, exhibiting the interplay between religious and non-religious factors (perhaps Max Weber's classical work in the sociology of religion comes into this category). Some proponents of the phenomenology of religion, have strongly upheld the autonomy of religious categories and therefore of the study of religion. This is a way of resisting a totally reductionist view of the scientific study of religion and has a certain justification, in my view; for whatever one might say about the genesis of, for example, the sense of the numinous, as depicted by Otto (see p. 181 below), there can be little doubt that this sense has to enter into some explanations of human conduct, etc., from the religious side. That is, religion has its own dynamic, even though it be affected, as we all know, by the dynamics of other aspects of human existence. Thus the study of religion needs to steer a course between a totally intra-religious body of explanation and a totally extra-religious one.

The foregoing discussion can be summed up as follows, by listing areas of enquiry. (1) There are histories of religions. (2) There is descriptive phenomenology of religion, aimed at cross-cultural typological classification. (3) There is speculative phenomenology of religion, concerned primarily with intra-religious explanations of religious phenomena. (4) There is sociology of religion. (5) There are anthropological data and theories important for explanatory purposes in relation to religion. (6) There is psychology of religion. In the ensuing, I shall attempt to give some guide to the material under some of these heads. For the sake of convenience, I shall conflate (2) and (3). I shall conclude with some remarks on the relevance of these studies in the theological and philosophical context.

HISTORIES OF RELIGIONS

Since the beginning of the nineteenth century, a vastly creative period in the development of scientific scholarship, there has been a remarkable explosion of historical work in relation to religions, stimulated in part by the rise of comparative philology and of great investments in the editing of the texts of the great religions. A signal monument of this endeavour was the *Sacred Books of the East* series, edited by Max Mueller. By the first part of the twentieth century, it was reasonable to say that Western scholars and general readers had available, for the first time in history, the basic materials to understand the great non-Christian traditions (though the literary, philological approach to other religions may have placed undue weight on scriptures —seeing other religions as having a relationship to scripture analogous to that of the Christian Church). There has also been in the last century and a half a vast amount of work done in archaeology and ancient history, yielding an understanding of great religious traditions now dead or virtually dead—for example, ancient Near Eastern religions other than Judaism; pre-Columbian religions in America; Greek and Roman religion and the mystery cults; and so on. Prehistorical re-searches and the fashion for evolutionary views of culture in the late nineteenth century helped, in addition, to stimulate enquiry into the origins of religion—an enquiry often linked to growing anthropological researches, on the principle that the modern 'primitive' might yield clues to primeval myth-making, etc.

It is perhaps useful to introduce here a classification of religions, to provide an inventory of the histories of religions. Beginning with the rough distinction between living and dead religions, one can list the former as follows: (1) Three major traditions springing from an overlapping Semitic background: Christianity, Judaism and Islam, together with various latter-day offshoots (e.g. Christian Science, Mormonism, the Baha'i, etc.). (2) Religions originating in the Indian sub-continent: Hinduism, Jainism, Buddhism, Sikhism (the last containing, however, Muslim elements). (3) Religions originating in China and Japan: Confucianism, Taoism, Shinto, together with latter-day offshoots (the new religions of Japan). (4) Ethnic/tribal religions: in Africa, the Americas, the Pacific and elsewhere, together with modern offshoots. The last group is often treated as 'primitive' or 'primal', terms which are open to objection. That a society is 'primitive' in the technological sense in no way entails lack of sophistication; and although 'primal' avoids the pejorative overtones of 'primitive' it suggests unnecessarily a sense of tribal peoples as standing, so to say, at the dawn of history—whereas it is platitudinously true that tribal religions have long histories (but ones which are not easily available to the scholar because of the usual lack of a written literary tradition).

Of the dead religions, the most important are as follows: (1) Ancient Near Eastern—Sumerian, Babylonian, Egyptian, etc.: these have attracted much attention not only because they constituted an aspect of the living milieu of Judaeo-Christian origins but also because of the strategic place of the ancient Near East in the growth of urban culture and civilization. (2) The religions of Indo-European speakers (other than those comprised under (1) and other than those which have continued in living form, e.g. Vedic religion): e.g. Celtic religions, Greek and Roman religions—and perhaps Zoroastrianism should be included here. The continued existence of a relatively small Parsi community gives Zoroastrianism a slight 'living' status. (3) Pre-Columbian religions of America—Aztec, Inca, Maya, etc. (4) The proto-historical religions of mankind, important in relation to problems about the genesis of religion.

These lists are not quite exhaustive, but map out the major areas of historical researches. It may be noted that the religions under (4) in the living category tend to be more widely investigated by anthropologists than by religionists.

Generally speaking, the main focus of interest among those concerned with Christian theology is in the so-called 'world religions' (usually held to include categories (1) to (3) in the first list, since these faiths provide both a challenge to Christianity and an opportunity of dialogue). From an ancillary point of view, the ancient Near Eastern religions are often linked to the study of biblical history and religion. I shall revert to the matter of world religions in the last section of this essay.

PHENOMENOLOGY OF RELIGION

The discovery of certain apparently recurrent patterns in religion has led to a series of attempts to bring the materials together in an ordered way. Sometimes such attempts have been connected to a theory or theories of a speculative character about the nature and genesis of religion, as in Sir James Frazer's work. Some themes, e.g. as to the nature of magic (prominent in Frazer's discussions), have also figured centrally in anthropological work. Some of the more ambitious exercises in religious typology attempt to cover the whole field of religious phenomena; others compare particular elements of doctrine, experience, ritual, etc. It will bring out the range of such studies best to mention some of the better-known authors and works in this field. These works are listed in the bibliographical section at the end of this chapter.

Of what we may call 'holistic' phenomenologies—covering the whole range—probably the best-known is Gerardus van der Leeuw's *Religion in Essence and Manifestation*; earlier attempts on the same scale include W. Brede Kristensen's lectures on phenomenology. Rather less wide in scope is Nathan Söderblom's *The Living God*, investigating basic forms of personal religion.

Perhaps the seminal work in the present century has been that of Rudolf Otto, who coined the term 'numinous' to characterize the basic religious experience which, in his view, is central to religion. Though his theory does not fit mysticism so easily, he was also an important modern pioneer of cross-cultural studies of the contemplative life, in his work comparing

Eckhart and Shankara. The topic of mysticism has generated quite a large literature, a significant and prolific recent contributor to which is R. C. Zaehner (though he does not always write from a strictly phenomenological point of view, since he works theological judgements into his descriptions). Otto also addressed himself to the problem of the relations between doctrines and experience, a case of intra-religious explanation—explaining one element of religion in terms of another.

Particular aspects of religion covered by Mircea Eliade include shamanism and yoga; but he is rather more widely known for his general theory of myth, which bears some relation to the psychology of Jung, though more oriented to the relation between time, history and responsible action. Thus Eliade holds that profane human acts are given cosmic significance through myths describing archetypal acts 'at the beginning of time' which are constantly repeated and recreated through ritual, etc. From this point of view, the idea of unrepeatable history, as expressed in the Judaeo-Christian revelation, represents a radical break with archaic, mythic thinking, so that the man who has no longer the security of the archetype is 'fallen'. (This part of Eliade's work is, naturally, speculative, but illustrates the way in which phenomenology may rise to theories bearing a theological significance.)

As well as many particular studies of such topics as the judgement of the dead in different religions, the mother goddess, the high god, prophecy, etc., the phenomenology of religion has naturally supplied material for various theories of the genesis of religion, as well as providing evidences for and against wider ranging theories in psychology, sociology and anthropology. This is very obvious when we consider that one of the seminal figures in the sociology of religion, Max Weber, made use of a typology, including such concepts as prophecy and charisma, in his works on Indian, Chinese and Western society, etc. As one of the few approximations to experimentation in regard to wide-scale sociological and psychological theories is to apply them to independent, or relatively independent, cultural histories, the phenomenology of religion must in principle play a crucial role here.

SOCIOLOGY OF RELIGION

Very roughly it is possible to divide approaches to the socio-logical investigation of religion into two kinds—the theoretical and the inductive. On the one hand, there are theories about the role of religion, or of particular aspects of it, in society; on the other hand, there is the gathering of data about religious behaviour, etc. As elsewhere, theories are fruitful in suggesting what data to look for; while conversely religious statistics may themselves suggest hypotheses to explain them.

On the theoretical side, the most influential figures have been Emile Durkheim and Max Weber. The former's functionalist theory of religion implied that religious rituals and beliefs fulfil a cohesive function in society: they correspond to men's needs to overcome the contingency and frustration inherent in their being subject both to the forces of nature and to the restraints imposed by social living. Despite the mythological and transcendental dressing concealing it, the true focus of religious activity is society itself. Such a functionalism is often taken to imply that religion is a necessary feature of man's existence. Weber's approach was subtler and more far-reaching than Durkheim's, and his thesis that religion can be a powerful element in social causation (notably worked out in his *Religion and the Rise of Capitalism*) went well beyond Durkheim's rather static functionalism. This is partly because of Durkheim's looking for his main models in 'primitive' societies, which possess a less fluid and plural character than more wide-scale cultures, such as that of Europe at the Reformation or India. Another significant contributor to sociology of religion was Ernst Troeltsch, whose distinction between church and sect—the former conserving, the latter protesting against, the given social order—has stimulated much recent investigation of sectarianism, for example in the work of Bryan Wilson.

Social changes in the twentieth century, and in particular the apparent secularization of some major industrialized societies, have posed questions about sociological theory—for instance, it casts doubt on functionalism. At the same time, religious thinkers and organizations have shown an increasing awareness of sociological determinants of religious behaviour. Hence the emergence of what might be called 'religious sociology', namely the investigation of the data, etc., with an ultimate view to remedying the decline in faith, etc. Conversely, secularization has stimulated a form of secular Christianity, as in Harvey Cox's *The Secular City*.

Meanwhile particular, more inductive studies multiply. Ultimately it is to be hoped that the theoretical and inductive sides can be welded closely together, for this has been the form of advance in other sciences. Necessarily, sociological theory has hitherto contained a heavily speculative element. Weber's programme of cross-cultural testing of theory remains important, and it is inevitable that the sociology of religion should be integrated with phenomenology and history of religions, and in such a way that it is not simply reductionist (see above, pp. 176, 178). This in principle is the view of the most important American theoretician, Talcott Parsons.

Needless to say, there is no strict boundary between anthropological and sociological approaches to religion (indeed a great deal of Durkheim's material was drawn from anthropology). The differentiation between anthropology and sociology is in part to do with the kind of society each tends to study (for example, the study of mortuary rites among the Wisconsin Winnebagos would tend to fall under anthropology; the mortuary rites of the citizens of Oshkosh, Wisconsin, would tend to provide material for sociological research).

ANTHROPOLOGY

The creation of modern anthropology in the nineteenth century coincided roughly with the vogue for evolutionary theories of human culture; so that not surprisingly much effort was devoted to evolving theories of early stages of religion by reference to newly discovered anthropological material. Thus E. B. Tylor, sometimes regarded as the founder of modern anthropology, saw the beginnings of religion in animism: belief in such spirits he explained somewhat rationalistically as due to primitive speculations about dreams, death, natural forces, etc. By contrast R. R. Marett emphasized the centrality of the experience of *mana*, a sacred, awe-inspiring force (he drew the word from Polynesia). Such a force can be looked at as magical and religious; but it is out of it that religious development springs. It was characteristic of the late nineteenth-century and early twentieth-century anthropological discussion that much weight was laid on the relations between magic and religion. Thus Frazer saw religion as emerging out of magic, finally to be displaced by science. In an important sense, both Tylor and Frazer could be described as reductionist—explaining religious phenomena in non-religious terms; while Marett, after a fashion, resisted such a reduction. Similar disputes, but in a different key, still operate. By reason of the natural concentration upon the *social* dimension of religion among social anthropologists there has been a strong tendency not to take sufficiently seriously the dynamic function of religion as a system of meanings. Nevertheless, there are also trends—for example in the work of Evans-Pritchard and of Clifford Geertz—towards a reappraisal of religious experience and symbolism, and one which is neither simply functionalist nor reductionist.

Somewhat at a tangent to these developments is the work of the French anthropologist Claude Lévi-Strauss, evolving a sophisticated way of looking at the structure of myth in terms of its formal properties and those of the social institutions, rituals, etc., with which myths are associated in a given society. In this, Lévi-Strauss hopes to show the logic of 'primitive' thinking. What he does not deal with much is the question as to the way religious meanings continue to have force though moving from one culture to another—for example, the story of the Incarnation and Resurrection retains something of a continued pattern of meaning through all the transformations of Christianity in its transitions from one cultural milieu to another.

Though there is a natural interplay between anthropology and the sociology of religion, there remains a certain lack of mutual fertilization between these studies and the history of religions and the phenomenology of religion. As yet there is no 'all-round' study of myth, for instance—the work of theologians, philosophers, sociologists, anthropologists and so on have not been integrated. This is a point to which I shall return in the concluding section.

PSYCHOLOGY OF RELIGION

The growth of modern psychoanalysis and psychology has inevitably raised questions about the origin and shaping of religious emotions. Freud's account, in *The Future of an Illusion* and elsewhere, has been profoundly influential. Though Freud himself considered that religious symbols were psychological projections of inner needs, there have been attempts to make use of Freud's general structure within the framework of a psychologically more self-aware Christianity. If Freud's theory is conflictual, in the sense that religion arises out of childhood conflict, Jung's is collective. For Jung, religious symbolism represents the uprush of primordial archetypes from the collective unconscious. The latter is, as it were, a storehouse of the experience of the human race, inherited as a common factor by each individual. To illustrate this view, Jung and his associates were at great pains to collect mythic and symbolic data from a variety of cultures, notably Eastern ones. Both for Freud and for Jung and for other psychologists with wide-ranging accounts of religion, there are problems about testing the theories from a statistical point of view; and there are also philosophical problems about concepts such as 'the unconscious' and 'the collective unconscious'. At the same time the relatively wide acceptance, in psychotherapy, of elements from Freudian psychology, has meant that a whole new concern has developed to relate religion to mental health. This in turn has produced, particularly in the United States, but to some extent in Britain, new ways of treating pastoral theology. Traditional ideas about the cure of souls have begun to suffer a sea-change in the wake of the new psychology (cf. p. 234f.).

Some classical studies of religious experience, for instance William James' *The Varieties of Religious Experience* and James Leuba's *The Psychology of Religious Mysticism*, overlap very considerably with phenomenology of religion; but they go beyond the descriptive aspect of the latter in so far as they offer explanations (whether favourable or unfavourable to traditional religion) couched in psychological theory. On the other hand, statistical attempts to check on theories of religion themselves are necessarily intertwined with work in the sociology of religion —as in Michael Argyle's *Religious Behaviour*.

Developmental psychology, and in particular the work of Jean Piaget, has recently made a strong impact on educational approaches to the teaching of religion, since there seems to be evidence that children's emotional and conceptual development is such as to preclude their understanding of certain kinds of religious teaching in the younger age-groups (intuitively obvious, perhaps, but a conclusion liable to have profound effects, when spelt out in detail, upon religious curricula, whether in the Church or the school context).

As in the case of sociological theory, it is hard to avoid the conclusion that psychological theories need cross-cultural testing. It may turn out, for instance, that Freudian psychology has a rather confined range of application—more plausible, say, for late nineteenth-century middle-class Vienna than for Nepal or Sicily. Here again the history of religions and the phenomenology of religion remain crucial.

THE RELEVANCE OF SCIENTIFIC STUDIES OF RELIGION TO THEOLOGY AND PHILOSOPHY OF RELIGION

The history of religions brings to light in a concrete and striking way the variety of religious beliefs and experience. It thus immediately confronts the Christian theologian with the problem of the appraisal of other faiths. Crudely, two types of attitudes tend to be manifested in the face of world religions (for it is they above all that supply a living question mark to the Christian faith). One is to stress the 'wholly-otherness' of the Christian Gospel. In recent times this attitude has drawn on the distinction between the Gospel (i.e. Christ) and human religion, as found in the work of Karl Barth—so that the Gospel stands in judgement upon all religions. This position was elaborated in a sophisticated way by H. Kraemer in his *The Christian Message in a Non-Christian World,* written just before World War II and of continuing influence in the mission field. (see p. 299f.). The other attitude is to recognize an overlap between Christian theology and practice on the one hand and the beliefs and practice of non-Christian religions on the other. From this point of view there is truth and illumination to be found in the world religions, even though of course for the Christian theologian the Christian faith is the highest. It is difficult to avoid the conclusion that there is overlap, from the point of view of the descriptive phenomenology of religion.

Reflection also shows that other faiths may adopt this second attitude in reverse—in effect this is the position of Sarvepalli Radhakrishnan, a chief exponent of modern Hinduism. This in turn raises the philosophical question of the problem of criteria of truth in religion. Put crudely and artificially, this question is: What grounds can there be for accepting the truth of one revelation rather than another?

A further relevance for philosophy of the history and phenomenology of religion is this: inasmuch as the philosopher of religion is concerned to delineate the nature of religious discourse (see Chapter 9), it is necessary to see the latter concretely in its varieties of manifestations. Christian discourse does not exhaust religious discourse.

We have seen that both in the phenomenology of religion and in anthropology, from rather different angles, there has been debate about the nature of mythic thinking. Here is an example of a search for understanding which is related to important tasks in modern theology. Rudolf Bultmann's project of demythologization (see p. 55), that is the re-presentation of the Gospel by penetrating to the inner, living meaning of New Testament myth and by discarding the outer shell of mythic concepts (such as the literal picture of Jesus' ascension upwards into heaven), depends upon a certain analysis of myth. This may have to be tested in a wider context. This must remain an abiding issue, in that the Christian theologian must always be re-presenting the Gospel afresh, and this must involve at one

188

end as rounded an understanding as possible of the cultural condition of the early Church.

We have noted that sociological and psychological theories of religion are sometimes reductionist, explaining away the transcendent focus of religious belief and action. In part this is a consequence of the fact that in the nineteenth century, the seminal century for scientific studies of religion, there was thought by many intellectuals to be a collision between scientific and religious thinking. The debate about Evolutionary Theory, for instance, often suggested that the Church was wedded to an anti-scientific literalism. But the question of the ultimate incompatibility between faith and science is highly complex, and essentially a philosophical question. Thus with regard to theories about religious experience, it is necessary to ask: Even though the psychologist may be able to speculate about factors predisposing a person towards a religious experience of a certain type, how does this affect the question of whether such an experience is of God? It might, for instance, be argued that God sustains the whole cosmic process and hence the factors predisposing a person to such-and-such an experience. For a proper investigation of such issues, it is necessary to have a clear understanding of the nature of a given experience (history and phenomenology of religion), a testable theory (psychology of religion), and a view about the conceptual relations between that theory and theology (philosophy of religion). The last of course presupposes a reasonably well defined theology, which itself may be affected by interaction with the scientific study of religion.

It can thus be seen that though scientific studies do not primarily have a theological intent, they supply materials which are necessarily of theological significance. The Christian theologian, if he is to be equipped to re-present the Gospel in the present (and future) situations of burgeoning knowledge and theories about religion, needs to take seriously the change in perspective brought about by seeing Christian belief in the context of world religions, in the context of sociology and in the context of modern psychology. Here are challenges which can only be met creatively—not be compartmentalizing the study of theology, but by opening it up to the new intellectual and cultural forces released by the nineteenth century's often fumbling but undoubtedly dynamic attempts to form a science of religion.

For further reading

1. HISTORY OF THE STUDY OF RELIGION:
Jan de Vries, *The Study of Religion,* Harcourt, Brace and World, New York, 1967.
John Macquarrie, *Twentieth Century Religious Thought,* S.C.M., London, 1963.

2. HISTORY OF RELIGIONS:
Trevor Ling, *A History of Religion East and West,* Macmillan, New York, 1968.
Ninian Smart, *The Religious Experience of Mankind,* Scribner's, New York, 1969.
Charles J. Adams, ed., *A Reader's Guide to the Great Religions,* The Free Press, New York, 1965.

3. PHENOMENOLOGY OF RELIGION:
Van der Leeuw, *Religion in Essence and Manifestation,* Harper and Row, New York, 1963.
Rudolf Otto, *The Idea of the Holy,* Oxford University Press, London, 1923, and Penguin Books, 1959.
Sidney Spencer, *Mysticism in World Religion,* Penguin Books, London, 1963.

4. SOCIOLOGY OF RELIGION:
Max Weber, *The Sociology of Religion,* Methuen, London, 1965 (with an introduction by Talcott Parsons).
Thomas F. O'Dea, *The Sociology of Religion,* Prentice-Hall, Englewood Cliffs, N.J., 1966.
Vittorio Lanternari, *The Religions of the Oppressed,* New American Library, New York, 1958.

5. ANTHROPOLOGY:

Robert A. Manners and David Kaplan, *Theory in Anthropology*, Routledge & Kegan Paul, London, 1969.

6. PSYCHOLOGY OF RELIGION:

Paul E. Johnson, *The Psychology of Religion*, revised and enlarged edn., Abingdon Press, New York, 1949.

Michael Argyle, *Religious Behaviour*, Routledge & Kegan Paul, London, 1958.

7. OTHER TOPICS:

Hendrik Kraemer, *The Christian Message in a Non-Christian World*, International Missionary Council, London, 1947.

Paul Tillich, *Christianity and the Encounter of World Religions*, Columbia University Press, New York, 1961.

Ninian Smart, *World Religions : A Dialogue*, Penguin Books, London, 1965.

Note: for some bibliographical and other advice, the author is indebted to his colleague, Stuart Mews.

9

PHILOSOPHICAL THEOLOGY

J. HEYWOOD THOMAS
Senior Lecturer, Faculty of Divinity, University of Durham

9

Philosophical Theology

After the publication of Tennant's *Philosophical Theology*[1] there was no text-book of philosophical theology published until a few years ago when once again there appeared several useful such books. One reason for the absence of text-books was the fact that the subject had been criticized by both philosophers and theologians with the result that many people suspected that it was an unjustifiable enterprise. It was even claimed by some that there was no such subject. If, however, one looks carefully at this claim it soon becomes clear that it is not one that can be settled by looking at university syllabuses or publishers' catalogues. So the question is one about the idea of philosophical theology (or philosophy of religion as it is more often called). The very question 'Is there such a subject as Philosophical Theology?' is thus the kind of question that is the subject-matter of philosophical theology, for the subject is not a factual but rather a conceptual treatment of religion. The same is true of the question 'Can we distinguish between Philosophical Theology and the Philosophy of Religion?' Though I should not deny that one could validly make such a distinction I do not see that there is much gained by making this distinction here; for a discussion of this would involve showing how our subject differs from theology in the sense of Christian Dogmatics (see p. 30). What I wish to do, however, is to try to show the need for a philosophical theology and explain its nature, showing how the task resembles the theologian's task and how the method one employs is philosophical.

Almost from the very beginning of Christian history there

have always been theologians who, like Tertullian, have argued that Jerusalem can have no dealings with Athens and that the Christian theologian must avoid producing a Stoic or Platonic Christianity.[2] In our own century the late Karl Barth is generally assumed to expound this kind of position and is labelled a theological irrationalist.[3] Whether this is an accurate exposition of Barth's position or not does not concern us, for our purpose is simply that of considering types of arguments.[4] The argument makes two points and not simply one. First, it argues that Christianity cannot have any dealings with philosophy because this would mean that Christianity becomes a philosophy. The other point is the very different argument that Christianity is the only source of truth, so that any relations with philosophy can only result in a loss of truth. These two points were not distinguished either by Tertullian or by any of the succeeding theologians who have adopted his position. Further, it is clear that this argument does not exhaust the possibilities in the relation of Christianity to philosophy. There is no reason why philosophy must engulf the Christian faith. It can be invoked as a tool to assist the theologian, or again it can be invoked as an equal partner in the business of thinking about the world. The appeal of the Tertullian-type of argument lies, however, less in its usefulness as a warning for theologians than in its passionate piety. Whether the Christian is interested in theological argument or not, he is always concerned to confess his belief in the redeeming work that God has achieved in Christ. If philosophical investigation of religion is for him a suspect enterprise it is because he feels that it is irrelevant and even impious. The reasons why he believes are not philosophical reasons; and to seek such reasons strikes him as an impious way of handling what he regards as God's gifts to him.

If the reasons for holding a belief are not philosophical, however, it does not follow that a philosophical investigation of these reasons is either impossible or irrelevant. Nor is such an enterprise necessarily impious. On the other hand, what does follow is that the starting-point of such investigation must be the very piety of the believer. The lesson that Tertullian and his like have taught us is the difference between saving faith and philosophical reason. The philosopher who imagines that he can start outside religion cannot produce a satisfactory philosophical theology. Likewise the philosopher who looks at religion as merely some kind of crude philosophy which is to be refined by philosophical theology is mistaken. The starting-point of philosophical theology is the fact of faith, and the starting-point of faith lies not in philosophical reflection but the area of experience that has closer affinities with aesthetic and moral experience.

It is one thing to say that there is no reason why philosophical theology should be said to be impossible, but it is quite another to say something about the nature of this enterprise. And it is when one tries to say what philosophical theology is that one becomes aware of the peculiar elusiveness of the subject. Prof. Wisdom in his *Paradox and Discovery* talks of the philosopher as one who tells us only what we already know.[5] This is exactly the kind of thing Plato tells us about the philosophical investigation of the concept of justice—the meaning of justice is there tumbling at our feet.[6] I think it is very important for us to remember this because one can be very easily misled by the cliché that the twentieth century has seen a revolution in philosophy. There is a sense in which the concern of the philosopher now is no different from Plato's. Clearly, however, one will be equally misled if one ignores the change that has taken place in philosophy.

Traditionally philosophy was concerned with questions such as "Is time real?" "Does matter exist?" The change began when Moore declared that he would not concern himself with these questions but with such questions as "What do we mean when we say that we know the external world?"[7] Already in 1914 Russell had said that he believed that the problem and method of philosophy had been misconstrued by all schools of philosophy.[8] By showing that the old metaphysical riddles vanished under logical analysis he sought to show that all philosophical problems, in so far as they are genuinely philosophical problems, are reducible to logical problems.[9] The revolution in philosophy had, however, only just begun; for the great advance that came with Moore was the appeal to ordinary language. As well as saying that philosophy is a matter of logical analysis of statements philosophers now said, by way of explanation, that the analysis of propositions is the translation of sentences. This way we see philosophy not simply as a matter of analysing the structures of propositions but as concerned with the plain matter of fact whether one would substitute a certain expression for another. This change from the logical mode to the linguistic mode must be seen for what it was. It was not a simple substitute of language for logic. The labels 'Linguistic Analysis' and 'Logical Analysis' were synonyms used indiscriminately to refer to the Cambridge philosophy or, as it was later called, the Oxford philosophy. Whereas a view of philosophy which made it a mere matter of logic might be said to be concerned with philosophy as analysis of propositions and definition, this view of philosophy was concerned with use and description (as distinct from definition). The traditional views of philosophy had interpreted it on the models of science. The revolution in philosophy had begun when Russell brought the whole realm of philosophy into logic. It was only complete when philosophy came to be viewed as essentially a linguistic study. The mood of the new era is aptly expressed by Prof. Wisdom's aphorism, "Philosophy begins where science vanishes into logic and logic grows into sentences."[10]. When we consider such a view of philosophy we can see that though philosophy has undergone a change it reappears as something as rich and strange as ever it was. The last condition of philosophy is not so different from its first. However we can no longer deal with the problems of philosophy as if they were scientific problems. So, although it is to those old problems of the structures of being that our linguistic analysis will finally lead us, it is this relatively humble task of linguistic analysis that is our starting-point.

We have seen that the critic who immediately objects to the demand for philosophical theology is mistaken in thinking that such a theology is an attempt to supplant theology of revelation by some so-called natural theology. The truth of the matter is that philosophical theology is not—at least initially—interested in developing any doctrines. A philosophical enquiry is seldom of any great relevance to the settling of the issues which form the subject-matter of the enquiry. Yet in the case of religion there is a possibility that the philosophy should engulf the religion. The philosopher is always tempted to domesticate the language of religion, as when he may say that talk about salvation being won by the cross is really expressing one's commitment to a specific kind of morality. Thus he may ignore the relations between the concepts of religion and the pattern of living in which they are found. The religious man sees this as a threat to faith because his faith depends on the awareness of the difference between the reality of God and that of things. However, it is precisely this which interests the philosopher, and so religious belief is not as far removed from philosophy as one might suppose. Philosophy and theology are always in contact. Is philosophical theology then a method of proving theology from philosophy? That is, what is the difference between philosophical theology and apologetic theology? We must be content with a short answer, which is that whilst the content of the argument may very well be the same in both cases the purpose of the argument is different. The apologist's purpose is to persuade his audience of the truth whereas the philosophical theologian, though just as much concerned with truth, is not concerned to persuade. His intention is not to convert but to classify and to understand. It is worth adding that the apologist's work will itself become material for the philosophical theologian to investigate. This will perhaps help us to understand why we must call philosophical theology 'meta-theology'. The primary function of the philosophical theologian is a critical rather than a creative one. He is not concerned to elaborate any doctrines or to make any religious assertions but primarily to criticize the samples provided him. So the direct concern of the philosophical theologian is not God but language about God. He studies religious language with a view to placing it on the language map. Consequently his first task is that of describing as carefully and exhaustively as he can the various forms of religious language so as to bring out their likeness to and difference from other forms of discourse. However, it ought to be added that the philosophical theologian will very

often undertake specifically doctrinal tasks. Not content with
the criticism of a certain interpretation of doctrine he will go on
to explain and re-interpret the doctrine himself.

In all this we have seen nothing of the kind of task that
philosophical theologians were traditionally expected to undertake. They set out to furnish proofs of God's existence and other
'philosophical bases of theism'. Theological conclusions were
thus drawn from non-theological premisses. This is a view that
dies very hard. One is still tempted to view philosophical
theology as essentially an investigation of the grounds for
religious belief and theological positions, these grounds being
the non-theological premisses by appeal to which the theological
positions can be justified. Now so long as philosophical theology
is thought to be concerned with proof this must be the way in
which it will work. Proof requires an appeal to something
independent and external. We have, however, learnt that
philosophy is not a matter of logic merely and so its method
cannot be that of proof. As F. Waismann says, "No philosopher
has ever proved anything. The whole claim is spurious. . . .
Philosophic arguments are not deductive; and therefore they
don't prove anything."[11] This is not to say that philosophical
arguments have no relevance. They do not compel, but they
do bring about conviction and a change of outlook.

The dismissal of the notion of proof may be thought very odd
in the case of a discipline which produced and often set great
store by the traditional proofs of God's existence. The proofs
were almost entirely the contribution of Greek philosophy to
Christian theology. True, St. Anselm in the eleventh century
displayed great originality by his formulation of the Ontological Argument as did St. Thomas in the thirteenth by his
formulation of the Five Ways, but both were heavily indebted
to Aristotle. It is impossible for us to discuss the problem of
their intentions, which is a matter of considerable debate
amongst scholars;[12] but we can state as an indisputable fact
that they were quoted as ways in which reason, unaided by
revelation, could know God. The importance of the proofs is
shown by Kant who, despite the fact that his general
epistemology renders a speculative theology impossible, yet

devoted considerable space in his *Critique of Pure Reason* to a criticism of the proofs.[13] In discussing the proofs it is necessary to see what gives them their appeal as well as what fallacies render them useless as proofs. It is impossible to do this at all fully here because we cannot hope either to discuss any of the proofs in detail or to give any account of the history of this 'natural theology'.[14] It could be said with justice to make its appearance with Plato's *Laws* where in Book Ten he shows that certain truths about God are demonstrable. The primary task of such a theology is to ask what grounds there can be found for asserting the existence of God. Clearly the domination of philosophy by the notion of proof is reflected in the concern of the philosophical theologian to found a valid proof of existence of God, as seems to have been the case in the life of St. Anselm. Furthermore, if one were to examine what St. Anselm meant by 'proof', and again what St. Thomas meant, one would be confronted with the problem of deciding how we ought to understand this notion of proof. One of the points made by St. Thomas against the Ontological Argument was that the assertion "God exists" is not self-evidently true, and so one might say that he rejected the method of logical proof while nevertheless seeking a philosophical proof. The possibility of proof is obviously very tempting. Nor is it as self-evident as some theologians have led us to assume that we must either deny God's transcendence or deny the possibility of proof. This can only be so if we make God's transcendence mean his being beyond proof. The theological slogan "A proved God is no God" thus becomes a tautology. More subtle is the rejection of proof in Kierkegaard's philosophy where proof is contrasted with faith and the notion of proof is shown to be applicable only in the case of non-existential propositions.[15] However, not even Kierkegaard suggested that the proofs were without interest or importance, and there is a great deal we can learn from a study of them. They reveal something of the metaphysical character of religious belief and the areas of experience where such belief can be said to be grounded. Each of the three classical arguments tells us something about the idea of God. Anselm's Ontological Argument, for instance, expresses the conviction that the God we meet in prayer is a reality than which there can be no greater; and this conviction is the only connection between the argument of the second and third chapters of his *Proslogion*. If we turn to the *a posteriori* arguments we find that the Cosmological Argument—which, as Kant said, has a certain persuasive force no less with the speculative than the common intellect—articulates the metaphysical intuition that there is a Power beyond the world on which the world depends; and the Teleological Argument seems to me to show not so much the way we come to know God as the way in which we confirm our belief.

The discussion of the proofs helps us to understand what kind of thing religious belief is. Because of the influence of the Logical Positivist movement (with its slogan "The meaning of a statement is the method of its verification") the question of God's existence was often discussed as if it were a question of knowing facts. So the methods of verification and falsification were invoked in the attempt to make clear what was meant by saying that God exists. However, the proofs make it quite clear that coming to see that there is a God is not like coming to see that there is an Abominable Snowman (though even this might turn out to be something other than knowing a new fact). Coming to see that there is a First Cause is to come to see the world as contingent and to see life as meaningful in the way in which we see the meaning of a garden when we see it as the work of the gardener. Coming to see that there is an infinite Designer is to come to see life as meaningful in the way in which we see meaning in designed activity. It is very tempting then to conclude that religion has no concern for matters of fact. The point of saying this would be to show these differences between an assertion of fact and the subjectivity which is religious truth. In the context of religion when we speak of belief, the theologian might say, we mean belief in God and not belief that God exists.[16] Whether religious belief does not also involve a belief that God exists and whether it could not be as misleading to identify it with a belief in God are questions which the philosophical theologian must ask.

To answer these questions one would need to analyse what

we mean when we speak of belief in X. Do we ever speak of belief in things or only of belief in persons? If to say that we believe in a person is to express our faith or trust in him, does not this give us too narrow a view of religious belief? The New Testament tells us that the man with the unclean spirit worshipped Jesus and said 'What have I to do with thee, Jesus, thou son of the most high God?'[17] A very much weaker form of this view is that which sees the contrast between belief-in and belief-that as one between expressive (or emotive) language and descriptive language. This was the positivist view that the theological assertions were not assertions at all but merely expressions of certain sentiments.

It is the business of the philosophical theologian to evaluate this view and this he does by discussing what it is to express something, and whether the family of linguistic acts which we call expressions are in the final analysis to be separated as sharply as this from assertions. Again the philosophical theologian may be tempted to make a slightly different distinction between religious faith and assertion of fact. He may argue that when people speak of God and Jesus Christ they do not really assert anything as to what is so. These statements, argues Prof. Braithwaite, for instance, are expressions of a commitment to a way of life.[18] His thesis is twofold. First, he argues that stories about God are to be interpreted either as disguised expressions of moral intention or as disguised statements of empirical fact (in which case there is usually no reason to believe them). Secondly, the function of the stories is not to provide reasons for the basic moral commitment which constitutes the religious conviction but rather to afford a psychological means of easily making and carrying through a decision. So the stories need to be entertained in thought though they need not be believed. This important contribution to recent philosophy of religion highlights the problem of religious belief precisely by its very failure to give a significant enough place to *belief*. Perhaps the most serious weakness in Braithwaite's argument is that it makes the relation of belief to Christian practice psychological rather than logical. Religious statements are reasons for the religious way of life, and this is possible only because they are believed by the religious man. He would regard the statement that we ought to obey God as an ultimate precept. For the philosopher the noteworthy point is that such a precept presupposes no intention but it does presuppose religious belief.

It could be said with some justice that the subject-matter of all philosophical theology is the concept of God. It is clear from what has been said that philosophical theology is an investigation of the domestic and foreign logic of certain conceptional schemes. However we analyse these schemes we shall agree that they are constituted religious schemes by their use in doctrinal assertions about God or in the language of worship and prayer. So it seems to me that all theological statements are about God in one or other sense of the word 'about'. At once the question arises—What is the logical status of the term 'God'? The word seems to name an individual as when one says "God created the world" which is, to all appearances, logically as well as grammatically parallel to "Mr. Berryman built this house". If this is so then the assertion that God exists becomes difficult to understand. It has become something of a dogma in logic that existence is not a predicate. The corollary of this is that in the statement "God exists" the term 'God' cannot be the subject of predication. Again it might be said that names do not mean anything whereas the term 'God' does have a content of meaning. Were this not so, it could be argued, why is the term translated from one language to another. 'de Gaulle' is referred to as 'de Gaulle' whether we speak French or English but it is not so with God. This is an important issue when we look at the problem of religious morality.

There are various ways in which this problem could be raised. For instance, a theologian might say that Christian ethics do not exist, that Christianity is the death of ethics as it is the death of religion. Now he does not mean by this paradox to deny that a Christian man is the kind of man who loves his neighbour, who regards charity as the primary virtue, who is forgiving, patient and benevolent. Nor does he mean to deny that these policies of action, this way of life, are derived from what he has said about God and Jesus Christ. He is in fact pointing to the very complexity of the language of religious morality which the philosopher may point to when, like G. E. Moore, he would argue that such statements or doctrines are guilty of the naturalistic fallacy,[19] i.e. of making value statements mere statements of fact. Whichever route is taken our destination is the problem of the inference of moral conclusions from religious premises. If in the assertion 'God is good' the term 'God' is the subject of predication then the statement cannot be necessarily true any more than the statement 'Wilson is good'. However, one of the peculiarities of religious morality is the absolute nature of the claim that God is good. If, on the other hand, 'God' is a predicative expression then we are not saying that when the religious man speaks of 'God' he does not mean to refer to a Person whom he encounters or One who claims him or who will be his Judge. This would surely be very odd. It is clear then that the question of the logical status of 'God' is of paramount importance and not least in trying to see the connection between religion and morality.[20]

There is another way in which philosophical theology is always concerned with the idea of God, and this is the problem of characterizing God. There are several aspects of this problem and we shall attempt little more than a delineation of them. It is by no means an idle piece of eloquence to say that paradoxical assertions play an important part in religious language. As Prof. Ronald Hepburn says, "paradoxical and near- paradoxical language is the *staple* of accounts of God's nature and is not confined to rhetorical extravagance".[21] It is easy enough to say that one would expect the language of religion to be odd and that the paradoxes are 'revealing improprieties', to use Prof. Wisdom's phrase. The problem is that of distinguishing between a mere contradiction or a piece of nonsense and a paradox which is the statement of a mystery.[22] This is not unrelated to the other more general problem of how we can make any valid predication of God. This was, of course, the problem to which St. Thomas long ago addressed himself when he developed his view of analogy. His point is simple enough: religious language uses words the primary meaning of which is empirical and the religious neither simply the same as, nor simply unrelated to, the primary meaning. His answer is that such language is analogical, so that one thereby has a rule for understanding his non-empirical use of empirical language. For St. Thomas it is therefore very important to distinguish between analogy and metaphor.[23] The analogical use of language is strict. Such a theory finds echoes in those views of religious language which speak of it as made up of parables,[24] or models,[25] or myths and symbols.[26]

The view that religious language is parabolic was put forward by Crombie as an answer to the problem of the possibility of theological statements (and for the moment one ignores the distinction between religion and theology). 'God', he says, is an indicating expression and the things that are said of God are parables, stories which express the truth. Rules can be laid down about their interpretation and so it is logically possible to "affirm the parables".

Dr. Ramsey's view is that the structure of religious language is to be seen as models whose particular meanings are revealed by accompanying terms which are their 'qualifiers'. The model is a situation with which one is quite familiar and it is here used to speak of a situation with which one is not so familiar. The use of models in religious and theological language cannot then be like that in situations where the model pictures the reality to which it refers. One function of the qualifier is to indicate that the model is not used in its normal context. "It is a directive which prescribes a special way of developing those 'model' situations. It suggests that . . . we . . . continue the story to build up a pattern of terms and relations until a characteristically different situation is evoked . . . when the light dawns, the penny drops, the ice breaks."[27] Finally it must be noticed that for Dr. Ramsey religious language has the twofold character of expressing a discernment and a commitment. The function of the model is to articulate the mystery, and he emphatically rejects any view of religious language which would over-simplify it. Our interpretation of this language must "preserve a faithful understanding of its own mysterious topic".[28]

There are important differences between Dr. Ramsey's

views and that of the late Paul Tillich, but these need not concern us now. What is interesting for us to appreciate at the moment is the way in which Tillich's view of religious language is very close to Dr. Ramsey's. Tillich was not, of course, at all interested in providing an answer to the challenge of empiricism; but it could be said that his phenomenological method led him to seek an empirical grounding to religious language. So he relates the concept of God to the situation of revelation in human experience. However, when he talks of the concept itself he offers an ontological definition of it. God is 'being itself' or 'the power of being whereby it resists non-being'. All other religious and theological assertions are symbolical and not literal in their meaning, though there may be an exception in the case of the statement 'God is the ground of being' which seems to hover between being an interpretation of the concept and a definition. However, when he calls this language symbolical Tillich quite steadfastly insists that he is thus rescuing the concept of symbol from the ruin which it had become in modern thought. A symbol is not a sign, he says, and unlike the sign it "participates in the reality" or "participates in the power" of what it signifies.[29]

Two points ought to be made before we move on from the concept of God to the consequential matters with which philosophical theology is concerned. First, we have tended to look at religious language as if it were a matter of discovering and communicating information about God. Nothing could be further from the truth. As Kierkegaard says, faith is subjectivity and passion; and so the language of religion will more often resemble that of the lover than that of the reporter. Thus we need to be concerned with that area of language where the active character of language is most evident, the language of promise and such, performatory language. It was Austin who made us aware of performative utterances by contrasting them with some true-or-false utterances.[30] Once again the details of the distinction and its refinement need not concern us. Sufficient for our purpose is that we appreciate that performative language can be classified as constative (which states something), commissive (more-than-verbal commitment), exercitive (which is an exercise of authority), behavative (which concerns social behaviour), verdictives (expressions of verdicts).[31] By his application of these results of Austin's work to the biblical concept of creation Prof. Donald Evans has shown how this concept of 'performative' is important for both the theoretical and the practical language of religion. That is, it not only helps us to understand what kind of language is the language of thanksgiving, praise, covenant and commitment but also how one can better understand such characteristically religious utterances as 'The heavens proclaim the glory of God', and 'By the word of the Lord the heavens were made'.

The second point is very different (though here too the notion of 'performatives' is relevant) and concerns the logic of characteristically Christian statements. The necessity of confining our attention to Christianity is self-evident, but it does raise problems about the relevance of other forms of religious language. However, the particular point that now concerns us is that Christian theology is essentially Christocentric. Since Barth this may be a cliché as it has also become a cliché to say that Barth's theology was thus essentially positivistic. There is in his theology a rejection of metaphysical speculation that is strongly reminiscent of the attitude of Logical Positivism. Similar too is their preference for the concrete statement instead of the abstract generalization. In both one discerns a feeling for logical economy. Yet, as Prof. Mackinnon points out in his important essay "Philosophy and Christology", Barth's standpoint is also strongly ontological. His thinking is governed by his sense of the primacy of what is over our thought of it, and in so far as our knowledge of God is in question this is dependent upon Jesus Christ. Prof. Mackinnon further points out[32] that Barth's very quarrel with the traditional method of Catholic theology is that it seems to give to something abstract (analogy) the role that belongs to Christ alone as the One who would say "he who has seen me has seen the Father". No analysis of Christian discourse is complete which ignores the cruciality of Christ for that discourse, and here again one comes face to face with the problems of factuality. To quote Prof. Mackinnon, "No theology whose axiom is the sovereignty of Christology can escape the problems of *history*."[33] If we speak of the fact of the Christ-event what kind of fact is it? What kind of facts are the stories the New Testament tells of His miracles? Is it enough to say that it is not history? Do we have to say too that it really did happen though the resurrection is not judged by men's senses? We can see how the fact of the Christ not only determines other parts of Christian doctrine (see pp. 24–5), but raises for the philosopher a whole host of problems.

In conclusion I want to indicate three problems that concern the philosophical theologian. Two of these have always been recognized as problems of philosophical theology. They are the problems of evil and immortality and finally that of Hell and Judgement. The problem of evil was formulated by St. Augustine as the dilemma: Either God cannot abolish evil or he will not: if he cannot then he is not all-powerful; and if he will not then he is not all-good. The problem then is J. S. Mill's "impossible problem", the reconciliation of infinite benevolence and justice with infinite power. Too often the problem of evil is trivialized by the assertion that it can only arise on the assumption that the world is created by an omnipotent and infinitely good God so that Christianity really creates the problem. The problem is posed by the fact of evil and constituted indeed by the belief that God is properly described as infinitely good and omnipotent. So the problem is that of finding a consistent way of talking about God and the world, using these models of goodness and power whilst nevertheless giving an adequate account of evil. We notice how the problem is thus a linguistic problem, though it is the same problem as that which hitherto had appeared to be a quest for the source of evil. To call it a linguistic problem, however, is not to say that we are not doing metaphysics; for if the traditional solutions of the problem were classified we should have to group them as either monistic or dualistic and either pessimistic or optimistic. Equally, calling it a linguistic problem is not to deny that it is primarily a problem of behaviour. Evil is a challenge, a cross to be borne by the believer, and not a problem to be solved. It is very important to realize this because we can be tempted into thinking that the problem of evil is the problem of evidence against God. But consider a typical problem of evidence, the problem of deciding a person's guilt in a court of law. So we might ask 'Can Dr. Adams be both competent and honest when we know that he gave some of his patients doses of morphia and heroin sufficient to kill them?' In both cases decision is necessary, but the place of decision in the legal sense is very different from its place in the theological case. We decide the prisoner's guilt on the basis of evidence, and the verdict of the court is reached by an argument concerning this evidence. In the case of the problem of evil the important thing is not the evidence but whether or not you will believe in God. Consequently the question is not a request for evidence. Let us return to the question. It is a question concerning God's attributes and, even more than goodness, omnipotence is the key to the problem. We might say that the problem is created by a wrong logical placing of the term 'omnipotent'. Certainly if we imagine that the statement 'God is all-powerful and so able to abolish evil' is a logical parallel of 'This man is a competent surgeon and so able to perform the operation' we shall be mistaken. Similarly questions about the power of God to control what he had made can be misleading. We might, for instance, be led to regard the problem of evil as the paradox that God's omnipotence is consistent neither with the assertion that he can make something which he cannot control nor with the assertion that he cannot make something which he cannot control. Here linguistic analysis dispels the problem; for we see that 'cannot' is here ambiguously used and that logical impossibility does not count against omnipotence. However, the problem of evil is no pseudo-problem and there is no easy way to answer it. It seems to me that we must balance the model of power with that of love. That is, we must make clear that when the Christian speaks of God's power he is referring to the person revealed in the suffering of the Son of God on the Cross. So he does justice to the fact of evil and yet claims that a world containing evil is the best of all possible worlds.

In a discussion of the problem of evil it would be necessary to classify things and situations which we call evil. One such would be that of death. It is a cliché that men have always refused to see in death the end of their activities, and indeed this is the basis on which it is sometimes argued that there must be an immortality. Once again it will be the philosophical theologian's task to make clear what kind of problem is posed by the question: 'Does a man survive his bodily death?' It seems to be a question of fact like 'Does a piece of copper survive when it is placed in nitric acid?' However, though there is perhaps a verbal difficulty about the *piece* of copper, this question is in the end easily answered by observation. The question of immortality is not so easily answered because it is a philosophical question, a question about the meaning of 'human survival of bodily death'.

First of all, it is worth noting that the assertion of immortality has an air of paradox about it. Strictly speaking, the word immortality is used to deny death. It applies in cases where death does not occur. If this is felt to be an unjustifiable quibble let me reflect that things are no better when we say 'What I mean is the belief that a man lives again after he dies, that he survives death'. This is equally odd because the word 'survive' is generally used to signify that we have escaped the jaws of death. We learn from the newspaper that there has been another air disaster and that only a certain number of people have 'survived'. To use 'survival' in cases where death has occurred is therefore to turn our back on the standard use of the term. Yet it is not difficult to see that this is a paradox to which we are driven by our language about persons, and in particular it is an essential part of Christian faith where the resurrection of Jesus is described as the 'first fruits of them that sleep'. This reference to Jesus' resurrection is very important because it tells us something about the nature of the Christian hope as well as its basis. One important implication of this is that this belief is not invalidated by refutations of arguments for the immortality of the soul. The arguments for immortality have often taken a dualist form ever since Plato. This dualist argument may be based on the soul's simplicity or its sub- stantiality or again on the fact that, though an entelechy of the body, in the case of the 'active soul' the soul can enjoy a separate existence. The weakness of all such arguments is their dualism, and so the question arises whether immortality can only be defended if we postulate such a view.

It is here that the argument from psychical research is so tempting. It could be argued that psychical research shows that some people do survive death, and ignoring such evidence is to look a gift horse in the mouth. But there are several difficulties here. In the first place, we need to be aware of the ambiguity in the use of key terms such as 'survival'. Secondly, no empirical evidence can be sufficient condition for the more-than empirical assertion which the religious man makes. That is, even if we know that Jones is having experiences though Jones is dead we still do not know that God had raised Jones from the dead. Nor again is the philosophical problem 'Is this really Jones?' settled by this empirical argument.

More promising is the argument from morality. This can take the crude form of an argument from an alleged necessity of reward and punishment and it needs neither great ingenuity nor great sensitivity to appreciate how fallacious this argument is. The classical exposition of the argument from morality is that of Kant. Immortality, he argues, is a postulate of practical reason, a necessary condition of the rationality of moral experience. Man, as compounded (a) of Reason which recognizes Duty and (b) of inclinations, is imperfect and lacks a holy will. In his pursuit of goodness man's will does not spontaneously conform to the moral law—it merely respects the law. The human will needs a longer life than the present to free itself from all impurities of motive and for all allurements of inclination to be brought under control. Every 'ought' implies a 'can'. Unless therefore human beings survive death the moral endeavour is irrational, and this for Kant is patently false. Despite the objections that can be brought against this, it remains an impressive argument; for if we do survive death then such existence must have connections with our present life. Furthermore, the Christian view is that Jesus Christ brought about our resurrection and that eternal life is to know him. Only by telling a moral story can we hope to gain some understanding of this belief and some justification of this hope.

Despite the fact that biblical scholarship had concerned itself ever since Schweitzer with the problem of eschatology (cf. p. 37 f.), modern philosophical theology had very little to say on this. However, recently the notes of some lectures which Wittgenstein gave on religious belief have been published. Here Wittgenstein is reported as having taken the belief in a Last Judgement as a paradigm of religious belief.[34] What is the logic of such belief? First, it cannot be too strongly emphasized that it is not a refinement of the belief in immortality. The Christian does not say, 'Well, since we are all agreed that man is immortal the little piece of information I should like to contribute is that there is a Last Judgement'. It is most instructive to consider carefully what Calvin says on the subject of predestination.[35] We see that for Calvin this 'comfortable' doctrine is learnt from Scripture and the fact of election is revealed in Christ. Also election is not an *a posteriori* phenomenon. Calvin is emphatic that election is to be distinguished from foreknowledge: it is "the eternal decree" whereby God has decided what he would do with each man. Again, by the Christocentric nature of his doctrine Calvin makes it clear that he is trying to talk of God's justice and mercy. As with the resurrection so with the judgement nobody who fails to take ethics seriously can hope to make any sense of it. Yet it is all too easy to take a simple view of God's justice and draw a conclusion about the necessity of a doctrine of Hell. It is tempting then to analyse such a doctrine as meaning the claim that God reveals himself in the situation of eternal loneliness.[36] I shall content myself with two more points here. First, there seems no way in which this description distinguishes Hell from Heaven, and it is suggested that we ought not to attempt such a distinction we are in fact revising our concepts of Hell and not analysing it. Secondly, this can only seem to work because some suggestion of judgement has been imported into 'reveal', as seems to be the case in 1 Cor. 3. However, it seems to me that in this as in the problem of immortality there is great illumination to be found in the writings of the existentialist philosophers. This may well involve a careful criticism of some such view as

Sartre's that hell is other people, but it is clear that here are philosophers struggling with the phenomenology of ethical decision.

At several points in the discussion we have met the problem of the relation of faith to morals. In much the same way there is a problem concerning the relation of faith to scientific investigation and results. For example, one could ask what relevance cosmological theory has for the evaluation of the Christian doctrine of creation, or what the relations are between the Christian view of man and systematics. Another problem which has not been discussed is the relevance of psychological theories to this Christian view of man, and indeed to the analysis of the attitude of faith. A discussion of views such as Freud put forward in *Totem and Taboo* or *The Future of an Illusion* is called for from the philosophical theologian and he would here touch more on a problem that has been mentioned but has not been discussed in this chapter. Similarly there are areas of religious experience (e.g. mysticism) which have not been discussed here but which will be the subject-matter of philosophical analysis. What I have tried to do is to show the need for a philosophical theology, what kind of thing it is and how it works.

For further reading

F. Ferré, *Language, Logic and God,* Eyre & Spottiswoode, London, 1962.

John Hick, *Evil and the God of Love,* Fontana Books, London, 1969.

H. D. Lewis, *Philosophy of Religion,* a Teach Yourself Book, English University Press, London, 1965.

T. H. McPherson, *Philosophy of Religion,* Van Nostrand Co., London, 1965.

E. L. Mascall, *He Who Is,* Darton, Longman and Todd, London, 1966.

Rudolf Otto, *The Idea of the Holy,* Penguin Books, 1959.

I. T. Ramsey, *Religious Language,* S.C.M., London, 1957.

I. T. Ramsey, *Freedom and Immortality,* S.C.M., London, 1960.

N. Smart, *Historical Selections in the Philosophy of Religion,* S.C.M., London, 1964.

N. Smart, *Philosophers and Religious Truth,* S.C.M., London, 1964.

IO

THE STUDY OF APPLIED THEOLOGY

J. E. NEWPORT

Professor of Applied Theology, Westminster and Cheshunt Colleges, Cambridge

The Study of Applied Theology

APPLIED THEOLOGY may be described as a contemporary and critical study of the practical application of theological convictions to the ministry of the Church. The name for such study is relatively new, and still competes with others for general recognition.

Of more traditional titles, Practical Theology has been used in Protestant churches since the early nineteenth century to delineate a fifth branch of theology, dependent upon the four main studies of Old Testament, New Testament, Church History and Systematic Theology (see pp. 29 ff.). It refers to the application of those studies to the life of the Church, with particular reference to preaching, worship, pastoral care, discipline and government. It suffers from the disadvantage that the word 'practical' has been devalued in common parlance, having come to mean not 'action derived from theory' so much as 'action independent of theory'. As a result, Practical Theology is in danger of being misunderstood as implying no more than the study of techniques.

Other recognized titles are the Cure of Souls, and Pastoral Theology. These cover only part of the field of Applied or Practical Theology. Neither title can be used without apology. 'Cure' (derived from the Latin *cura*) is now an archaism, used in this context only to denote 'oversight'; 'soul' might be misinterpreted by some as a reference to the immortal spark within a man rather than to the whole human person.[1] The term 'pastoral' has not changed its meaning, but the changing structure of society, today increasingly urban, makes the reference to the work of a 'shepherd' less meaningful to many than formerly; moreover, the use of language which apparently divides the Church into clerical shepherds and lay sheep creates an unfortunate image of paternalistic domination which modern industrial man is likely to resist.[2]

Although names for this kind of study have varied, the themes for discussion have remained substantially the same. Today, however, the treatment of them must differ considerably from that of other times. The main reason lies in changes in interpretation of 'the ministry of the Church', brought about by three factors: (i) a re-appraisal by the Church of its own life and purpose; (ii) a reconsideration of the relationship of those designated 'ministers' to other members within the Church; (iii) a recognition of the changed and changing patterns of society in which the Church must work. Although these factors have inter-acted upon one another, it will be convenient to consider them in this order.

I THE LIFE OF THE CHURCH

In the liturgical and ecumenical movements of the twentieth century (see Chapters 11 and 13), the Church has undertaken a thorough reappraisal of its own life. In particular, it has taken seriously into account its experience of unity, and as a result the doctrine of the Church has undergone a radical change. The Roman Catholic church (see p. 305 f.) has been led to refer to "ecclesiastical communities outside the Catholic Church" as "Churches", whose members "share with us in . . . some true union in the Holy Spirit".[3] The Lund Faith and Order Conference (1952) went further. Its members had no doubt of the fact of the unity already given by God in Christ and of the participation in it of every Christian.[4] But they clearly recognized that the experience of 'unity in Christ' has produced a paradox which involves all Christians: "We differ, however, in our understanding of the relation of our unity in Christ to the visible Holy, Catholic and Apostolic Church". This posed the urgent question how Christians may be united in Christ and disunited as churches, and on one level of discourse it seems impossible to find an answer. Nevertheless, the doctrine

of the Church at a profounder level has fully recognized the
existing unity, even though it has also been constrained to
recognize that the Church which "is already one in Christ"
must "become one in Christ".[5]

The doctrine of ministry has been involved in the same
paradox. This may be seen in more than one scheme for the
re-union of churches, in which an affirmation of the unity of
ministry in the Church is followed by specific proposals for
unifying the ministries of the divided churches. In this chapter
we shall give our attention to the fundamental affirmations
which have increasingly received acceptance in ecumenical
gatherings, rather than engage ourselves with the niceties of ecclesiastical negotiation. Three such heads of agreement stand out.

Firstly, the source of ministry in the Church is the ministry
of Jesus Christ himself. The New Testament evidence is clear;
"the Son of Man came not to be ministered unto but to
minister" (Mark 10: 45), and his ministry is the pattern for
members of his Church (cf. 1 Peter 2: 21). From this derives
the call to Christians to serve their fellow men. But the ministry
of Jesus Christ meant more than loving service; he "gave his
life as a ransom for many", he undertook the whole work of
man's redemption. As Son of Man, he identified himself with
the human race which he came to reconcile to God. Other
titles given in the New Testament remind us of the varied
aspects of this work of reconciliation. He was Prophet, Teacher,
Rabbi, Witness, the speaker of God's Word who was the Word
of God. He was Priest, Shepherd, Pastor, standing between
God and men as the mediator, who brought divine life to men
and led men to God. He was King, Bishop, Judge, whose law
was love, the commander of the destinies of his people, who
came not to condemn but that the world might be saved.
Of these titles, three have become especially significant in
Christian tradition, Prophet, Priest and King; the others may
be seen to be implicit within them.[6] The New Testament titles
are not to be restricted to past history, as if they applied to a
Christ whose work ended with his earthly ministry and has lost
any further relevance (see p. 54); he who was, still is and shall
be Prophet, Priest and King within his Church.

Secondly, the ministry of Christ in the contemporary world is the task of the whole people of God through the Holy Spirit. The Spirit gives assurance of the divine presence in the Church, since the Spirit is God, one with the Father and the Son. All ministry in the Church, therefore, is God's ministry, Christ's ministry. To the Church, that is to those who share his life, has been committed the ministry of Christ in our world. This ministry belongs to the people of God as a whole. It is wrongly restricted to a particular group within the Church if thereby the ministry of all God's people is explicitly or implicitly denied. In recognition of this emphasis, the part of the laity in ministry has been re-affirmed. The *laos* are God's people. The Roman Catholic church, for example, has encouraged the setting up of a 'lay apostolate' (a juxtaposition of two words which in earlier theological systems would appear quite paradoxical). The Second Vatican Council significantly stressed the common priesthood of the faithful, the people of God (cf. p. 307), and their share in Christ's prophetic office, before it spoke of the church's hierarchy and episcopate.[7] Although one cannot claim that the practice of the Church accords everywhere with its theory, in non-Catholic denominations any more than in the Roman Catholic church,[8] yet in this generation as never before 'ministry' has been recognized as the task of the Church as a whole in and to the social order in which it is set.[9]

Thirdly, ministry is always to be exercised in terms of 'servantship'. This must be so, since ministry in the Church must always be the ministry of Christ, offered to the Church and to the 'world' in his name. Christians in South East Asia have spoken of "the nature of the Church as the People of the Servant, sharing God's total ministry", and they have called for "a fresh understanding of the Church's role and calling in the world as the People of the Servant following the Servant style of life".[10] If this is true for lay members of the Church, how much more for those called to exercise leadership! They must ponder the dictum, "servantship training is more important than leadership training". In the past, leadership has been expressed in terms of authority, sometimes only too bluntly. In our time, there is still a proper place for the exercise of authority, but this must be expressed not magisterially but ministerially, in submission to him who came "not to be served but to serve". Those who share allegiance to him should acknowledge willingly and corporately an authority within the Church based upon mutual love and trust; if this authority of servantship proves ineffective, there is nothing to replace it, no legal enactments, no sanctions, if the true nature of the People of the Servant is to be preserved (see below pp. 226 f.).

Thus it may be seen that the Church itself has challenged its concept of ministry far more radically than social forces could possibly do; this new vision comes with theological backing based on biblical insight. It must illumine our study as we consider the exercise of ministry both within the Church and within society.

II MINISTRY WITHIN THE CHURCH

(a) Aspects of ministry

Within the Church, various aspects of ministry may be delineated. We may study their past and present manifestations with reference to the traditional threefold office of Christ.

Christ as Prophet calls his people to a ministry of *prophecy*. The New Testament tells of the proclamation *(kērygma)* of the apostle or evangelist, which evoked a response of faith and established a Church. Within this early Church, prophecy *(prophēteia)*, teaching *(didachē)* and exhortation *(paraklēsis)* were exercised by members endowed with the relevant gifts of the Holy Spirit.[11] The revelation disclosed by the prophet called for commitment to action. Teaching filled out the content of proclamation, demanding the constant renewal and deepening of the quality of living. Exhortation offered strength and comfort to those hardpressed by persecution or labour. With regard to the Church today, it would be almost impossible to make a hard and fast distinction between proclamation, prophecy, teaching and exhortation; these may be accepted collectively as a ministry of prophecy, which is rightly termed the ministry of the Word of God. Now as in New Testament times it depends upon the initiative of Christ the divine Word, to which God's people are called to respond.[12]

In the history of the Church, the ministry of the Word has attained greater importance at certain periods, particularly during the Reformation and the Evangelical Revival. Churches originating in those periods have virtually identified the ministry of the Church with the preaching of the Word; this ministry has been entrusted to gifted individuals.[13] The scholarly minister expounding the Scriptures to an attentive congregation Sunday by Sunday in an atmosphere of expectant devotion stimulated and nourished the faith of generations faced with the questionings of the Age of Reason and the upheaval of the industrial revolution.[14]

In our own day both the content of the Scriptures and the vehicle of exposition have undergone re-assessment. The ministerial monologue in the confessional assembly which "provides an impoverished setting for preaching" may need to give way to the "prophetic fellowship" in which "this work will have to be carried on through group processes of biblical reflection".[15] Nevertheless, ministry of the Word of God remains essential within the Church, since the people of God have been entrusted with the ministry of the Word to the world.

Christ as Priest calls his people to a ministry of *priesthood*. Worship is the ministry of the Church to God in adoration, praise and self-offering, as a response to the sacrifice of the divine Saviour who offered himself for the sake of his people. There is a sense in which the whole ministry of the Church, the service of man as well as the service of God, may be described as worship. More narrowly, the ministry of worship is performed within the liturgical assembly by the priesthood of believers, and is consummated in the Church's sacraments, particularly in the eucharistic liturgy.[16]

The priestly ministry of the Church, like the prophetic, is not restricted to life within the Church. Just as Christ is both Priest and Shepherd, so membership of the Church implies not only communion in the sacrifice of Christ the Victim who offered himself in obedience to his Father, but fellowship in the reconciling ministry of Christ the Good Shepherd who laid down his life for his sheep. There is a strong tradition in the Church that this ministry should be exercised both sacramentally and pastorally by those to whom the title 'priest' has been accorded. The intense discussion since the Reformation as to the nature of the ministerial priesthood of individuals in the Church need not obscure agreement upon the calling of God's own people to be a royal priesthood (1 Peter 2: 9–10).

Christ as King calls his people to a ministry of *oversight*.[17] Anarchy has never been a Christian ideal; God is a God of order as well as of liberty. Within the early Church the presence of the Holy Spirit was recognizable in the fellowship of the community, directing its devotion and action; there was corporate oversight, although apostles had pre-eminence. Later in the New Testament, oversight came to be the responsibility of certain men set aside by the Church, called variously by the titles of *presbyteros* and *episkopos*, exercising corporate authority. During the first three centuries, the title of *episkopos* ('overseer') came to be reserved for the most honourable or presiding officer; from it is derived the Latin *episcopus* and the English *bishop*. The title *presbyteros* ('elder') became attached to a subordinate minister, who performed both governmental and liturgical functions under the bishop. During the same period, those holding the office of *diakonos* ('deacon' or 'servant') came to be recognized as a third order of ministry within the Church.

The Reformation reaffirmed the corporate nature of *episkopē*. At Geneva oversight was shared by the body of elders. The more radical reformers maintained that it was the prerogative of the whole membership of the Church. During succeeding centuries oversight has been exercised in different branches of the Church either by one man within a pyramidical structure of organization, or by a corporate body of elders meeting in courts of the Church with clearly defined mutual relationships, or by the Christian community accepting no other authority than the lordship of Christ mediated by the Holy Spirit in the local gathered fellowship.

Today it is recognized that all three types of structure have a part to play if the oversight of Christ the King is to be effective within the Church. There is a theological necessity for the

Church to combine both episcopal, presbyterian and congregational elements. The people of God need their congregational assemblies through which the will of the Spirit may be made known to the gathered community and its individual members. The people of God need the guidance of the common consensus of 'presbyters' whose lives have been attested among them. The people of God need the consecrated leadership of episcopal persons, not "lording it over them" but manifesting the image of Christ crucified and risen for the sake of the world to whom the Church's mission is directed. It is precisely because we now realize again that ministry belongs to God's servant people as a whole that we cannot rest content with any single traditional characteristic ecclesiastical structure.

Oversight is expressed by the Church in the discipline and in the deployment of its members. *Discipline* has been a preoccupation of the Christian community from the earliest times. St. Paul had to give an account of his faith and practice to the apostles and elders at Jerusalem, and himself called to account the members of the churches founded by him.[18] Discipline later became more formalized. In the Middle Ages a comprehensive system of canon law developed in the Western Church, parallel and comparable to the civil law both in theory and practice;[19] it brought to mediaeval society a cohesion which would otherwise have been lacking. In our own day the Church cannot invoke the support of the 'secular arm', and the ecclesiastical sanction of excommunication has lost much of its terror for the laity. In practice, therefore, the exercise of canon law is largely restricted to the discipline of the clergy, with the exception of the regulation of marriage among its members. The Reformers reacted against canon law, but nevertheless established a rigorous system of ecclesiastical discipline, notably in Calvinist Geneva. The name 'Puritan' has come to be associated (not altogether justly) with a negative attitude to human pleasures and cultural pursuits, but the positive value of the Puritan approach lay in the concept of the Church as a corporate body within which the faith and morals of any member affected the health of the whole.

226

Today all branches of the Church need to re-assess together their attitude to the discipline both of individuals and of groups. The reaction against an oppressively authoritarian approach partly reflects the permissive nature of modern society, but it results too from the new understanding of the nature of ministry within the Church. The problem for all churches, not only for those whose approach has previously been 'magisterial', is that of combining a proper care for the standards of their members with the offer of freedom in Christ which is the birthright of every Christian.

Deployment of the Church's members and resources for service and mission was undertaken under the guidance of the Holy Spirit in the New Testament Church. As with discipline, effective oversight of strategy in subsequent times has chiefly been concerned with the clergy. During more than one epoch of church history even those professionally engaged in its ministry have resisted any attempt to dislodge them from the green pastures in which they found comfortable livings. As a result, from time to time para-ecclesial societies have sprung up to fulfil the mission in which the Church was failing; one might cite the preaching Orders of the Middle Ages, the Society of Jesus, the Methodist Societies of the Evangelical Revival and the Salvation Army. That some of these societies developed into separate denominations, leading to further division in the Church, is a warning to the Church of our day to give heed to the work of the Spirit. In the past the strategy of deployment has sometimes been highly authoritarian,[20] but persuasion and co-operation have also proved fruitful methods.[21] The Protestant churches, if no others, need to impress upon all their members today their calling to be at the disposal of the Church for its work of mission and service, and to find effective machinery within their understanding of the doctrine of the Church to deploy these servants to the best advantage.[22]

(b) *An ordained ministry*

Within the Church, ministry has traditionally been associated with a particular group of church members, known variously as

227

'clergy', 'priests', 'ordained ministers' or (in England, affec-
tionately or scornfully) 'parsons'. The concept of ministry has
often been restricted to members of the group. The fresh
recognition in our own time that ministry belongs to the people
of God as a whole, deriving from the ministry of Christ, has
called in question the limitation of ministry to a group of
professional, full-time servants.[23] On the other hand, it is still
generally accepted that there is a place in the Church for a
special ministry exercised by individuals separated and
ordained to that office within the total ministry of the Church.
Discussion centres around the criterion by which those who
exercise it may be distinguished from other members of the
Church, and the significance of the ordination by which they
are set apart for their office.

In the past such ministers have normally been distinguishable
from 'laymen' by the fact that they are committed to the
ministry of the Church as a profession, and derive their liveli-
hood from it. Some Christian communities have never made
such a distinction; their 'tent-making ministries' have claimed
apostolic precedent (Acts 18: 3). In recent years experimental
ministries of worker-priests or their equivalent have made it
clear that professional, full-time, salaried service is no criterion
by which to distinguish the special ministry.[24] Neither may we
look to a traditional 'clergy-line', which in most denominations provides an instinctive criterion by which a minister may
be recognized. Bishop John Robinson has noted its arbitrary
nature, since it is drawn at different levels in different denominations, and claims that it is 'neither native nor essential to the
Church'.[25] The criteria which we shall establish are connected
with the threefold aspects of ministry to which attention has
already been drawn.

The ministry of *prophecy* stems from the call of God to a man
or woman to utter the Word of God. The authority to act as a
minister of the Word is inherent in the call, stemming from the
prophetic consciousness of the inward compulsion of the
Spirit. Such a call was received by the great prophets of Israel
and Judah, by St. Paul on the Damascus road, by Luther,
Wesley, Booth, in varied ways. The Church has not always

recognized the charismatic gifts which such servants possess, so that schism has sometimes unhappily accompanied the exercise of the prophetic gift. In some branches of the Church this is the ministry *par excellence*. Where a church recognizes the divine call to one of its members in our own day, it provides training for the nurture and development of the gift, and by ordination confers authority to exercise it.

The call to preach however cannot be the only criterion of special ministry; in more than one denomination 'laymen' who have received such a call are authorized to perform the ministry of the Word, either as auxiliaries to those who have been ordained to the full ministry of Word and Sacrament, or in their own right. But even if the ministry of the Word is not restricted to the special ministry, those who have been ordained must give high priority to the tasks of prophecy, witness and education, to proclaiming the Word of God to members of the Church, and undergirding the work of God's people through whom the ministry of the Word to the world must effectively be performed.

The ministry of *priesthood* receives a different emphasis in different branches of the Church, in all of which the minister plays a leading role in worship, but in different ways. During its formative years the early Church developed a concern for order in worship,[26] and by the second century control of worship was given to a leader, 'president' or 'bishop'. The threefold order of bishop, presbyter and deacon is specifically linked with the liturgical life of the Church, and the development of a profusion of sub-orders shows the extent to which ministry came to be equated with liturgy. Ordination in this context means the giving of authority to perform certain liturgical functions; even those churches which do not acknowledge the threefold order accept this significance of ordination, although some churches (notably the Congregational and Baptist) would not restrict the leadership of worship, or even the celebration of the sacraments, to ordained ministers.

The development of the doctrine of eucharistic sacrifice led to the identification of leadership in worship with a Christian priesthood, shared by bishops and, somewhat later, by presbyters, who acquired the title of 'priest'. As a result, churches in the Catholic tradition conceive of ordination specifically as the power of consecrating the elements and offering the bloodless sacrifice of the Mass. The questioning of this doctrine at the Reformation meant that ordination to priesthood ceased to be a universal criterion of ministry within the Church. In the Lutheran and Reformed churches the concept of the pastor replaced that of the priest.[27] The office of pastor reflects other aspects of the Catholic tradition of priesthood, particularly the giving of sacramental absolution. The Reformed pastor is called to watch over the spiritual health of his people no less than the Catholic priest, and has received authority through the Church to proclaim the word of forgiveness to the penitent, but there is nevertheless a subtle distinction, both with regard to the criterion by which he differs from the layman and to the authority conferred by his ordination. To risk over-simplification, the pastor's powers are never personal to himself, but always exercised on behalf of the Church whose minister he is; the priest enshrines in himself the priestly power of the Church, to such an extent that one might until recently have been justified in supposing that the priesthood was the Church.[28]

The same difference of opinion has been reflected with regard to the ministry of *oversight*. Those who hold a high doctrine of priesthood usually affirm that such priesthood is transmitted in the Church by succession through the episcopate. Even where (as in the Church of England) there is not unanimity over the theological significance of episcopal ordination, undoubtedly the practice of ordination by the laying on of episcopal hands demonstrates unequivocally the separation of the special ministry from the laity. Ordination, even episcopal ordination, might be accepted by most member-churches in the World Council of Churches as a necessary and helpful criterion of such setting-apart for special service in the Church; the continuity of episcopal ministry from a very early period, and the fellowship of a world-wide episcopal community at any given point of time, point to episcopacy as a unifying factor within the life of the Church, down the ages and across the world.[29] But further discussion is undoubtedly necessary before there can be a consensus throughout Christendom concerning the significance of episcopal ordination, the grace conferred by it, and its efficacy in transmitting a priestly power distinct from that shared by other members of the Church.

(c) *An ecumenical ministry*

Such discussion is an interesting academic exercise. It can become agonizing during negotiations between denominations seeking to unite, each of which sees its traditional doctrine threatened. One might ask whether the attempt to 'reconcile' different forms of ministry may not be a cul-de-sac, since the 'catholic' doctrine of eucharist and priesthood appears to be fundamentally different from the 'protestant' doctrine of Lord's Supper and ministry of Word and Sacrament. But even such differences as these are transcended by the manifest unity in Christ which the separated churches have already recognized. Might they not therefore continue to exist in a United Church which made no attempt to claim an identical status for all its ministers *vis-à-vis* the doctrine of episcopal and priestly orders? Such a suggestion is not outrageous when it is realized that this is precisely the situation which prevails within the Anglican Communion.

In such a case, it would still be necessary to define the criterion by which those exercising a special ministry were distinguishable from other church members, and the significance of ordination, within the United Church. The Church needs servants who will represent Christ to the Church in order that the Church may represent Christ to the world. Their ministry will be *prophetic* as they proclaim the Word of God, not only in the formal worshipping assembly, but to individuals and groups of God's people, standing behind them to train and encourage them for the Church's ministry to the world. Their ministry will be *priestly* as they mediate the grace of forgiving love, not only in the traditional sacraments but wherever their presence effectively communicates to God's people, collectively or individually, release from the weight of guilt and the joyful assurance of power to obey God's will in the apostolic mission of the Church. Their ministry will be *episcopal* as they undertake in Christ's name the guidance of his people in that mission, giving oversight to the tasks to be performed and to the deployment of his servants, sometimes working with fellow-members of the Church in their mission, and from time to time going ahead of them into the secular structures to experiment in new forms of service or to demonstrate what might be done by a Church whose members were fully trained and equipped. The criterion of their ministry would be the recognition by the People of God of their call to this significant service; ordination would confer the confirmation of their call and the authorization to act as servants of the servants of God.

III   THE CHURCH'S MINISTRY WITHIN SOCIETY

Since the Church in the fourth century acquired a position of favour in the Roman Empire under Constantine, it has envisaged its life as having a 'normal' form within a Christian society in which the truth of its teaching was recognized, opportunities to promote social well-being were offered, and even temporal power or prestige was accorded. When, during the sixteen centuries from Constantine to the present, the Church has extended its work into a missionary situation, it has worked not only as a converting but as a civilizing agency for the establishment of the 'norm'.[30] But during the last three centuries a transformation in attitudes has been taking place; the Age of Reason has led Western man via the questioning of the eighteenth and nineteenth centuries to the contemporary acceptance of a secular, scientific culture with the resultant disturbance of the Church's cherished position.

As a result, the Church and its teachers have lost the magisterial position in the field of thought and culture which they held in the West during the Middle Ages and Reformation; the study of dogmatics (see pp. 30 and 156) may still be pursued within the Church, but the Church no longer has the right or the ability to impose its dogmatic teaching upon society as a whole, scarcely upon its own members.

In the field of social caring, too, the Church's monopoly has been breached. Until comparatively recently the Church was the main dispenser of alms, an amateur welfare organization with its agent in every parish. Now these functions of the Church have been overtaken by the development and application of the sciences of psychology, sociology and education. The growth of professional agencies sponsored by governmental or voluntary organizations for the well-being of all citizens has left no role for the Church but the filling of the few gaps in the welfare state.

At the same time the Church, in lands where formerly it could claim privileges within the State, is finding its position crumbling under its feet. Some churches may still be recognized as 'established', but they are wise not to trade upon their establishment. If the Church is to be accorded any eminence, it is on the same basis as any secular institution; its service will be assessed by reference to its social value, upon grounds chosen by humanists rather than theologians.

There is no reason to think that the traditional setting of the Church in the social order will return. Hope springs rather from signs that the Church is learning to find a new relevance in a situation in which tradition is questioned, change is normal, and security is to be found no more in secular structures but only in Christian faith (see pp. 23-6).

In this setting the Church must re-assess the ministry of *witness*. In the tradition of the West, the Church's proclamation has been offered in the residential community, and in schools, colleges and hospitals, many of its own foundation. Today the educational or medical institution is dependent upon a secular authority, with its own communal life which means more to those who work in it than the more tenuous residential parish in which they sleep. Thanks to its previous work in these fields, the Church has been able to maintain its witness, partly through the work of laymen involved in these structures, but also through the official recognition of ordained chaplains. The success of their work has depended upon their ability to demonstrate convincingly their willingness to serve the community 'without strings', so that those who may not accept the Church's beliefs, or even hold anti-Christian or anti-clerical views, are persuaded of the value of their service.

The Church has learnt from this experience to extend its witness to other social structures on the same basis. Like the school and hospital, the industrial firm or commercial company plays a greater part in the life of its employees than the parish; here too witness by lay workers or by chaplains has proved effective. In a slightly different way the Church has extended its witness to the mass-media of communication, in which above all it has discovered that it must experiment constantly and learn from the professional practitioners. In other and varied ways, too, Christian influence has been brought to bear in political and governmental structures at the local, national and international levels. From these experiences the Church has received new insights for its work in the traditional field of parochial ministry within a residential community.

In all these areas the criterion of effective witness is likely to be service which is recognized as helpful by those to whom it is offered, whether employees or managers. The Church must be willing to be judged by the world's terms. This does not mean that in its ministry it is restricted to an untheological pragmatism. The university or industrial chaplain will indeed be judged in the working community by the value of his service to the community, but he will receive no recognition if he is indistinguishable from the welfare officer or psychiatrist. Even those who reject the Christian faith expect from the Church's servants a ministry which springs from faith and offers faith—a faith which takes account of the stresses imposed by the secular environment, but nevertheless transcends its baser values as it points to the eternal Gospel of reconciliation.

In the same setting the Church is called to the ministry of *care and service*. Traditionally this 'pastoral' ministry has been exercised by the parish priest or minister who relied upon sanctified common sense, an instinctive feeling for the needs of his 'flock', and the experience gained through a long ministry. During this century psychology and sociology have proved valuable allies; the good pastor, no less than the good psycho-therapist, must listen rather than speak, support rather than exhort, understand rather than condemn. All who are ordained to ministry in the Church should receive training in counselling; no less is demanded of management trainees in industry. Some will go further to acquire specialist qualifications in 'pastoral psychology', sometimes described as 'clinical theology'. The servants of the Son of Man should come to terms with the reactions of the human mind to the normal stresses imposed by everyday life at work and at home, and to the additional strain associated with insecurity and unemployment, illness and old age, birth, marriage and death. They may study the behaviour not only of individuals but also of groups, and of individuals in relation to groups, through the experience of membership of different kinds of groups and reflection upon it. But when the Church has learnt all that it can from the secular sciences, it retains its responsibility as representative of the mediator between God and man. Frank Lake, while dealing exhaustively with the medical and psychiatric causes of mental ill-health, says forthrightly with regard to treatment, "A clinical theology stands or falls by the faith of Christians that the resources, as outlined by Paul in the Ephesian letter . . . , are still available within the corporate life of the Body of Christ."[31]

Finally, the Church is called to the ministry of *judgement*. Its members must still be the conscience of society. Perhaps the fear of a Puritan image has inhibited the Church from this function towards society, for the same reason that mutual discipline of its own members has become atrophied. But judgement need not be censorious. R. A. Lambourne has written of the ministry of 'visitation', linking the visitation of the sick to the visitation promised by God to his people, seeing it as the offering by the Church of the life of Christ, so that the sick person is joined to the Body of Christ.[32] The Church's visitation must similarly be directed to the strong, those in positions of responsibility and leadership in their professions, who are conscious of the problems imposed by a society which they did not create but must seek to control. Such visitation involves not only comfort but judgement,[33] proffered indeed in a spirit of understanding rather than of condemnation, an understanding stemming from faith in a God whose self-giving love does not contradict, but comprehends, the fullness of purity and righteousness. The Church's ministry within society, exercised in all humility, is to point members of society away from their own environment to the transcendent Father of love.

While human nature remains human, the Church and its ministry will not be redundant. Society may change. A pluralist, permissive society will require from the people of God a pluriform ministry, which may well be exercised by those who earn their living in industry and commerce, specializing within a team in different aspects according to their qualifications, some serving a gathered congregation or residential parish, but others going out into economic, political or social structures to meet their fellow-men where their interests lie. It may prove as daunting to come to terms with a pluriform ministry as with the pluralist society which it is designed to serve.

But however much the structures of the Church change, the theological basis of Christian ministry will remain. The needs of men and women, within the Church and beyond its bounds in the social order, will always demand the ministry of the people of God, called to be servants of him who came not to be served but to serve, as Prophet, Priest and King.

For further reading

GENERAL

J. T. McNeill, *A History of the Cure of Souls*, Harper, New York, 1951.

Frederic Greeves, *Theology and the Cure of Souls: an Introduction to Pastoral Theology*, Epworth, London, 1960.

Martin Thornton, *The Function of Theology*, Hodder, London, 1968 (Dr. Thornton gives to 'Applied Theology' a definition different from that on p. 219 above).

MINISTRY WITHIN THE CHURCH

K. Carey (ed.), *The Historic Episcopate in the Fullness of the Church*, Dacre, London, 1954.

J. E. L. Newbigin, *The Household of God*, S.C.M., London, 1957; 2nd ed., 1964.

Daniel T. Jenkins, *The Protestant Ministry*, Doubleday, New York, and Faber, London, 1958.

David M. Paton (ed.), *New Forms of Ministry*, Edinburgh House, London, 1965.

The Shape of the Ministry; the report of a working party, British Council of Churches, London, 1965.

S. C. Mackie (ed.), *Ministry, I–VI,* Proceedings of a study on patterns of ministry and theological education, mimeographed, World Council of Churches, Geneva, 1965–6.

S. C. Mackie, *Patterns of Ministry*, Collins, London, 1969.

THE CHURCH'S MINISTRY WITHIN SOCIETY

Gibson Winter, *The New Creation as Metropolis*, Macmillan, New York, 1963.

Harvey Cox, *The Secular City*, S.C.M., London, 1965.

Bryan R. Wilson, *Religion in Secular Society*, Watts, London, 1966.

David Martin, *A Sociology of English Religion*, S.C.M., London, 1967.

PASTORAL PSYCHOLOGY

E. N. Ducker, *A Christian Therapy for a Neurotic World*, Allen, London, 1961.

R. A. Lambourne, *Community, Church and Healing*, Darton, Longman and Todd, London, 1963.

Frank Lake, *Clinical Theology*, Darton, Longman and Todd, London, 1966.

I I

THE STUDY OF WORSHIP

J. G. DAVIES

*Edward Cadbury Professor and Head of the Department of Theology,
Director of the Institute for the Study of Worship and Religious
Architecture, University of Birmingham*

11

The Study of Worship

INTRODUCTION

WORSHIP, AT least in the Christian and Jewish traditions, is primarily a thanksgiving to God for his action in history and, at the same time, a means of participation in that action. So the Jewish festivals, possibly of Canaanite origin (cf. p. 65 above), were eventually linked with Yahweh's mighty acts of deliverance so that the Passover, for example, was both an expression of gratitude for the redemption from Egypt and for the establishment of the covenant and the means of re-engaging within that covenant.[1] Similarly, the Christian eucharist is based upon God's action in Christ and is both a thanksgiving for that act of redemption and for the new covenant that it established and a means of participating in the fruits of that deliverance and of renewing the covenant bond between God and his people.

Christian worship is not, therefore, a method of cajoling God, of inducing him to do something, which was often the case with more primitive forms. So it is to be contrasted with the sacrifice offered by Elijah on Mount Carmel (1 Kings 18). Elijah's concern was to bring an end to the prevailing and disastrous drought and thereby demonstrate the power of his God; the water that he poured upon the sacrificial victims was an act of sympathetic magic to induce Yahweh to perform in like manner and pour down rain from the skies. According to the report, Elijah was successful, but his act of worship was little short of magic and to that extent is to be distinguished from what Christians believe and do when they assemble to worship their Lord.

R 241

Christian worship, too, like its developed Jewish counterpart, is understood as an action in which God takes the initiative. Thus the sacrificial system which bulks so large in Exodus and Leviticus is represented as being detailed by Yahweh himself, and the eucharist is also understood in the New Testament to have been instituted by Christ. This does not deny the human element; God does not worship himself, but he does provide the means whereby mankind can worship him. Hence Christians regard the basic structure of the eucharist—the taking of food and drink, the blessing of God over them and their distribution and consumption—as unalterable because it is in accordance with the divine will, revealed in their authoritative scriptures, but the particular form that this structure may assume, the words accompanying the action and the setting, can obviously change from age to age and culture to culture. The study of Christian worship therefore comprises the history of its different forms throughout the centuries, and to this must be added an examination of its meaning in general and of the rationale of particular services, all undertaken in the light of its setting, which includes sociology, theology and architecture. Textual study is also necessary, especially for the period before the printed book, in order to determine exactly what was said and done.

The study of worship is an exacting historical discipline and this is a necessary prolegomenon to another element in the whole subject, viz. the provision of relevant and meaningful forms at the present day. Because Christianity rests upon what God has done in past history, a knowledge of the Church's worshipful response throughout the centuries is essential to safeguard its liturgical inheritance and to provide some guide lines for contemporary revisions and reforms. But because God continues to act in history, there must be a continuing dialectic between tradition and the modern situation. To throw away the past completely is unthinkable for Christianity, but to allow the past so to dominate the present that new forms of response are made impossible is to be guilty of historicism, not to say archaism, and to deny the inner dynamic of Christian faith as it finds expression in worship (cf. pp. 54 ff.). Certainly, within the Patristic period, we find a continuing development of worship but one that never loses its roots in the New Testament record.

WORSHIP IN THE NEW TESTAMENT

Whereas the first Christians, being Jews, continued to attend services in the synagogues (Acts 22: 19) and, if in Jerusalem, went to the Temple to pray (Acts 2: 46), they also had their own cultic acts, of which the most important was the breaking of bread (Acts 2: 42) or the Lord's Supper (1 Cor. 11: 20). Initially a complete meal, following the pattern of the Last Supper, which whether a Passover or not had a paschal context,[2] it began with the breaking of bread and concluded with the cup of wine and it had a threefold reference: first, to the past event of God's saving action in Christ; second, to the experience of the contemporary fact of his coming in the gathering; and third, to his coming again at the final consummation. Past and future thus found a creative meeting in the present. In addition to the consumption of food, there is evidence that a homily was delivered (Acts 20: 7), that letters from leading Christians were read (Col. 4: 16), that a collection was taken for charitable purposes (1 Cor. 16: 2) and that the worshippers exchanged a kiss of peace as a sign of their solidarity (1 Cor. 16: 20). It is probable that petitions were made and intercessions offered and there may have been lections from the Old Testament. The meetings took place at night and, although it is impossible to determine how frequently in the earliest days, it soon became the practice to hold them once a week, early on Sunday morning, being the day of Christ's resurrection, and it is possible that the day became known as the Lord's day because it was the occasion of the celebration of the Lord's Supper.[3] The community assembled in the house of one of its members, presumably in the dining-room; so at Ephesus they gathered in that of Aquila and Priscilla (1 Cor 16: 19) and at Laodicea in that of Nymphas (Col. 4: 15).

Baptism in the apostolic age was perhaps scarcely an act of worship, although it was later to undergo liturgical elaboration.

Among the precedents that influenced the practice must be included the lustrations of the Jews, the ritual baths of the Qumran community, proselyte baptism and the baptism of John, together with Jesus' own example in submitting to the latter. Water was used, either that of a river (Acts 16: 13 ff.), or a wayside pool (Acts 8:36). The laying on of hands, a Jewish sign of identification, often accompanied the water rite (e.g. Acts 19: 6), and references to unction and to the putting on of Christ (1 John 2: 20; Gal. 3: 27) have been understood of the anointing and the clothing with white garments that were features of the ceremonial in the second century, but there is no certainty about this.

Within the New Testament there is little evidence of gatherings for worship other than at baptism and the eucharist, but it is reasonable to suppose that Christians did meet simply for prayer and Bible study. Certain of the elements may be listed by Paul when he says that 'each one hath a psalm, hath a teaching, hath a revelation, hath a tongue, hath an interpretation' (1 Cor. 14: 26). There was also manifest a tendency towards the use of fixed liturgical forms, including the Lord's Prayer (Rom. 8: 15), benedictions (1 Cor. 16: 23), doxologies (Rom. 1: 25) and the singing of hymns (Col. 3: 16).

WORSHIP IN THE SECOND AND THIRD CENTURIES

The study of worship from the close of the apostolic age involves an examination of the steady elaboration and enrichment of the New Testament forms. Justin Martyr in his *Apology* of *c.* 150 reveals how the meal has been dropped, thus bringing the bread and wine together, and how a preparatory ministry of the word, probably modelled on the synagogue liturgy and consisting of readings and a sermon, has been added to the sacramental action (cap. 65). Hippolytus, in his *Apostolic Tradition* of *c.* 217, gives a very detailed account, including an offertory or the bringing up of the bread and the wine and a model eucharistic prayer, although he is emphatic that the latter is not *de rigueur* and that extempore prayer is still widely practised (caps. 4, 23). References in Cyprian's letters indicate a similar shape in North Africa in the mid-third century and there is some slight evidence that the *sanctus* may have been used in Alexandria.[4]

Both Tertullian and Hippolytus provide descriptions of baptism[5] and they indicate that there has been added to the rite a blessing of the water, questions relating to the candidates' beliefs, an exorcism and the continuation or introduction of unction.

The meal proper of the Last Supper, dissociated from the eucharistic bread and cup, was by now a quasi-religious gathering of the faithful, known as the agapé or love-feast.

THE DEVELOPMENT OF THE CLASSICAL LITURGIES

If the development of the eucharist hitherto had been steady and unspectacular, various factors now combined to accelerate the process. Of primary importance was the acceptance in the West of Latin as its liturgical language. The immediate effect of this was to create a distinction between Eastern and Western rites. Further, within the areas differentiated by language, there also took place a rapid growth of local forms of worship, issuing in families of liturgies.

A whole series of texts now demands the student's attention. Beginning with the *Euchologion* of Serapion of Thmuis, *c.* 350, which provides evidence for the Egyptian eucharistic rite,[6] they also include for Jerusalem the *Mystagogical Lectures* usually attributed to Cyril (*c.* 350) but possibly by his successor John (*c.* 386),[7] and for Syria the so-called Clementine Liturgy contained in Book 8 of the *Apostolic Constitutions* (*c.* 375).[8] In the West the Milanesian liturgy can be largely reconstituted from two works by Ambrose—*On the Mysteries* and *On the Sacraments,*[9] and the African rite from references in the writings of Augustine.[10]

Gradually the various families of liturgies emerged. In the East there was the Syrian, which may be sub-divided into West Syrian, including the Melkite, the Jacobean and the Maronite, and the East Syrian comprising the Nestorian, the Chaldean and ultimately that of Malabar. In Egypt there were the Greek liturgies of Mark and Basil and the Coptic rite of Mark. To these must be added the Ethiopic and finally the Byzantine. The latter ultimately predominated in two forms—the liturgy of St. Basil, still celebrated by the Eastern Orthodox churches on a few days each year, and that of St. John Chrysostom which has continued in general use.[11] From the West we have the Ambrosian rite of Milan, together with the Gallican, Celtic, Mozarabic and finally the Roman. It was this last that ultimately became predominant in western Europe and provided the form of the mass against which the Reformers were to react in the sixteenth century.[12]

Eastern and Western liturgies also grew apart because of a dissimilarity in the way the offertory was performed. In the West it was the custom for the bread and wine to be brought up by the individual worshippers during the service ; in the East the gifts were handed in beforehand, and from this two practices were to develop peculiar to the Eastern liturgies: the rite of the prothesis and the Great Entrance. The former was an elaborate preparation of the eucharistic species before the service proper began, while the Great Entrance was the carrying in of the elements to the high altar. A rationale was developed to connect these features—in the rite of the prothesis Christ is slain in a figure by the piercing of the host with a miniature lance; at the Great Entrance the dead Christ is solemnly borne to his altar-tomb, and finally at the Epiclesis, or invocation, the Spirit is invoked to raise the dead Christ who is then present as the living Lord in the midst of his worshippers. In this way there was created a divergent ethos in East and West, which also affected the doctrinal understanding of the eucharistic action. This showed itself particularly in relation to consecration, associated in the West with the words of institution and in the East with the Epiclesis. However as regards such concepts as the eucharistic sacrifice and the real presence, there was in the main agreement, although the belief in transubstantiation was primarily of Western origin.

Baptism also underwent considerable development, issuing in the West in the final supremacy of the Roman form, while in the East there have survived a host of local orders, differing slightly from each other in small details—these include the Armenian, Chaldean and Maronite.

Non-sacramental forms of worship also underwent considerable development. During the third and fourth centuries, Christians were expected to offer prayer at certain hours; this practice however was a private exercise for individuals and their families. The history of the transformation of this cycle of private prayer into a cycle of public worship is by no means clear, but from the late fourth century two of these hours, morning and evening, were conducted publicly day by day in the large churches. The main impetus to further development came from the monastic movement. Living together as a community, the monks said prayer in common at various hours of the day and this issued in the regulated offices of Benedict which became the pattern for the Western Church, there being ultimately eight hours. Their structure was not altogether uniform but all included canticles, psalms and prayers.[13]

The Middle Ages also saw the creation of a great number of other services, e.g. for the consecration of churches,[14] for ordination,[15] for marriage,[16] burial[17] and the churching of women. All these were given a setting in time by the creation of the Church's Calendar or Year,[18] and in space by the building of special churches, and often separate baptisteries, from the basilicas of the days of Constantine to the vast cathedrals of the twelfth to fifteenth centuries.[19] Treatise after treatise on the meaning of the mass, baptism, etc. were also produced, thus adding to the large amount of material to be studied if a comprehensive knowledge of worship is to be obtained.

In addition to the doctrinal studies, the mediaeval period was rich in service books. For the West these may be divided into four main groups. First, there were those required for the Hour Services; these included at least fourteen separate volumes, such as the *Ordo,* which regulated the relative precedence to be given to Saints' Days, Sundays, commemorations and week-day services, and the *Hymnarium,* containing metrical office hymns. For the eucharist some ten books were needed, such as the *Comes,* which helped the priest find the lessons for the day. Most important of all the mass books was the *Sacramentarium,* a comprehensive collection of all forms belonging to the rite, e.g. the variable portions, the ordinary or unchanging parts and the canon of consecration prayer. Study of these involves determining their date and the character of their contents, and the two most important sacramentaries requiring attention are the Gregorian, which was the official book in Rome at the time of Gregory the Great, and the Gelasian. The latter has been preserved in two forms—the older from the end of the seventh century and the later or Frankish Gelasian from the first half of the eighth century.[20] The third group of service books concerns the occasional offices, such as confirmation, the anointing of the sick and the burial of the dead. The final series is a varied one, including the *Benedictionale* or episcopal blessings and the *Ordines,* an important series from the sixth to the eleventh centuries, of which over fifty have been preserved.[21]

The inconvenience of having to use so many books led to their being grouped together, the two principal comprehensive collections being the Breviary, which assembled all the material for the daily offices, and the Missal, which was used for mass.

The Eastern churches produced a parallel series of books, but these cannot be easily divided into groups as many contain sections for different services. Moreover no one-volume collection has been made, the chief development being the issuing of abridgements. Some, such as the *Euangelium* or Gospel Book, have direct counterparts in the West, while others, such as the *Diakonikon,* comprising rules for the deacon's part in the eucharist, lauds and vespers, are peculiar to Orthodoxy. No student of worship in the Middle Ages can progress far without familiarizing himself with this rich and varied literature, and to complete the picture he needs to know something of the musical accompaniment of worship,[22] which necessarily involves the history of hymnody, and of the various means used to enrich the services, such as the development of the ritual of Holy Week[23] and the wearing of vestments.[24]

WORSHIP IN A DIVIDED CHURCH

Despite the Great Schism, which divided East and West in the eleventh century, the general evolution of the forms of worship up to the Reformation is not too difficult to follow, since, despite local differences, there was a general homogeneity. With the Reformation however and the coming into being of a number of separate churches or denominations, the study of worship becomes highly complex, since each Christian communion developed its own forms and its own ethos, and also tended to adapt its architectural setting to its own particular understanding of the cultus.[25]

Luther's *Formula Missae* of 1523 was a conservative revision, following the mediaeval Roman rite closely, but with the omission of the offertory and any references to sacrifice—a key subject in the sixteenth century theological debate. Two years later he issued his *Deutsche Messe* in the vernacular, but again made no important innovations. However between 1523 and 1555 no less than 135 Agendas or church orders were issued. These had a certain similarity in that, while stressing the unity of Word and Sacrament, they tended to stress the sermon above all else and the prayers were of a didactic nature.[26] While all this was going on in Germany, other Lutheran churches were producing their own services. So from Sweden we have the *Red Book* of 1574, replaced later by the order of 1614,[27] while in the United States a significant landmark was the *Mühlenberg Liturgy* of 1748.

Under the influence of Farel and Calvin numerous eucharistic and baptismal rites were devised for the Reformed or Presbyterian Churches.[28] Meanwhile the Church of England was drawing up its *Book of Common Prayer*, the 1549 edition being conservative and the 1552 more Protestant in intent,[29] which became the basis for similar books in all the provinces of the Anglican Communion.[30] While the Methodists in the eighteenth century largely followed their Anglican parent,[31] Baptists and Congregationalists preferred to devise a 'free' and non-liturgical tradition, and such books as emanated from them were intended to provide guidance for the individual minister.[32]

249

The forms of worship which stemmed from the Reformation have certain common characteristics, although one or other of these tended to receive greater or less emphasis by the different churches. Henceforth all services were in the vernacular (cf. p. 287), the use of Latin being repudiated as an obstacle to full participation with understanding in worship. The attempt was also made to remove mediaeval accretions which had obscured the basic structure. This effort in the sixteenth century was by no means successful, since the Reformers were often greater heirs of their immediate past than they were able to realize. All these churches also wished to return to what they believed to be the purity of New Testament worship. Sometimes this took the form, as far as the eucharist was concerned, of a deliberate reproduction of a supper. So the order drawn up in 1550 by John à Lasco for Dutch refugees in England requires the pastor and all the worshippers to sit around a table. This became part of the basis of the Reformed liturgical tradition in Holland, where to this day many new churches are planned with large eucharistic tables, and it influenced the Reformed practice in Scotland, where for centuries the eucharist was celebrated around 'God's board'.

A further common feature of the Protestant services was the emphasis placed upon the sermon; this stemmed directly from the doctrinal stress upon the Word of God. While in the thought of Luther, Calvin and the Anglican Reformers this was not to be separated from the sacrament, in the course of time the latter was celebrated less and less frequently and the ministry of the Word, with accompanying readings and prayers, became all important (cf. p. 224). Also at the doctrinal level the Reformers reacted strongly against any association of sacrificial ideas with the eucharist. Structurally this led to the dropping of the offertory; verbally it issued in the removal of all liturgical phrases which could be interpreted to refer to it. Debate about the real presence was long and heated and very diverse views were adopted. United in rejecting trans-substantiation, the Reformers often disagreed about what to put in its place and their different positions affected the pattern of their services.

THE LITURGICAL MOVEMENT

If the Reformation resulted in the production of a multitude of liturgical forms, the other great movement of the sixteenth century, the Renaissance, was ultimately to have an adverse effect upon the worshipping life of the churches. The excessive individualism that it encouraged, when combined with the rationalism of the Enlightenment (see p. 17), issued in the virtual destruction of corporate worship and the assumption by the devotional life of a largely subjective and private character. Participation, the key note of the early centuries, was replaced by formal attendance. Reaction against this began within the Roman church with Dom Guéranger in particular, who refounded the abbey of Solesmes in 1830. Although his interests were chiefly mediaeval and indeed 'archaeological' he was successful in arousing interest in liturgical studies and so began a movement that was ultimately to affect all churches. Its remarkable advance can be assigned to the combination of at least five factors.

In the first place is to be counted the development of the study of worship itself. Although the modern scientific study of liturgies had begun in the seventeenth and eighteenth centuries with the collections of texts by such men as Mabillon (1632–1707)and Tommassi (1649–1713), it is only within the last fifty years that its fruits have begun to be garnered, partly through sustained and patient study, partly through the fortunate discovery of fresh original documents. In 1873 the *Didache* was found, being published ten years later; in 1884 the *Pilgrimage of Egeria* was brought to light; in 1899 the Greek text of the *Euchologion* of Serapion of Thmuis was issued, and there was also printed the Syriac text of the *Testament of our Lord*; in 1916 Dom R. H. Connolly demonstrated that the 'Egyptian Church Order' was the supposedly lost *Apostolic Tradition* of Hippolytus. The revolution that these discoveries have brought in liturgical studies will be immediately apparent when it is recalled that until the closing years of the nineteenth century scholars believed that the so-called Clementine liturgy, in Book 8 of the *Apostolic Constitutions*, either was or represented the universal primitive rite of the apostolic age. This late fourth-century academic exercise, with its doctrinal peculiarities and its developed structure, can now be set in its proper context; the history of early Christian worship can be reconstructed in its main outlines with reasonable accuracy; the influence of different ecclesiastical centres can be estimated; additions to the primitive pattern can be detected and evaluated; mediaeval accretions can be isolated and their origins largely determined. Thus, whereas the Reformers desired to return to the practice of the primitive Church and were in large measure unable to do so, we today in large measure could, if we so desired—whether we should so desire is another question. But this new knowledge has brought with it dissatisfaction on the part of many with existing forms of worship.

In the second place account must be taken of the emergence of biblical theology, with its emphasis upon the inner unity of the Scriptures and its recognition that the authors did not write as individuals in isolation but as members of the chosen people for their fellow members. For the appreciation of the Bible therefore numerous questions had to be faced: what is it that constitutes the chosen people? What is the nature of their election? How are we to understand the covenant that unites them to one another and to God? What, in other words is the meaning of the Church? So these questions resulted in the third factor, which was the rediscovery of the doctrine of the Church (cf. p. 220). But biblical theologians do not live in a world apart. Their studies led them to ask the same question that was being forced upon them as Christians by the contemporary situation (cf. p. 162) and in particular by the emergence of Marxism with its eschatological doctrine of an ideal community or a perfect society.

In the fourth place after liturgical studies proper, biblical theology and the rediscovery of the doctrine of the Church, must be included the ecumenical movement, which was compelling attention to the same question—what is the Church? (see Chapter 13). Faced by persecution under Communist rule, by the Church struggle under the Nazis, by the scandal of a divided Christendom, Christians saw that

Renaissance individualism was not enough and they began to appreciate anew the Pauline doctrine of the Church as the Body of Christ. "We, who are many, are one loaf, one body: for we all partake of the one loaf" (1 Cor. 10: 17).

This Pauline quotation focuses attention upon worship, as not only the central act of the Body, but the very means whereby it realizes its own true nature. The importance thus given to the cultus has also been emphasized by biblical studies in general. If we turn to the Old Testament, we find modern scholars drawing attention to the cultic background not only of the psalms but of many passages that are now deemed to have been recited at annual festivals. If we turn to the New Testament, we find the theses being advanced that Matthew's Gospel was specially compiled for reading aloud at the gatherings for worship[33]; that the fourth gospel was written to show the connection between the historical Jesus and the sacraments which actualize his saving presence;[34] that many of the Pauline epistles were intended to be made public at the eucharistic gatherings; that 1 Peter is to be closely related to baptism,[35] and that the Book of Revelation sets the drama of the last days in the context of the Lord's Service on the Lord's Day. It is possible that not all these will continue to be maintained, but the importance of the cultus to the people of God and its forming part of the background of the Bible cannot be gainsaid. Hence the centrality of worship comes in as the fifth element fostering the Liturgical Movement.[36] All this does not mean that it is concerned with worship as a means to an end or that it seeks to enliven worship in order to induce people to be present. It sees the eucharist as something at the very centre of the life of the Church which is truly in accord with the mind of Christ. The idea of the Church is primary; it is the nature of the Church which compels the adoption of a new attitude to worship. Consequently no student of worship can avoid coming to grips with this remarkable phenomenon, and in so doing he cannot afford to neglect its architectural expression.[37] The population explosion of the twentieth century and the devastation resulting from two world wars have been the occasion for an immense programme of church building. While revivalism and monumentality have influenced not a few of these structures, which therefore are 'new' only in date and not in concept, other churches have directly mirrored the various stages of development of the Liturgical Movement. Thus some of the earliest buildings were intended to facilitate participation, upon which the Movement has always laid supreme stress. They therefore took the form of 'offertory churches', i.e. long, narrow plans, emphasizing the offertory procession, with the altar visible from all corners. The participation was thus primarily visual. Later, under the impact of the stress upon the unity of the worshipping assembly, plans were followed which grouped the faithful around the altar. So by studying the visible embodiments of the various concepts formulated by the Liturgical Movement, one is enabled more fully to appreciate its development.

LITURGICAL REVISION IN THE TWENTIETH CENTURY

Scarcely any Christian body has escaped the influence of the Liturgical Movement and, as a result, the present century is very much a period of liturgical revision. Whether we look at the various provinces of the Anglican Communion,[38] or the possible results of the constitution on the liturgy of the Second Vatican Council,[39] or the abundance of service books issued by Lutherans, Presbyterians and others, we are confronted with the same phenomenon: a certain dis-ease with inherited forms and a desire to produce patterns of worship suitable for the twentieth century.

In general it may be said that most revisions to date are historically conditioned, i.e. the task of producing modern forms has been largely dominated by the historical study of liturgies. So, for example, *The Book of Common Worship* (1963) of the Church of South India represents an attempt to combine Protestant, Catholic and Eastern Orthodox elements in a series of services the details of which have been mainly determined by reference to past liturgical tradition.[40] The same may be said of the experimental rites devised by the Church of England.

Any critical appraisal of these new orders—and this is an

essential part of the study of contemporary worship—must rest upon some appreciation of principles. Amongst these are to be included the following:

1. Liturgical revision should rest upon a comparative study of all liturgies, both ancient and modern, both Eastern and Western. The history of Christian worship is not that of a series of mistakes best forgotten; it has much to teach twentieth-century man, whether he be aware of it or not, and in an attempt to meet the contemporary situation the riches of former ages should not be neglected. [41]

2. Liturgical revision should be ecumenical. In the present atmosphere of ecumenical debate to take as in any sense fundamental a particular service devised in the past by a particular Church is to manifest a narrow parochial spirit. One should not be restricted by too close an adherence to any one tradition, but should seek to be informed by the fullness of Christian belief and practice as it is preserved fragmented in the separated branches of the Church (cf. pp. 28, 309).

3. Liturgical forms should have a close association with the Bible. Since Christianity rests upon certain specific acts of God in history, recorded, and given classic interpretation in the scriptures, no act of worship should be severed from this basis.

4. The services produced should be intelligible and should not take the form of esoteric rites using archaic language and embodying outmoded concepts.

5. The services should be corporate. Many existing liturgies give little expression to this, being predominantly monologues uttered by the minister in the presence of a passive congregation. Liturgical revision which does not grapple seriously with the problem of making worship truly corporate, all having a part to play, would be better not undertake at all.

6. The forms produced should be flexible, i.e. they shoul contain both fixed and free elements. Each has its dangers and advantages. Fixed forms can become vain repetitions uttered by rote. Free forms can become clericalized and

restricted in their scope to the individual taste and capacity of the leader. Fixed forms can provide balance and breadth and bring something to the worshipper in addition to what they bring themselves. Free prayer can be spontaneous, relevant and congregational. Either may exert a tyranny; a judicious use of both can help to revitalize worship.[42]

7. Attention should be paid to the need for a multiplicity of patterns. Liturgical revision is not just the production of a single rite for every occasion; in a pluriform society many forms will be needed.

8. Liturgical revision should be undertaken within the context of mission, i.e. the missionary, outward-looking, character of worship must be rediscovered. In the past the understanding of Christian worship has been defined mainly in one direction, i.e. inwardly, but the time has come to develop a complementary interpretation, i.e. outwardly, in terms of mission.[43]

9. Revision must rest upon an appreciation of the secular nature of Christian worship. Instead of understanding worship as a drawing apart from the world to enter into the sphere of the holy and there encounter an other-worldly reality, contemporary insights compel us to recognize that worship is itself a worldly activity which is primarily concerned with how the holiness of the common is made manifest. Worship, in other words, is an activity that springs out of life in the world and is a celebration of that life; it is a coming to awareness of and a response to God in and through what is human and secular. If this aspect is lacking in liturgical revision, the forms devised will be irrelevant to modern man.[44]

CONCLUSION

This final emphasis upon the secular nature of Christian worship raises acutely the doctrinal question of the relationship of the sacred and the secular. This question is also basic to one's understanding of Christology and of the Church's mission. So the ramifications of the study of worship are immense.[45] The question too has a bearing upon the architectural setting of worship. If one regards sacred and secular as essentially distinct, then churches must be set apart from everyday life and reserved exclusively for 'holy' activities. But if one regards the two as twin aspects of a single and unified reality, then churches may be planned for multi-purpose use, where liturgy and life are celebrated together.[46]

The study of worship is not just a circumscribed area of detailed analysis; like any other branch of theology it is associated with all other branches of theology (see Chapter 1). Herein lies perhaps its difficulty but also its interest and fascination.

For further reading

G. P. Beasley-Murray, *Baptism in the New Testament*, Macmillan, London, 1962.

G. J. Cuming, *A History of the Anglican Liturgy*, Macmillan, London, 1969.

J. G. Davies, *Worship and Mission*, S.C.M., London, 1966.

J. G. Davies, *The Secular Use of Church Buildings*, S.C.M., London, 1968.

J. D. C. Fisher, *Christian Initiation: Baptism in the Medieval West*, S.P.C.K., London, 1965.

A. J. B. Higgins, *The Lord's Supper in the New Testament*, S.C.M., London, 1952.

J. A. Jungmann, *The Mass of the Roman Rite*, Benziger, New York, 1951–55.

J. A. Jungmann, *The Early Liturgy*, Darton, Longman and Todd, London, 1960.

W. D. Maxwell, *An Outline of Christian Worship*, O.U.P., London, 1939.

A. A. McArthur, *The Evolution of the Christian Year*, S.C.M., London, 1953.

C. F. D. Moule, *Worship in the New Testament*, Lutterworth, London, 1961.

H. H. Rowley, *Worship in Ancient Israel*, S.P.C.K., London, 1967.

M. H. Shepherd, ed., *The Liturgical Renewal of the Church*, O.U.P., Oxford, 1960.

J. F. White, *The Worldliness of Worship*, O.U.P., New York, 1967.

12

CHRISTIAN ETHICS

N. H. G. ROBINSON

*Professor of Divinity, St. Mary's College, University of
St. Andrews*

Christian Ethics

MORALITY IS something of a mystery. It is the task of
ethics to try to elucidate this mystery and of Christian
ethics to do so in the light of Christian convictions.
What is the nature of this sign-post in human life which tells
me that I ought to do this rather than that whether I want
to or not, and which condemns as atrocities, for example, the
happenings of Belsen whether or not they could be vindicated
by national strategy? What is the source and explanation of
this sign-post?

Some have found the underlying principle of morality in the
pursuit of pleasure (eudaemonism), but others in quite the
opposite direction in self-denial (asceticism). Some have looked
to a law governing human life but have sometimes found it
difficult to say what this law ordains, and so have tended
towards formalism (law without content). Others, again, have
laid all the weight upon what is somehow natural to human
beings, so that, just as scissors are for cutting, likewise sex is for
the propagation of the species and birth-control is therefore
wrong. This latter view might be called naturalism because it
depends so much upon what is supposed to be 'natural'; but
taken as the whole truth it might suggest that even self-control
is wrong, and so naturalism would become actualism (content,
or life, without law) and the virtual denial of morality. Some
carry the investigation so far and then come to a halt at the
blank wall of some authority which they blindly accept and
are not prepared to question (what I am going to call a *de
facto* authority); but there is a serious difficulty in this kind of
theory because it has no answer to the question why it should

accept this *de facto* authority rather than that. Such a theory would also be called a heteronomous one because it finds the law of morality quite outside man's life, whereas an autonomous theory would understand it as in some sense self-imposed, for example, as the law of a man's own reason.

These considerations are common to general ethics and Christian ethics, but Christian ethics has its own peculiar difficulty. Part of this difficulty stems from the fact that in Christian ethics two diverse traditions come together. One of them is the religious Hebrew-Christian tradition with its unmistakably moral teaching, from the Ten Commandments through the prophetic messages of Amos and Micah, Hosea and Isaiah, to the life and teaching of Jesus Christ. The other is the explicitly ethical and philosophical discussion of the good life in ancient Greece at the hands of men like Socrates, Plato and Aristotle. In the latter the moral question is plainly posed and a variety of ethical possibilities (such as asceticism and eudaemonism) is explored. In the former a divinely authoritative answer is enunciated and insistently clarified against, not the confusions of human thought, but the compromises of human practice. Yet the unique authority of the moral claim seems to imply that there cannot be a double standard here, that the claim is single, self-consistent and quite categorical.

It is not to be expected that the problems raised by the conjunction of these two traditions should be immediately and clearly envisaged. In ethics as in theology discussion was bound at first to be *ad hoc* and piecemeal in character. It is probably not unjust to regard in this light the rules for Christian living enumerated by Basil of Caesarea in the fourth century and even the more extensive treatment offered by Bishop Ambrose of Milan under the title "Concerning the Duties of Ministers" *(De Officiis Ministrorum)*. Such discussion produced what has sometimes been called a situational ethics (cf. p. 51) and what might well be described, less ambiguously for the contemporary mind, as an occasional ethics, that is, one which tries to answer particular moral questions about what to do in this situation or in that, rather than answer the general question about the curious nature of morality itself.

Over and above this inevitable feature, however, there was early operative a circumstance which served to present the moral question in one particular form, and so to obscure what might turn out to be the basic issues. This was the fact that the moral question tended to arise within the context of the institutional Church and in the form imposed upon it by that Church in its search for perfection, and in its claim and concern to save its members from sin and accordingly to regulate its administration of the sacrament of Penance. In other words, the moral question arose within an ultimately authoritative Church, in relation to an ultimate *de facto* or visible authority. As a result of this the investigation flowed along two different channels—ascetical theology concerned with the means necessary for the attainment of perfection, and moral theology concerned to rule and guide the actions of a frail humanity which had to be held in with bit and bridle.

Thus in the development of moral theology an extensive system of casuistry was established, within which the ethical thought of Christianity was almost imprisoned. In this development attention was chiefly paid to particular cases or problems, but nevertheless questions of a more general character also arose eventually and were debated from the sixteenth century onwards. Such was the controversy which produced the schools of thought known as probabilism, rigorism or tutiorism, and probabiliorism. The first of these views weighed the scales between the freedom of the individual and the law in favour of the former, on the ground that an uncertain law, even if probable, cannot bind and is in fact no law. The second weighed the scales in favour of law, holding that freedom must always be sacrificed to the safety of law. The third tried to achieve a balance by maintaining that that must be favoured, freedom or law, for which the case was the more probable. Most significantly, however, all three theories dealt with the general problem of morality as one concerning the relationship between the freedom of the individual and a *de facto* authority which must not be questioned.

So long as the discussion was thus cut short by the blank wall of a *de facto* authority and more basic issues were obscured,

Christian ethics could not properly take shape. Yet in the background, behind the development of moral theology, some attempt was made to grapple with those more fundamental problems which give to Christian ethics its peculiar character. Even in the ancient period St. Augustine endeavoured to bring philosophical and Christian ethics into contact by super-imposing his Christian insight upon the ethical outlook of Platonism. He identified virtue with "the perfect love of God", and held that the virtues recognized by Platonism were varying forms of this essential virtue. For St. Augustine "the happiness which is the aim of human endeavour consists," says John Burnaby,[1] ". . . in a relation of knowledge and love which binds the soul to the one immutable Reality"; and he is quite emphatic about the strong Platonic influence which lay behind this identification of the Good, and behind St. Augustine's other-worldliness which was but the other side of the same coin. "No Christian Father is more uncompromising," he says, "in his other-worldliness than is St. Augustine. But his other-worldliness is not a piece of traditional homiletic: it can only be appreciated in its intimate connection with his Platonic metaphysic."

It was, however, in the ethical thought of St. Thomas Aquinas in the thirteenth century that a fully articulated system of Christian morality was attempted. The name of Aquinas is for many associated, so far as morality is concerned, with his theory of natural law; and it is true that St. Thomas maintained a fourfold conception of law, as eternal, natural, human and divine. According to this scheme the eternal law is that which governs the whole creation, and natural law is the rational, free and responsible creature's participation in this eternal law. Thus by law fire burns and cannot avoid doing so; and no less man is subject to law which, however, in his freedom he may obey or disobey. Human law, in turn, is the application of natural law to the varied circumstances of diverse societies, while the divine law is the specially revealed guidance by which divine grace seeks to lead man beyond his proper natural end to what is by that same grace his *supernatural* end, friendship with God.

None the less, this teaching on law is only a part of the Thomist treatment of morality; and the distinguished scholar, Etienne Gilson, is almost apologetic in introducing the topic of law at all. He holds that "Thomist morality is unquestionably autonomous" and that the will remains "master of itself" even "when external legislation imperiously prescribes its end."[3] In fact the autonomous character of Thomist ethics quickly reappears when it is seen that the ultimate law is to do good and to avoid evil; and further, that the good of any being belongs to its nature and can virtually be read off from its natural constitution. It is from this good that the various moral laws are to be rationally derived, such as those which ordain the duty of self-preservation and govern the propagation of the race. Moreover, it is in relation to this good that the different virtues are to be recognized as distinguishable dispositions to act according to reason—the intellectual virtues of understanding, knowledge, wisdom and prudence, and the moral virtues of justice, temperance and fortitude which, together with prudence, constitute the 'cardinal virtues'. In all this there is a fundamental naturalism which subsequent ages of ethical debate were bound to question, in respect of its underlying principle as well as its application to particular moral problems, such as that of birth-control, and the emphasis in this sphere upon what is deemed objectively natural.

To this point, however, the treatment of morality does not specifically claim to be Christian. It does so only in so far as St. Thomas recognizes beyond man's natural good his quite literally supernatural end, "friendship between man and God", and in relation to this an area of divine law and a number of 'theological virtues', faith, hope and charity. In this way, by attending to both natural and Christian morality in a single system, both man's natural good and his supernatural end, St. Thomas introduces his readers to Christian ethics properly so called. It is to be noticed, however, that by and large he achieves this system by a process of simple addition, erecting Christian morality upon natural morality as a further instalment, or another storey. It is therefore only in a very limited sense that St. Thomas reaches an integrated view of the single field of morality as a whole.[4] The cleavage, the firm line drawn, between nature and grace seems to bar any more complete integration; for if the conception of man's natural good is self-contained and self-sufficient it is not logically possible to hold that it is modified and transformed by the recognition of a supernatural end.

The Reformation effected several important changes in the Christian ethical outlook, although it did not immediately pave the way for an equally thorough-going and more adequate conception of the Christian ethic. For one thing, it placed a question-mark against the whole tradition of moral theology (see pp. 263f. above). Secondly, it tended in greater or less degree to assume the primacy of the will rather than the intellect, and to think of God as sovereign will rather than as supreme *being*. At the same time, thirdly, it called in question any self-contained and self-sufficient concept of man's natural good,[5] and taught instead that as a result of the Fall human nature is virtually corrupt and totally depraved. Fourthly, more or less explicitly it saw the ethical situation in the light of an ultimately *de facto* authority, the infallible word of Scripture. These are all elements or tendencies in the outlook generated by the Reformation, and perhaps they are most clearly and instructively seen in John Calvin. For one thing, there is in his thought a streak of fundamentalism which when separated off yields an ill-grounded conception of the Christian life. It leads him to suggest that "it will be profitable to assemble from various passages of Scripture a pattern for the conduct of life in order that those who heartily repent may not err in their zeal."[6] Calvin can indeed speak of conscience as "holding before us the difference between good and evil",[7] but he considers that because of our pride and self-love we do not profit from this witness and require a written law. What Calvin chiefly finds in Scripture is God's law as one of self-denial in which he finds the sum and substance of the Christian life, and he holds that Scripture "gives us commandments of which our mind is quite incapable unless our mind is previously emptied of its natural feelings".[8]

What is important for the present survey, however, is not the precise way in which the various elements are respectively weighted and fitted together by any individual theologian of the Reformation, but the elements themselves which are conjoined. These are, we have seen, the tendency to think of God as sovereign will and so of man's primary obligation as obedience (the positive side of Calvin's self-denial); the tendency to reject any self-contained concept of man's natural good and to replace it by some form of a doctrine of total depravity; and the tendency to see man's moral life exclusively under the *de facto* authority of God's revelation contained in Scripture. Moreover these tendencies, however conjoined in detail, implicitly abandon the Thomist idea of a potentially good nature which may by divine grace be crowned by a 'super-nature'. Instead they substitute the notion of an evil nature to be *replaced* by one that is renewed and good. Yet if the Thomist account failed by reason of its lack of final integrity (combining, as it attempted to do, a thoroughly autonomous morality with one that must in the end be deemed heteronomous, being by definition beyond nature and its highest good), Protestant ethical thought was inherently unstable, being in the most radical way quite heteronomous throughout. Accordingly it was almost bound to provoke from within itself an opposite reaction. This reaction involved Protestant thought in the tantalizing dilemma, either fundamentalism or liberalism, that is, either an ethical outlook for which the words of Scripture are an ultimate *de facto* authority, or else one in which the moral aspirations of natural man have moved to the centre in place of the command and the grace of God.

Certainly on Protestant soil there has flourished the modern enterprise of philosophical or natural ethics which has proved in certain periods a ready ally of religious thought, and which has often found in Jesus Christ (not the orthodox incarnation of God, but) the embodiment of the highest human moral insights. This alliance may not have been without its dangers. If fundamentalism is ethically inadequate, liberalism may well be religiously immature. Yet by the nature of the case Christianity and morality belong together. An a-moral interpretation of Christianity would *ipso facto* be a misinterpretation and certainly un-Biblical. In the Bible the moral and the trans-moral are inextricably intertwined. The evidence for this is to be found on almost every page of the Bible, and it rises to an impressive height when St. John declares that "this is the work of God, that ye believe on him whom he hath sent"[9] and when St. Luke suggests that Christ "ought to have suffered these things and to enter into his glory."[10] It is noteworthy that Karl Barth, who in one context could classify morality with chance as an arbitrary factor in human life, was driven in another context to declare that "the doctrine of God . . . is at every point . . . *ethics*".[11]

Accordingly Christian ethics can never be indifferent to the neutral investigation of morality and its independent doctrine of ethics; and indeed the eighteenth and nineteenth centuries produced a variety of schools of thought. Some thinkers, such as the Earl of Shaftesbury (1671–1713) and Bishop Butler (1692–1752), concentrated their attention upon the motives and dispositions which lead to action. In consequence they outlined a theory of virtue in which the place of altruism and a disinterested regard for the welfare of others was emphasized, to give the lie to those like Thomas Hobbes (1588–1679) who would have argued that the individual can act only with a view to his own benefit. Others found the significant feature of morality elsewhere, in the quality of actions themselves, such as the keeping of a promise. Such writers formed a school of intellectualism and intuitionism which maintained that the difference between right and wrong, the fact that certain acts are right and others wrong, was perceived by reason so that the denial of any such affirmation was no less absurd than the denial of a mathematical axiom. Men like Ralph Cudworth (1617–1688), Samuel Clarke (1675–1729) and John Balguy (1686–1748) helped to articulate this ethical outlook, emphasizing at the heart of morality an insight of reason rather than a benevolent disposition or even a moral sentiment of approval.

The greatest intellectualist of the eighteenth century, however, was the German philosopher, Immanuel Kant (1724–1804), who regarded morality as consisting in that kind of action which alone befitted a rational being. Such action he variously described as acting on a maxim which could without contradiction be made a universal law; as acting towards rational beings always as ends in themselves and never as means only; and as acting on those maxims which would "harmonize with a possible kingdom of ends."[12]

Yet already in the eighteenth century another type of ethical theory had appeared which paid attention, neither to motives nor to the quality of action, but to the nature of the consequences. This utilitarian brand of theory was to prove highly influential in the nineteenth century through the work of Jeremy Bentham (1748–1842), James Mill (1773–1836) and John Stuart Mill (1806–73). In the earlier century however it appeared mainly in a far from profound form of theological utilitarianism according to which, in the words of William Paley (1743–1805), duty differs from prudence as involving some consideration of "what we shall gain or lose in the world to come".

The later utilitarianism had in itself no explicitly theological reference but simply declared those acts right which in their different situations were calculated to produce the greatest happiness of the greatest number. Yet this thesis, along with other variations on the theme of an independent doctrine of ethics, has at times appealed in greater or less degree to the Christian consciousness as a satisfactory expression of its own ethical outlook. Immanuel Kant himself considered that morality as he understood it was the true gateway to religion, for it demanded God, freedom and immortality as necessary postulates of the moral and practical reason; and many have found in his ethic an acceptable articulation of the Christian spirit. As such an articulation his respect for personality seems to excel, for example, Albert Schweitzer's reverence for life as such. John Stuart Mill for his part thought that his own ethic did not depart from the Christian outlook and indeed that "in the golden rule of Jesus of Nazareth we read the complete spirit of the ethics of utility".[13] Bishop Butler too in the eighteenth century declared in his *Analogy of Religion* that Christianity is a republication of natural religion. In the twentieth century Bishop Herbert Hensley Henson (1863–1947) echoed the moral side of this theory when he maintained that "Christian morality is, in unique and plenary sense, natural, the expression of natural theology."[14]

This is not to say that other forms of more specifically Christian ethical teaching were not prevalent in the period; but, where they did not provide a non-Roman version of moral theology which posited the *de facto* authority of the Church (as in the work of such Caroline divines as Robert Sanderson (1587–1663) and Jeremy Taylor (1613–67) in the seventeenth century), the central ethical emphasis fell upon faith either as free from all law—as in the various types of antinomianism—or else as bound by the law written in Scripture, thus positing another *de facto* authority. Protestant thought therefore found it exceedingly difficult to devise a serious alternative to liberalism other than fundamentalism.

Indeed it was a changed and sobering experience of life in the twentieth century which was to prove a major factor in driving Christian ethics forward to a more profound grasp of its proper province. Already, however, in the nineteenth century, as part of the general theological revolution that was taking place and that was to continue vigorously into the twentieth century, the way was being prepared. One of the first notable figures in this forward movement is that of Friedrich Schleiermacher (1768–1834) in whom the investigation called Christian ethics made a significant advance. On the one hand, Schleiermacher could not disown the general philosophical enquiry into morality. He appeared in the wake of Immanuel Kant, but he did not follow slavishly the great German philosopher. On the contrary, he thought that he found a greater ethical adequacy in Plato, although he brought to the Platonic understanding a sense of history and of social historical existence which were simply not available to the thought of ancient Greece. On the other hand, he recognized a parallel enquiry, that of Christian ethics. The peculiarity and profundity of his view derive from the fact that, while acknowledging the non-identity of these two enquiries, he found himself affirming the one in affirming the other. It is this comprehensiveness and integrity in general and in principle which assures Schleiermacher his place in the development of Christian ethics, and which leads one commentator to characterize his position as dia-parallelism in contrast to the revisionism of St. Augustine and the synthesis of St. Thomas Aquinas. For Schleiermacher, he says,[15] "there is an internal attraction and repulsion of each toward and away from the other which give to the parallelism between them a dynamic rather than a static significance." The position is certainly not without its difficulties, which are in some respects intolerable and of some of which Schleiermacher himself was aware. It may well be significant that in the last resort the plane on which these two lines of enquiry were held together as parallels seems to have been the human consciousness, "the innermost life of the spirit", for this would so far support the charge of subjectivism which over a wide front has been persistently preferred against Schleiermacher.

In the aftermath to Schleiermacher in the nineteenth century his parallel lines did not survive unscathed, but in different quarters they suffered different fates. On the one hand in Albrecht Ritschl (1822–89) and his very influential school they coalesced. It is not quite true to say that this school simply surrendered to Kant. Certainly the liberalism which pervaded it is not to be ignored, but in men like Wilhelm Herrmann (1846–1922) and Theodor Haering (1848–1928) the explicitly theological element must be recognized. Their ethics claimed from the outset to be Christian. It is largely true, however, that by this school as a whole ethics was not thoroughly integrated with theology and retained a relative independence. The specifically theological element consisted not of religious reality but of mere presuppositions and ideas, and thus was immobilized. The overlordship of Christ tended to be conceived as an assumption rather than an encounter; and the basic character of this way of handling the subject comes to the surface in the declaration that Christian ethics is a branch of philosophical ethics.

On the other hand, in Sören Kierkegaard (1813–55) Schleiermacher's parallel lines are swung round as it were and placed across man's path as two of the three levels of life recognized by Kierkegaard—the aesthetic, the moral and, above all, the religious. This arrangement rendered the position of ethics highly ambiguous and seemed to make morality little more than a psychological gateway to the higher realm of religion. Nevertheless it has exercised an incalculable influence on twentieth-century thought. And certainly Kierkegaard himself was fond of referring to Abraham's readiness to sacrifice Isaac, as if in religion morality was virtually left behind.

In the twentieth century itself there is no doubt that the outstanding figure has been Karl Barth (1886–1968). At an early stage in the articulation of his thought he was prepared, after the fashion of Kierkegaard, to treat morality as a natural and psychological gateway to religion. A further development in his position however consisted precisely in the elimination of every element of existentialism, as Kierkegaard's type of thought was called, and this new emphasis in Barthian theology often seemed to carry with it a paradoxically scornful attitude towards morality. Yet as the development continued it became clear that Barth's scorn was reserved for natural morality. To Christian morality he assigned a quite central place of unqualified dignity. "The doctrine of God," he said,[16] ". . . is at every point . . . *ethics*"; but, he also insisted,[17] ethics "has its basis in the knowledge of Jesus Christ", and apart from occasional statements with somewhat ambiguous implications this remained his fundamental thesis. As known in Jesus Christ, God is the Maker and Lord of the covenant of grace of which there are two elements, divine election and divine command, and Barth was always perfectly clear that neither could arise independently of the other. To treat the Christian ethic of obedience to the God of the Gospel as a theological answer to a more general, non-theological question, the question of philosophical ethics for example, is at once to infringe the Godness of God.

The peculiar difficulty of Christian ethics, we have suggested, derives from the fact that the Christian moralist enters upon a ground already occupied; but Barth had a short and direct way of dealing with this situation which he pictured as that of

Israel entering the land of Canaan. The various ethical systems appear, he held, "as a result and in prolongation of the fall",[18] and consequently there is only one right attitude to them, one of aggression. Any wavering in "this offensiveness" can only destroy theological ethics itself. In Barth himself there was certainly no wavering on this point, although there is the difficulty of reconciling it with the suggestion he made from time to time that natural man is not immune from the ethical question but is exposed to it from the outset. At any rate Barth was emphatic that Christian ethics could not assimilate itself to general or philosophical ethics, nor could it agree to divide the field and proceed along parallel lines. No more could it follow the example of St. Thomas and treat natural ethics and Christian ethics as belonging together. Even a modern apologetic approach was not properly permissible or even possible. The only correct attitude to general or philosophical ethics on the part of Christian ethics is to be found in a deliberate policy of "annexation", and "there must be no armistice with the peoples of Canaan and their culture and their cultus".[19]

Furthermore this theological ethic must represent the Christian life as one of *obedience* to the command of God, in a choice in which we have no choice because it is we who are chosen; and it must represent it as one which *corresponds* to the command of God which is also the grace of God, in that the basis of the divine claim is the action of God in Christ in whom he renders what he demands. Accordingly Barth can also say that the distinctive quality of this command is that it is a 'permission'. On the other hand, that to which the Christian renders obedience and with which his action corresponds is not an objective and manageable content like a general principle, nor is it to be found exactly in the words of Scripture. Rather, according to Barth, it is not a reality but an event, not static but active, not general but supremely particular.

There are difficulties in this view and especially perhaps two. The first is that of understanding how it can be said *both* that man as such is exposed to the ethical question *and* that ethics has its basis in the knowledge of Jesus Christ. The second is that of understanding how the supremely particular command

T

273

can be recognized as divine and distinguished from any and every natural impulse. Accordingly on its deepest level Christian ethics has been driven on in search of a more adequate basic conception. Thus Emil Brunner (1889–1967), recognizing a general revelation behind the special revelation in Christ, could more plausibly treat man as such as basically a moral being. Nevertheless, perhaps under Barth's influence, Brunner regarded natural morality as sin itself, and general ethics as a rebellious attempt on the part of reason to produce a standard out of itself. This attempt, he taught, was doomed to frustration in the dilemma, either law without content or life without law, either formalism or naturalism (see p. 261). Moreover, holding that "the Good has its basis and its existence solely in the will of God",[20] that "nothing is good save obedience to the command of God, just because it is obedience"[21] (although, as it happens, that means loving one's neighbour), and that indeed "the goodness of man can be no other than letting himself be placed within the activity of God",[22] Brunner's treatment ran into the same difficulty as Barth's in indicating what is the path of the Christian. This difficulty he tried to avoid by recognizing certain divinely ordained 'orders', or forms of community, such as marriage and family, labour, government or state, culture, and the Church, each with its own guide-lines. Yet it is true, and curious, that Brunner regarded these as 'technical' rather than moral, and somehow as external to the true life of faith—a contention which rules out the possibility of an integrated view as effectively as did the Thomist cleavage between nature and grace (see further p. 278 below).

It would seem that in both Barth and Brunner the old dilemma between fundamentalism and liberalism has been effectively transcended and the discussion advanced into a new phase. And yet, if the command of God is no longer seen as a *de facto* authority identical with either the teaching of the Church or the word of Scripture, the question remains how it is to be recognized. Further, if it is held that the command of God makes its own self-authenticating impact, there is still a question how the individual himself can be sure that it is a divine command and not something else altogether, like a private hunch. As it stands the conquest of the dilemma between liberalism and fundamentalism results (to use terms already explained on p. 262) in a radical 'heteronomy' which, so far from being stable, seems bound to provoke a no less radical 'autonomy' and so produce for Protestant thought still another dilemma.

In fact, on the wing of modern Protestantism associated with the name of Rudolf Bultmann (b. 1884), this is precisely what has happened, and the emphasis upon determination by the divine has yielded place to a new emphasis upon man's free decision of faith (cf. p. 55). Further, although in this contemporary existentialism the word 'obedience' continues to be employed frequently, analysis makes plain that what is really meant is openness in love to each concrete situation or encounter with one's neighbour. Moreover, this love knows of no precise definable content, no law, no preformulation, but is said to make known its requirements in the concrete encounter of the moment. What love is and what it involves are to be seen only in the particular situation as it arises. Faith "realizes itself," Bultmann tells us,[23] "in knowledge of what one has to do or not to do in the specific instance". Where for Barth and Brunner the *form* of obedience was everything, for Bultmann the *content* of love is all-important—and all-sufficient.

Here the argument approaches the very core of the contemporary debate in Christian ethics. This core does not consist of a single issue, and certainly not of the dispute between those who take a traditionally Christian view of sexual morality, for example, and those who would prefer to lay much greater weight upon charity than upon chastity. It does not consist even, more generally, of the dispute between what is called "act-agapism" and "rule-agapism"—whether love operates with law or without it. The divergence is even more fundamental and vastly more complex.

The very definition of Christian ethics is by no means beyond question. It is no longer plausible to say that Christian ethics is a branch of philosophical ethics. But Brunner's definition that Christian ethics is "the science of human conduct as it is determined by Divine conduct"[24] is question-begging as a definition of any kind of ethics. Perhaps we can say that Christian ethics is the systematic account of human life as given over in faith to the overlordship of Christ as containing within himself the whole duty of man.[25] Yet if much is thus uncertain, at least the Christian moralist can no longer proceed in terms ultimately of a merely *de facto* authority such as the teaching of the Church or the dictum of Scripture. This perhaps is the grain of truth contained in the slogan that God is dead. There is certainly no factor left in man's world that is plainly and unambiguously identifiable with God or his will.

None the less difficult and far-reaching problems remain. For one thing, it is clearly the case (see p. 262) that Christian ethics enters upon a field already occupied; and its relationship to philosophical ethics, and to the natural morality it seeks to understand, must be clarified. In Protestant thought, where it is not content to assimilate the Christian ethic to natural morality, there is a persistent hostility to, or rejection of, the latter which none the less remains highly ambiguous.

Perhaps the most striking exception is to be found in Reinhold Niebuhr's articulation of the Christian ethic in terms of his contention that "the eternal is involved in every moral judgement".[26] Thus a positive relationship is established with natural morality. At the same time Niebuhr maintains that every moral achievement inevitably comes under the divine judgement, while in every human situation the ethical ideal—although in that situation its realization is not possible—remains relevant. It is as if in all their moral aspirations men were seeking "a city which hath foundations, whose builder and maker" is yet God. In this way, by recognizing the possibility of significant achievements in history, Niebuhr avoids both the other-worldliness of St. Augustine (who confined history A.D. to only one of his seven ages), and the incipient anti-worldliness of Barth and Brunner, who ambiguously place the Christian life somehow beyond and out of relation to the life and standards of the world. Yet by continuing to recognize the place of divine judgement even in relation to man's greatest achievements Niebuhr refrains from taking an unduly positive view of natural morality, and so avoids both Thomism and liberalism. Moreover this positive but critical account of natural morality seems to foreshadow the possibility of a thoroughly integrated view of morality both natural and Christian, and to require in theology some doctrine of general revelation.

Alternatively, the Christian moralist may be attracted by recent developments in philosophical ethics, and, in particular by the linguistic or prescriptive theory of morality. This theory finds the uniqueness of morality, not in any mysterious intrusion into human life, but in one particular use of human language, namely that whereby we *prescribe*. The theory seems to surrender any truth-claiming element in the moral judgement. It finds the apparent objectivity of moral standards exclusively in the fact that the standards I accept may have been accepted by my father and my grandfather.[27] It thus substitutes the conservatism of the moral consciousness for the coerciveness of the moral claim, and it traces the ultimate source of morality to a decision of the human will to adopt this policy of life rather than that.[28] Accepting such a theory the Christian moralist might then be prepared to agree with Brunner's curious view of the aim of philosophical ethics, as "the erection of a standard for the will and for conduct which can be established in accordance with reason".[29] He might then go on to maintain that in Christianity, and in Christianity alone, there is a prescription which is objective because it is not human but divine. Even so he may then have to reckon with the question whether, on his interpretation of their situation, the original inhabitants of the land he has come to occupy are real men or only shadows on the wall.

On the other hand, and in the second place, it may be the lack of a positive element in its attitude to natural morality which drives Protestant ethical thought into the dilemma already noted between a sheerly heteronomous ethics and one that is almost as sheerly autonomous. This soon reveals itself as a dilemma between formalism on the one hand and actualism or naturalism on the other, between law without content and life without law, between obedience as such to the command of God and openness as such to the reality of one's neighbour. On the one side, there is the emphasis upon obedience as such in both Barth and Brunner. It is significant that the latter, in order to fill the resultant life with content, resorts to the various 'orders' of creation, such as marriage. Yet he treats these orders as 'technical' rather than moral. For example, he seeks to derive the lifelong union of one man and one woman from the bare facts that "every human being is irrevocably the child of one man and one woman"[30] and that "those who love each other do feel the intrusion of a third person to be intolerably disturbing".[31] So far as he regards such considerations as 'technical' he may be thought to avoid what has been called the naturalistic fallacy, that of deriving the moral from the natural, the normative from the factual. If those considerations are deemed relevant, however, it would seem that at some stage this illicit transition must be made.

On the other side, we have the insistence (even when the word 'obedience' is used) on openness in love. Such insistence carries with it "an extraordinary emphasis on the autonomy of man",[32] and is apparently irreconcilable with a "a system of ideas, as a structure of laws, which," it is said, would "seek to impose themselves on the forms of a society to which they are fundamentally alien".[33] This actualism, or naturalism, seems to be echoed in Dietrich Bonhoeffer's reiteration of his thesis that the world "is always already sustained, accepted and reconciled in the reality of God".[34] It is evident too in Paul Lehmann's emphasis upon what God is doing "to make and to keep human life human",[35] and in his substitution of an indicative for an imperative ethic so that "I am to do what I am".[36] This naturalism is present also behind the stress, by Lehmann[37] and many other writers, upon maturity rather than morality. It is, however, difficult to believe that maturity is not a much vaguer concept than morality, which requires to borrow from the latter whatever substance it may have. Nor is openness in love, without the guidance of something like law, in any better case. I ought to meet my neighbour in the total openness of unrestricted love in the concrete encounter of the moment, it may be said. But does it not make a difference if on this occasion my neighbour happens to be, as it were, my neighbour's wife? Brunner's 'orders' (and perhaps Bonhoeffer's 'mandates') may be too inflexible, as well as being assigned to the non-moral and technical (or by Bonhoeffer to the penultimate); but human life is more than a discrete series of concrete encounters, it is a complex network of personal relationships.

The problem of autonomy and heteronomy is indeed a difficult one, of which philosophical ethics is not unaware;[38] but in theological ethics it is by the nature of the case even more intractable, since God is no mere function of the human. In a sense it is the problem of integrating a 'vertical' and a 'horizontal' conception of the divine action, and certainly no solution is possible in static terms. What is required is a conception which will correspond in ethics to Brunner's idea of dialogical, rather than monological, truth in theology. We need a conception, that is to say, of a bi-polar autonomy within which there is room for passing elements of heteronomy, within which not even a man's surest standards are quite inviolate, but within which he is called to love as the fulfilment of the law and of all his standards, which are really historically conditioned and at the same time sinful apprehensions of God's standard. Moral autonomy thus conceived would be the autonomy, not simply of a rational being, but specifically of a creature summoned to be a fellow-worker with his Creator. Perhaps at this point Christian ethics requires the idea of vocation for its adequate articulation. Appropriately too the kingdom of God in Christ must be seen as both the leaven operating in human society and as the divine judgement upon human society in all its terrestrial forms.

There is, however, a further problematical element in contemporary Christian ethical thought, and that is the demand for *particularity*. Barth, we have already noted, insisted that that to which a Christian renders obedience, and with which his action corresponds, is not a reality but an event, not static but active, not general but supremely particular. Brunner too concluded his discussion of marriage by referring to the "will of God, which here and now requires nothing of me save that I should meet my neighbour in the spirit of responsible love. But," he added, "no universal law can anticipate what this means in a world confused and corrupted by sin", so that "no one can teach another person what God demands from him in this situation, not even in matters connected with marriage."[39] Likewise existentialist theology has laid the greatest stress upon the concrete encounter of the moment and its concrete demand, independent of all pre-formulated standards and general laws. Lehmann too holds natural morality to be abstract, preceptual, and so defective, because it leaves an unbridgeable gap between the insight of judgement and the act. The suggestion is that the gap between general principle and particular act can only be bridged by logic, so that the particular act is nothing more than an instance of a general type (e.g. helping this unfortunate person is only an instance of alms-giving); whereas "ethics is a matter not of logic but of life, a certain kind of reality possessed by the concrete."[40]

Yet the cult of the sheerly particular is a wild goose chase; and presumably this '*kind* of reality' is conceptualizable and recognizable. The trouble arises, not with natural morality as such, but with the articulation of it in terms of laws which have simply to be applied. That is indeed, as Lehmann alleges, a matter merely of logic. The metaphor of *law* in morality may well be a misleading one, especially in an age of change; but it would be an error to throw away the normative in human life along with fixed norms in the form of statable laws. The normative in all its elusive complexity, and in its independence of private wish and desire, remains and keeps human life human. It is this complex normative that is creatively and imaginatively realized and fulfilled in love. Without it love would be empty or arbitrary. It makes its impact in all the different spheres of life, in love, marriage and family, in work, industry and commerce, in community and country, in questions of race and international relations. But just because it demands a creative response in each situation, that response cannot be read off beforehand in some mechanical fashion. Sometimes the normative appears in the shape of established institutions, such as marriage—not moral absolutes nor yet merely human conventions, but the moral achievement of many generations. Sometimes it appears as the social goals of a given generation—such as the advancement of undeveloped countries and the solution of the problem of race. Thus the normative underlies the so-called middle axioms (for example, desegregation in the U.S.A.) which J. H. Oldham described as "an attempt to define the directions in which, in a particular state of society, Christian faith must express itself".[41] Because it demands a creative response it is unpredictable and unprescribable; but, because it is the demand it is, it is recognizable and in its own way rational. For the Christian, moreover, it demands the creative response of the creature (his vocation) in his own situation within the reconciling work of the Creator's love in Jesus Christ.

It is worth noting too that in this conception of the Christian ethic older divisions in Christian ethical thought and other divisions in philosophical ethics may be overcome and transcended. Sometimes in the past the Christian ethic has been represented as an ethic for the individual, and at other times emphasis has fallen on the social implications of the Gospel. In the light of this discussion both appear as partial insights. Similarly, in philosophical ethics, utilitarianism which stresses the consequences of acts, and theories which emphasize the quality of an action, tend to appear as rival conceptions. But again in the light of this discussion of the Christian ethic (which sets the individual's decision in any particular situation within the context of a divine act of reconciliation on the scale of history itself) both appear as partial expressions of the truth.

Finally, it must be said that the Christian love which fulfils the normative is a responsive love to the divine, to the reconciliation of man to man and of man to God in Jesus Christ. It is arguable that apart from this reconciliation the command of love, to love even one's enemies, to love the evildoer, fails to make sense. The Christian love which fulfils the normative thus corresponds to the divine reconciliation; and consequently the divine command may be seen, in Barth's words, as a 'permission'. Accordingly for the Christian, love does not stand alone but is inextricably interfused with faith and hope. The theological virtues are not added to the good life as separate virtues; they do not crown it, they constitute it.

For further reading

J. Burnaby, *Amor Dei*, Hodder & Stoughton, London, 1938—on St. Augustine.

E. Gilson, *The Christian Philosophy of St. Thomas Aquinas*, Victor Gollancz, London, 1957.

D. J. O'Connor, *Aquinas and Natural Law*, Macmillan, London, 1967.

R. S. Wallace, *Calvin's Doctrine of the Christian Life*, Oliver & Boyd, Edinburgh, 1959.

T. Haering, *The Ethics of the Christian Life*, E. T., Williams & Norgate, London, 1909.

P. Ramsey, *Basic Christian Ethics*, Charles Scribner's Sons, New York, 1950.

R. Niebuhr, *An Interpretation of Christian Ethics*, S.C.M., London, 1941.

R. Niebuhr, *Moral Man and Immoral Society*, Charles Scribner's Sons, New York, 1941.

K. Barth, *Church Dogmatics*, Vol. II, Part 2, E. T., T. & T. Clark, Edinburgh, 1957.

E. Brunner, *The Divine Imperative*, E. T., Lutterworth, London, 1937.

D. Bonhoeffer, *Ethics*, E.T., S.C.M., London, 1960.

P. L. Lehmann, *Ethics in a Christian Context*, S.C.M., London, 1963.

T. C. Oden, *Radical Obedience*, Epworth, London, 1965.

H. Cox, *The Secular City*, S.C.M., London, 1965.

J. Fletcher, *Situation Ethics*, S.C.M., London, 1966.

G. F. Woods, *A Defence of Theological Ethics*, Cambridge University Press, Cambridge, 1966.

13

THE ECUMENICAL DIMENSION IN THEOLOGY

STEPHEN NEILL

*Formerly Professor of Ecumenical Theology and Missions,
University of Hamburg*

13

The Ecumenical Dimension in Theology

Introduction: DIVIDED CHRISTENDOM

FROM THE time of the apostles the Church of Jesus Christ
has been threatened by the spirit of division. In every age
there have been Christians who have made it their aim to
maintain or to restore the unity of the Church.

Modern research has made it plain that none of the great
reformers of the sixteenth century wished or intended to
divide the Church.[1] But one notable figure of that time stands
out above all others as the apostle of unity—the gentle and
tolerant Desiderius Erasmus.[2] He saw clearly amid the clash
of opinions that what the opponents held in common was far
stronger than that which divided them; he hoped that by
concentrating on that central core of obedience it would be
possible to mitigate dissensions, and so to bring men to a better
mind and to reconciliation in the one Church.*

Erasmus was the author and only-begetter of a long line
of eirenical writers, who over a period of more than two
centuries tried to get behind the differences to the underlying
unity, which needed not to be created but to be revealed.
Typical of these writers is George Calixtus (1586–1656), who
worked with the principle of the agreement of the Church in
the first five centuries (*Consensus quinquesaecularis*), and popu-
larized, if he did not invent, the idea of the "Fundamental
Articles".[3] Not all articles of the Christian faith are of equal
importance; on those which are essential all Christians are

---

* This was the theme of his two eirenical works—the *Prayer to the Lord
Jesus for the Peace of the Church*, 1532, and the tract *On Restoring Concord in the
Church*, 1533.

agreed; if it were possible to bring them back to the simplicity of Scripture and of the agreed articles, union would be on the way. This concept reappears from time to time, and in different guises even today.

The trouble is that we all experience whatever form of religion we profess as a whole. It is possible to draw up a list of particular doctrines and to show the wide range of agreement between separated churches. But this amounts to nothing at all, since each doctrine is conditioned by the context in which it is set, and agreement in detail weighs little against the fundamental disagreements through which churches have come into separate existence.[4]

One of the first to grasp this fact was J. A. Moehler of Tübingen, who gave to his most important work the title *Symbolics: or, an Exposition of the dogmatic differences between Catholics and Protestants in the light of their official confessional Documents.*[5]* It was not the aim of Moehler to go back to the polemical theology of ancient days. But, as he assumed that the Roman Catholic church in the first third of the nineteenth century was the sole standard of unity and truth, the inevitable result was the opening of a renewed period of controversy. Moehler's Protestant colleague at Tübingen, Ferdinand Christian Baur, felt it necessary to answer him with *The Difference between Catholicism and Protestantism according to the Principles and main Dogmas of the two systems of Doctrine.*† The repercussions of this controversy between two outstanding men continued to be felt for the best part of a century.

The nineteenth century, in fact, presents the spectacle of an increasingly divided Christendom. The victory of ultramontanism (i.e. the centralizing of authority and influence in the papal court) meant that Rome withdrew even further from contact with the Christian world as a whole; in consequence for a century there was little in Roman Catholic theology, other than the writings of the Modernists condemned by the Church, that anyone outside the Roman Catholic fold could be con-

Symbolik oder Darstellung der dogmatischen Gegensätze der Katholiken und Protestanten nach ihren öffentlichen Bekenntnisschriften.

†*Der Gegensatz des Katholizismus und Protestantismus nach den Prinzipien und Hauptdogmen der beiden Lehrbegriffe.* (1836).

cerned to read. The Protestant world was the scene of ever new divisions—the Old Lutheran movement in Germany, which led to the formation of the highly confessional Lutheran Church-Missouri Synod in the United States; the Disruption of the Church of Scotland in 1843;[6] the fragmentation of Methodism; the emergence of the Disciples of Christ as a separate entity;[7] the Old Catholic split at the time of the first Vatican Council in 1870.[8]

The lack of a common language has often been noted as one of the causes that led to the final split between the Eastern and the Western sections of the Church.[9] The dominance of Latin from Iceland to Sicily in the early middle ages was an immense source of strength to the Western Church. But this process had hardly reached its climax before the treasure began to become a wasting asset. The reversal began with Dante, who still felt it necessary to defend himself for writing in a contemporary tongue—Italian was all right for light verse, but anyone who had anything serious to say ought to say it in Latin. The change was carried much further in the period of the Reformation through the translation of the Bible into every European language, the translation in many cases forming the foundation of a vernacular literature. Bishop Jewel wrote his *Apology of the Church of England* (1562) in Latin;[10] Hooker wrote his *Ecclesiastical Polity*[11] in his own lapidary English.

A further blow was dealt the unity of the *Corpus Christianum* in the West by the almost total loss of Latin as a common language at the end of the eighteenth century. Until that time scholars had been accustomed to correspond with one another in slightly pompous pseudo-Ciceronian Latin. It was a portent of change when Herbert Marsh in 1817 began to lecture on theology at Cambridge in English. No doubt this was much better for the students than the dreary Latin to which they had been subjected; but it indicated a certain withdrawal of England from the fellowship of the Christian world. The peoples of the West were tending to draw away from one another into the isolation of a new nationalism.

It is possible, of course, to point to many exceptions. Adolf von Harnack (1851–1930) was well acquainted with English work on the New Testament, and himself took the initiative in translating a number of English books. Conversely there was a spate of translations from German into English. Yet Schleiermacher's *On Religion: Speeches to its Cultured Despisers* was not Englished until John Oman took the task in hand in 1893; and his most famous work of all, *The Christian Faith*, had to wait for the twentieth century before its turn came.[12] The famous Hauck-Herzog: *Realenzyklopädie* contains no article on Frederick Denison Maurice, and the American theologian Horace Bushnell is not even mentioned in the Index.

With so much divergence, where was any principle of convergence to be found? It is to be noted, in the history of the Church as elsewhere, that practice usually precedes theory; action comes before reflective thought; habit before theology. New movements invariably produce new forms of theology; it does not always follow that new theological ideas produce new movements. It will not therefore surprise us to find many tendencies of ecumenical convergence in practice before it becomes possible to speak of anything like an ecumenical theology.

I. ECUMENICAL BEGINNINGS

It has long been noted that the origins of the modern ecumenical movement are to be found in the missionary movement of the nineteenth century, and that in so far as the ecumenical movement can be said to have had a birthplace, that birthplace was the first World Missionary Conference held at Edinburgh in 1910.[13] It must not, however, be forgotten that Edinburgh had a long tradition of mutual understanding and co-operation on which to build.

The modern missionary movement was the child of the various revivals which shook the countries of Europe in the eighteenth and early nineteenth centuries. Pietism[14] has always possessed a strong international sense, and a feeling of fellowship which has transcended national and linguistic boundaries. One of the manifestations of the new spirit was the Mission

House at Basel, many of the sons of which went into the service of the English-speaking missionary societies. In 1816 the Basel Missionary Society began to publish the *Evangelisches Missions-magazin,* a periodical which still appears, in order not merely to record their own affairs, but to educate the German-reading public on the whole course of modern missionary history. Thus, to take at random a single volume, that of 1880, we find eight articles on the spiritual life of the Chinese, three on the work of the Norwegian missions in Madagascar and South Africa, two on the 81st anniversary of the Church Missionary Society, one on Swedish missionary effort, as well as a monthly survey of missionary progress in Asia and Africa, and reviews of books in a number of languages.

A second periodical of the same kind was the *Allgemeine Missionszeitschrift,* started in 1874 by Gustav Warneck,[15] who is generally regarded as the founder of the science of missiology. Here also the wealth and variety of material assembled is astonishing. Of course the writers retained their right to be critical. These two journals had little to say that was good about the Roman Catholic missions—ecumenism in the nineteenth century could not extend so far. Warneck did not like high Anglicans. He criticized ruthlessly the current slogan "The evangelization of the world in this generation".[16] For all that, the non-Roman missionary enterprise was held to be one single campaign. David Livingstone was revered everywhere on the continent no less than in his native Scotland.

Those who planned the Edinburgh Conference were extraordinarily fortunate in securing John R. Mott[17] as chairman and J. H. Oldham as secretary. The Conference was extremely well prepared for. Every attempt was made to gather an assembly that would be as fully ecumenical as possible. It is important to note the limits that were accepted at that time as inevitable. No Roman Catholic was present. It does not appear that any representatives of the Orthodox churches were invited, though the famous mission in Japan under Archbishop Nicolai[18] was flourishing at the time. Latin America was not represented, since Europe, in contrast to North America, did not recognize nominally Roman Catholic countries as missionary territory. Otherwise the representation, territorial and confessional, was remarkably complete.

It is often said that Edinburgh 1910 neglected the role of the Church in the mission, and that it had no specific theology. The first affirmation can be maintained only through disregard of the documents. The second rests on a misunderstanding. It is true that questions of Faith and Order were excluded from the programme of Edinburgh 1910, which was a conference of churchmen but not of the churches. It is also true that the Conference did not spend its time discussing questions of theology, not because theology was regarded as unimportant, but because there was such widespread agreement that discussion seemed hardly necessary. The theology of the majority of those gathered at Edinburgh was biblical, pietistic, evangelical and conservative. They were agreed on all the main doctrines of the Christian faith as set forth in the Scriptures and in the classic creeds of the Church. They accepted literally the command to go into all the world and preach the Gospel to every creature. Though far from being starry-eyed optimists, they looked forward to an ever-increasing penetration of the world by the Gospel. In view of all these agreements, what was there left to discuss?

Edinburgh 1910 was hardly troubled at all by the question of liberalism in missions. There had been a controversy in the United States in 1893 as to the terms on which missionaries should be admitted to missionary service.[19] In Germany the General Missionary Union *(Allgemeine Missionsverein)* had been founded in 1885 by those who could not approve of the rigid confessionalism of most of the German missions.[20] J. N. Farquhar, who arrived in India in 1891, was generally regarded as a liberal.[21] Twenty years later the situation was entirely different; the tension between liberal and conservative was one of the main issues in the missionary world. The question had to be decided whether ecumenical advance was to be tied to one particular theological formulation, or whether some other basis for it could be found. It may be thought that even in 1910 there should have been far more awareness of this problem than apparently there was.

At one point, however, Edinburgh 1910 had taken one step of cardinal importance for the future of ecumenical theology. Evangelicals, the majority of missionaries among them, on the whole regarded confessional differences as an irrelevance or a misfortune, and experienced little difficulty in working with one another. Other Christians, however, regarded confessional allegiance as an essential part of Christian obedience. On this ground high Anglicans and strict Lutherans had refused to be drawn into any of the numerous forms of co-operation which had been growing up between Christians in the non-Christian countries.[22] The British Student Christian Movement had in the meantime worked out a new formula, under which a student's loyalty to one Christian confession was to be regarded not as a limitation or an irrelevance, but as a treasure which he would contribute to the common stock.[23] The importance of this new approach cannot be exaggerated. It was the application of this principle which alone made possible the presence of the Society for the Propagation of the Gospel at Edinburgh 1910. All later ecumenism, in the main line of development, has been based on this theological understanding. This has made possible the gradual accession of the Orthodox, also originally via the Student Christian Movement, and later still of the Roman Catholic church, to ecumenical contacts with the other churches of Christendom.

II. CHRISTIAN SOCIAL CONCERN

The missionary movement set the ball rolling. There was another principle of convergence which had been quietly at work for sixty years before it became evident to all eyes—the growing concern of Christians for their environment, and an increasing sense of the social responsibility of the churches.

It is not the case that in earlier times Christians had been lacking in a sense of social concern. But this had usually taken the form of personal help and service within a framework which was generally regarded as unchangeable. The industrial revolution brought about a new form of human enslavement. At the same time it made it evident that poverty was not a necessary accompaniment of human life through all ages.

The first Christian to realize that it is the business of the Church not merely to alleviate poverty but to change the face of society was perhaps Frederick Denison Maurice.[24] His prophetic influence lived on through such disciples as B. F. Westcott, Charles Gore, Henry Scott Holland and William Temple; a direct line of succession can be traced from the Christian Socialists of 1848 to the Conference on Politics, Economics and Citizenship of 1924.

England was not alone in this awakening. German Roman Catholics can point to Bishop Ketteler (1811–77), Protestants to Friedrich Naumann (1860–1919). In France, Tommy Fallot (1844–1904) found eager successors in Elie Gounelle and the group which made of *Le Christianisme social* one of the best of all Christian periodicals. In Switzerland, Leonhard Ragaz (1868–1948) exercised a profound influence on the young Karl Barth.[25] America came along a little later with the Social Gospel, powerfully propounded by Walter Rauschenbusch (1861–1918), a far more prophetic and theologically grounded movement than was generally admitted by the neo-orthodoxy which prevailed from 1930 onwards.[26]

These movements differed among themselves, but they had much in common and were beginning to discover one another. It needed one great figure to draw all the streams into one channel. The hour was matched with the man. In 1914 Nathan Söderblom was appointed, by what might appear almost as a freak of fortune, Archbishop of Uppsala and Primate of the Swedish Church.[27]

This many-sided man first came into prominence in connection with abortive efforts on behalf of peace during the First World War. Though these failed, Söderblom remained convinced that after the war the churches must together lift up their voices on social issues, and in particular in denunciation of war as a means of settling international rivalries. With persistence, ingenuity and passion he set himself to convince the churches. His first great success was in securing the interest of the Orthodox. His second was in linking the British movement which led up to the COPEC[28] Conference of 1924, at which the Archbishop appeared briefly in person, to the movement that he was himself propagating, so that this conference was regarded as the British contribution to the preparation for the international conference which Söderblom had proposed for the following year.

Each new conference seems to start by forgetting everything that has ever been done before. What we do today is less new than we sometimes imagine. Anyone who takes the trouble to look up the twelve preparatory volumes of COPEC is likely to be astonished at the range of subjects dealt with and the contemporary relevance of much that was written at that time. It is particularly notable that up till a late stage in the preparations there was full co-operation from Roman Catholics; the ground on which they felt it necessary to withdraw was the liberal attitude taken up by some of their colleagues on what were then the new problems of contraception.

Stockholm 1925 was Nathan Söderblom. He had seen the vision. Throughout the conference he radiated power. More than any other Christian conference this was the expression of the personality of a single man. In many ways his work has endured; but in later times one of his essential principles has all too often been forgotten—that a true ecumenical theology can grow only out of the fellowship of prayer and adoration.

Two problems, both ecumenical but one more strictly theological than the other, had to be faced at Stockholm 1925.

The concerns of the conference were both social and international. There was in existence a body which in 1915 had taken the name of the World Alliance for Promoting International Friendship through the Churches.[29] This was a fellowship of concerned individuals, in which the Quaker influence was strong and the tendency towards a pacifist position was marked. As President of the Swedish branch of the Alliance Söderblom was placed in a dilemma: should the Alliance be allowed to play a considerable part in the preparations for and the conduct of the conference or should it be kept at a distance? Stimulated by Bishop E. S. Talbot of Winchester, behind whom stood the formidable figure of Randall Davidson, Archbishop of Canterbury, Söderblom took the prophetic decision; Stockholm 1925 was to be a conference of the churches; as far as possible those who attended should be the accredited representatives of the Christian churches of the world. This was crucial; what distinguishes the ecumenical movement of the twentieth century from all that have preceded it is that it is a church movement, for which the churches of the world as such have increasingly accepted responsibility.[30]

The second problem arose out of a difference of theological understanding of the nature of the Kingdom of God. In the opening sermon Bishop Theodore Woods had suggested that the bringing in of the Kingdom of God upon earth was a task of which at least a share had been put into the hands of men by God himself. Bishop Ihmels of Saxony retaliated by the affirmation that the Kingdom of God was the affair of God alone, and that all that men could do was to wait patiently for its appearing.[31] The rift ran deep through all the deliberations of the conference. The Continentals accused the "Anglo-Saxons" of theological superficiality and naïve optimism in face of the calamities of world history. The Americans, in particular, accused the Germans of disregarding the great forces of renewal that God has let loose in the world through the Gospel. This, one of the deepest of ecumenical divisions, has continued to perplex men of goodwill as they meet one another. It almost completely frustrated the committee charged with the task of drawing up an agreed statement on the Christian hope for the second Assembly of the World Council of Churches in 1954.[32] Not until Jürgen Moltmann published his work *The Theology of Hope*[33] was the German theological world prepared to take seriously the idea that the world is there to be transformed and not merely to be endured—and Moltmann came to his views via Karl Marx rather than directly through a reconsideration of biblical truth.

III. THEOLOGICAL CONSIDERATIONS

Stockholm 1925 met under the influence of the slogan

"Doctrine divides, service unites".[34] It was not, of course, possible to live by this principle. As the Epistles of Paul show, even the most practical aspects of Christian action have to be traced back to their deep theological roots; and a theology which does not lead on to action hardly deserves the name of theology. Nevertheless this was a view widely prevalent in the liberal age. The third wing of the ecumenical movement, Faith and Order, came into existence on precisely the contrary principle—that theological confrontation is what is needed, and that the churches must learn to meet and talk at exactly those points at which differences are most clearly evident, and at which sensitive feelings are most likely to be hurt.

If Stockholm 1925 was Söderblom, for many years Faith and Order was Charles Henry Brent.[35] At Edinburgh 1910 Brent, who was at that time Bishop of the Missionary District of the Philippines (American Episcopal), while not questioning the ruling that questions of faith and order were not appropriate for discussion at a missionary assembly, saw clearly that the time had come at which the churches must have the courage to take the theological bull by the horns. When at last the first World Conference on Faith and Order met at Lausanne in 1927, it was universally felt to be right and proper that Brent should be the chairman.

The times were not propitious for such an attempt. The old habit of 'theological colloquies'[36] had almost completely died out. There were few signs of any progress towards theological agreement. The somewhat strident tones of Karl Barth and the dialectical theology were shaking the citadel of liberalism. The total failure of the ageing Adolf von Harnack and the young Karl Barth to understand one another was typical of an age in which theological exchange had become more and not less difficult.

In the circumstances the holding of the conference in 1927 was a notable achievement. Representation was comparatively wide, and on the whole official. Both Orthodox[37] and Lutherans found it necessary to hand in separate statements, and agreements could be stated only in the most general terms. But the tone of the conference had been friendly. The basic principles of ecumenical confrontation—absolute freedom of speech for all, and courteous respect for opinions which one does not share—were beginning to appear.

The first thing that became evident was that the churches still lived in splendid ignorance about one another. The classic instance was Orthodox support for a Lutheran proposal that a reference to the invisible Church should be added at a certain point in one of the documents of the conference, the Orthodox supposing that the reference was to that part of the Church which has passed the frontier of death and is now in glory, whereas the Lutheran concern was to guard against any complete identification of the Church with any of its visible forms. Accurate knowledge of the churches of Christendom is a necessary prerequisite for every form of ecumenical understanding, and for any advance towards agreement in the truth.

One result of the Faith and Order movement has been the appearance of a new kind of *Konfessionskunde*.* Moehler's work was based on a comparison of the dogmatic and confessional statements of one church with those of another. It now came to be realized that this was not a fruitful approach. The life of the churches consists of far more than doctrinal statements (p. 27 f.). Anyone who tried to understand the Church of England on the basis of the Thirty-nine Articles of Religion alone would not advance very far; Anglicans have been correct in saying that the best manual of Anglican theology is the Book of Common Prayer. It is now realized that the life of every communion is a unity; if it is to be understood, account must be taken of traditions and customs, of worship, of social attitudes, and of relationships with other Christian bodies and with the world. To compile a work genuinely descriptive of the various churches in the Christian world is immensely difficult. When a variety of contributors are asked to write each on his own church, there is no unity of presentation or point of view. If one man sets out on the gigantic task of depicting all the churches of Christendom, it is unlikely that

* Descriptive surveys of the various confessions within the Christian world.

what he puts out will be accurate at every point. Yet some works of this kind have attained to a high degree of comprehensiveness and accuracy. As examples it is possible to cite from the Roman Catholic side the *Konfessionskunde* of K. Algermissen, of which the 7th edition appeared at Paderborn (Bonifacius Druckerer) in 1957; on the Protestant side the work of the Norwegian Einar Molland: *Christendom,*[38] and the *Ökumenische Kirchenkunde* of Peter Meinholde.[39] We have now come to see that the whole Christian spectrum must be considered; it is not easy to determine exactly where the line should be drawn, but on the whole it is better to include even the groups such as Christian Science and the Church of the Latter Day Saints (the Mormons), the claims of which to be part of the Christian family are at least dubious.

One of the merits of Faith and Order was its recognition of the fact that the recovery of Christian unity can only be a long-term process, in which theological elements must play the leading part. Commissions were kept in being. A series of international meetings of Christian scholars was held. Out of these emerged two volumes of considerable merit, *The Doctrine of Grace* (1932), and *The Ministry and the Sacraments* (1937), to each of which a number of eminent scholars contributed. But in each of these volumes little more was achieved than the setting side by side of a number of individual viewpoints; there was very little sign of anything that could be called an ecumenical consensus. And, during the years between 1937 and 1948, the productivity of Faith and Order seemed to grow less and less; a truly ecumenical theology remained a vision for an apparently indeterminate future.[40]

IV. PRACTICAL STEPS TO UNITY

The authorities of Faith and Order made it clear that their movement was theological and theoretical in character, and that it had nothing directly to say in that area of applied theology which has to do with the actual union of churches.[41]

Yet the period of development of Faith and Order was also the period in which the movement for visible church union was setting in with a power unknown in any previous century. There had been some small unions of churches in the nineteenth century, usually through the coming together of fragments from the same confessional tradition. The wider movement for church union is a phenomenon of the twentieth century.

Between 1910 and 1960 fifty unions of churches came about in various countries of the world.[42] Many of these took place within the limits of a single confession, as in the case of the many movements of unity among the Lutherans in the United States. But a considerable number—Canada and Japan, the Philippines, China, South India—leaped over the borders of the confessions and arrived at the establishment of a wider range of unity.

In a mainly non-Christian country Christian union has obvious practical advantages. Not unnaturally the purely pragmatic element plays a considerable, though varying, role in these many plans and projects of church union. But none of them was merely pragmatic. Each group of negotiators found themselves faced with a number of theological issues which could not be evaded. In the course of these many negotiations there was hardly a problem in the whole theological encyclopaedia which did not sooner or later come to be considered.

It is greatly to be regretted that so little scientific study has been directed to this vital area of ecumenical theology. For only two of these inter-confessional movements—Canada[43] and South India[44]—have we standard works of merit equal to the greatness of the theme.[45] Each union brought to light a vast array of problems, personal, sociological and theological. To trace these out requires more than mere diligence; it makes considerable demands on insight and imagination. Yet the reward in understanding should more than compensate for the labour involved. For instance, the process by which the divided forces of French Protestantism were brought together again in 1938, if fully recorded, would be of interest far beyond the limits of France and of the world of continental Protestantism. Even the little union in the Canton of Neuchâtel in Switzerland, in which not more than 150,000 Christians were involved, reveals intensity of conviction and passion not unworthy of a Greek city state in the age of Pericles. Here is a vast field for research which lies open to the ecumenically-minded student; in most cases the sources and documents are not difficult to find.

If detailed studies are lacking, still more do we stand in need of the comprehensive study which would attempt to answer the question, Why at this moment of Church history and no other did the divisive forces in Christendom appear to be checked, and to be replaced by a movement towards actual and visible unity on a scale never previously seen in Christian history?[46]

V. NEW SOURCES OF CONTROVERSY

But had the divisive forces really been so effectively checked? An ecumenical theology which took the form of a success story would involve extensive falsification of the realities. As Paul warned us long ago, unity is not easy to attain, and at least as difficult to maintain. We have already noted one area of ecumenical disagreement; this is the appropriate point at which to look at another.

The year 1932 may be taken as the highest point of the liberal influence on the missionary work of the Church. In that year the long labours of the Laymen's Foreign Missions Inquiry were crowned by the publication of the book *Rethinking Missions,* in which the distinguished American philosopher W. E. Hocking put forward in an extreme form the liberal view of Christian missions. The task of the missionary is not to attempt to convert anyone, but to co-operate with the best forces making for reform in the non-Christian religions, the worth of which appears to be assumed, as valid though perhaps imperfect forms of the truth.

It was to be expected that such a statement would call out a vigorous reaction from the side of the orthodox. The reaction was not long in coming. As preparation for the third World Missionary Conference, held at Tambaram-Madras in 1938, Dr. Hendrik Kraemer, then in Indonesia, had been asked to prepare a book, *The Christian Message in a non-Christian World*. Kraemer had come profoundly under the influence of the Barthian theology. His book, probably the best that he ever wrote, turned out to be a point-by-point refutation of everything for which the liberals stood. Kraemer does not deny outright that God may have spoken to men through other religions; but the stress on discontinuity, on the uniqueness of God's word in Christ, is so strong, that it is hard to see how any measure of truth can be ascribed to any other form of religion (cf. pp. 187 f.).[47]

Something of the vigour of the discussion that ensued can be traced in the first volume of the Tambaram Series, *The Authority of the Faith,* a collection of essays by various authors, with a further contribution by Kraemer himself. Then the Second World War intervened, and for the time being the debate languished. But the issues that arose in the 1930s made it clear that ecumenism cannot be understood simply in terms of adaptations and encounters within the Church; the world is always present as the extra dimension, and this may be interpreted either as the world of the non-Christian religions, or as the technological world which in the main has decided that it can dispense with God. After thirty years it is still necessary to speak of an area of ecumenical confusion rather than of ecumenical conviction. It will be convenient to consider the problem under three heads:

1. *The Christian attitude towards non-Christian religions.* In the main the swing of the pendulum has been away from the rigid attitude maintained by Kraemer, though this attitude still has its supporters especially in conservative circles.

In these years leaders in the Younger Churches have had their say. In the year of the Tambaram Conference, 1938, a group of Indian Christians produced a book called *Rethinking Christianity in India,*[48] in part in conscious reaction against the views of Kraemer. These thinkers were prepared to affirm that much of value for the understanding of the Christian faith is to be found in the ancient classics of India, and that these classics can fulfil for the Asian churches the same function that was fulfilled for the early Church by the Scriptures of the Old

Testament. African Christians similarly claim that the missionaries were wrong in sweeping away everything in the African tradition; there are beauties and treasures to be recovered from the past of the African peoples.

No subject is more vigorously debated among young people all over the world than the claim of any religion to uniqueness. The flow of books on the subject continues.[49]

2. *A positive affirmation of the world.* Many Christians have been distressed at the secular attitudes increasingly prevalent throughout the world. One school of theologians, of whom F. Gogarten[50] in Germany was among the first, put forward the view that this secularization is something that has come about largely as a result of the preaching of the Christian Gospel, and is something for which Christians ought to be thankful. The old magical and mythological view of the world is decaying, and this opens out before man the possibility of entering into that sovereignty over the world which it was always the will of God that man should have. Thus the Christian is able to look out on all the processes of world history as part of the plan of God, and to see God at work far beyond the limits of the Church.

3. *A new understanding of Christian missions.* The old antithesis between the Christian West and the non-Christian East has entirely broken down. The Christian mission as carried on in the nineteenth century was a reflection of the imperialistic attitudes of that age. We have to recognize that the mission is always God's mission, that the lordship of Christ has been established over the whole world, and that we must expect to find Christ at work even in the most unexpected places.

This new way of looking at things may be summed up in four brief paragraphs:

1. We are as likely to find God at work outside the Church as within it; in fact we may have to go outside the Church in order to find out where God is really at work.

2. We must not suppose that we go to 'take Christ' to some situation where he is not. We go to find him already there. We may have more to learn from the non-Christian than he has to learn from us.

3. We must speak of 'mission in six continents'; otherwise we shall fall back into the old idea that mission is something that the Christian world carries on in non-Christian countries.

4. God is on the side of the weak and the oppressed. In a revolutionary situation Christians should not be afraid of the use of violence, if this is the only way in which justice can be established.

Such views were strongly expressed at the Conference of the Division of World Mission and Evangelism held at Mexico City in 1963,[51] at the Conference on Church and Society at Geneva in 1966 and at the fourth Assembly of the World Council of Churches at Uppsala in 1968.[52] It need hardly be said that such views meet with violent opposition in conservative and orthodox circles; this is still one of the points at which theological divergence rather than ecumenical convergence is to be observed today.

VI. A COUNCIL IN BEING

For the moment we have departed from chronological order. We must now go back to the turning-point in ecumenical history which was marked by the formation of the World Council of Churches in 1948. It has been right to mention the forces making for division; nevertheless it is possible to see that, in view of the many lines of convergence, the coming into existence of the Council and its integration with the International Missionary Council in 1961 were parts of an almost inevitable and irresistible process. This is not to deny the courage and determination of the individuals through whom the Council came into being; without William Temple and W. A. Visser 't Hooft, Samuel Cavert, Kathleen Bliss and a thousand others, there would have been no World Council.[53] But these pioneers had been working with the stream of the times and not against it.

In the end the Council came into being very simply, as a "fellowship of Churches which acknowledge Jesus Christ as God and Saviour".[54] Still incomplete, since the great churches of Rome and Moscow, and some large churches on the Protestant side, were absent, it yet represented a larger range of churches wishing to be permanently associated with one another, to "stay together", as the Message of Amsterdam expressed it, than had ever before been seen in the history of the Church. Here was a new phenomenon. How was it to be understood?

Ecumenical theology is far from being exhausted by the theology of the World Council of Churches. Yet that the existence of the Council presents a new theological problem cannot be denied.

The twentieth century is the century of councils—local, regional, international, worldwide; permanent, highly organized; not claiming to be churches, and yet fulfilling many of the functions of churches. What is the theological status of such bodies? The only theologian who has so far seriously tackled this new problem appears to be H. P. Van Dusen, who in his book *One Great Ground of Hope* (New York, 1961), strongly defends the *churchly* character of such councils.[55]

Before the Council came into being Dr. Visser 't Hooft, General Secretary of the Provisional Committee, attempted to assess the theoretical significance of the projected council in an essay published in one of the preparatory volumes for the Amsterdam Assembly—"The Significance of the World Council of Churches". He starts with the question put by Dietrich Bonhoeffer: *"Ist die Ökumene Kirche?"*, a phrase which cannot be exactly translated into English. It is clear what Bonhoeffer meant—"Is this a merely pragmatic attempt to bring the churches nearer to one another, or is it a serious theological attempt to realize the true nature of the Church?" Dr. 't Hooft concludes that the Council is an "emergency solution", the best solution possible in the circumstances resulting from the failure of the churches to be true to their vocation as the body of Christ.[56]

The most important theological statement made by the World Council of Churches about itself is the document entitled "The Church, the Churches and the World Council of Churches", accepted by the Central Committee of the Council at Toronto in January 1950. Here it is emphatically stated that the Council is not a church, much less a super-church, and that it has no intention of ever becoming a church. Its function is to be the servant of the churches, helping them to be true to their great vocation and so serving the cause of Christian unity.[57]

The Council has been very careful not to issue instructions to the churches, or to tell them what kind of unity they ought to seek. But at New Delhi in 1961 it committed itself to the view that local unity is the ideal, as "all in each place" are able both to find and to express their oneness in Christ.[58] At the same time it was careful not to lay down any rules as to how that unity was to be reached, or in what institutional form it was to be expressed.

The problem of the World Council of Churches is that it cannot serve the churches unless it continues itself to be in a state of movement. But how can that which has come to be an institution remain in movement? This is the greatest problem in the ecumenical world today.

VII.   THINKING OUT WHAT IT MEANS

We have already noticed that some of the Orthodox churches had accepted the call to ecumenical co-operation as early as 1920. But the great church of Moscow, for reasons which it endeavoured to make plain, held back.[59] It was a real triumph for patient ecumenical diplomacy when that church, together with other churches more or less dependent on it, overcame hesitations and presented themselves at New Delhi 1961 as candidates for membership in the Council.

What does it mean to an Orthodox church to take part in a venture of this kind? Neither Orthodox theology nor Orthodox practice are entirely consistent; but it is clear that in principle the Orthodox regard all other Christian bodies as voluntary societies of laymen without grace and without sacraments; even baptism administered by non-Orthodox bodies is not always accepted as valid.[60] How, then, can an Orthodox Christian co-operate with those whom he can only doubtfully recognize as Christians? In the ecumenical encounter he is compelled to recognize that those whom he meets are living by the grace of Christ; in his official theology he cannot admit that the grace of Christ is present with them as it is with him.

Two writers, Leo Zander[61] and Paul Evdokimov,[62] have specially wrestled with this problem, distinguishing between the empirical reality as the plane on which the ecumenical encounter can take place, and the eschatological realm, in which alone unity will finally be possible. It may be, however, that our greatest Orthodox illumination will come from America, where a younger generation of scholars such as Alexander Schmemann and John Meyendorff, both Russians brought up in France, are re-thinking Orthodoxy in a Western and basically alien situation. It will be interesting to see how loyalty to Orthodox tradition can be combined with the new revolution of ecumenical thinking.[63]

The problem for the Roman Catholic was scarcely less difficult. The official attitude of the Roman church, as set forth in the Encyclical of Pius XI *Mortalium Animos*[64] was as negative as it could be on the subject of ecumenical co-operation; this attitude remained unchanged for twenty years. But this is only one side of the picture. In a brilliant essay Professor R. Aubert of Louvain has shown us how often great movements in the Roman Catholic church start on the periphery, almost unnoticed, not infrequently disapproved; and then move in to the centre until at last their power causes them to be recognized by authority.[65] Beginning with the epoch-making work of Fr. Yves Congar, *Chrétiens Désunis* (1937),[66] ecumenical interest was slowly spreading, mainly in France and Belgium, but also in Germany and to a lesser degree in the United States. Rome might attempt to control and direct this movement; it could not extinguish it. And so in the end Rome itself was faced with the fundamental problem of ecumenical theology—What am I to think of Christians of an allegiance other than my own?

The question is that of "the limits of the Church".[67] By Roman Catholic definition only those can be saved who are in communion with the Bishop of Rome, and so are in the one true ark of salvation. But is this the sole and final answer? Both honesty and charity compelled Roman Catholics of good will to recognize that it is far more difficult to define the boundaries of the Church than had been supposed. The way was wide open for a radical re-consideration of that most neglected area of theology—the doctrine of the Church.[68]

Not much might have happened outside the narrow limits of the academic world, had it not been for the tense election, at the end of which Angelo Cardinal Roncalli emerged as Pope John XXIII. Even his unexpected and apparently spontaneous decision to hold a council would not necessarily have been followed by extensive ecumenical consequences. It was the decision to throw the council open to the whole world, and to invite observers from the various confessions and from such bodies as the World Council of Churches, that made the council a great event in ecumenical history.[69]

For ecumenical study three documents of the Second Vatican Council will afford material for many years yet to come—the *Decree on Ecumenism,* the *Declaration on the Attitude of the Church towards non-Christian Religions,* and above all the *Dogmatic Constitution on the Church.*[70] On Ecumenism the council had many kind things to say, recognizing all that the non-Roman churches of Christendom have retained of Christian substance, and attributing to them a churchly character far more fully than in any official document of the Roman Catholic church in earlier times. Whereas traditional Christian theology has had little that was good to say about the non-Christian religions, Rome has now intervened decisively on the liberal side in the debate, recognizing not only the common substance of faith in Judaism and Islam, but also speaking with deep sympathy of the aspirations of those who in any religious form seek after the Father of all. But more than any other document it is the *De Ecclesia* that introduces the new ecumenical atmosphere.

Roman Catholic ecclesiology had tended to be hierarchic—mainly concerned with the status and authority of the Pope, and of the hierarchy of which he is the head. Here a different wind is blowing. The treatment is biblical in the extreme.

Even the term 'mystical body of Christ', though not entirely abandoned, is not regarded as fully adequate to the task. The Church is set forth primarily as the 'people of God'. By the constant stress on the pilgrim character of this people, the council restored that eschatological tension between the 'already' and the 'not-yet' (see p.38 above) which Protestant scholars have so often felt to be lacking in Roman Catholic theology. The notable thing is that at point after point the Fathers at the council are seen to be tracing the same road as has been followed by the best Protestant theology in recent years. It is this more than anything else that has made possible such fruitful dialogue as has been unknown since the days of the Reformation.

CONCLUSION

We come back to the question, In what sense, if any, is it proper to use the term 'ecumenical theology'.

In one sense, it may be said that never in the whole history of the Church has there been such total agreement as would justify the use of the term. Modern scholarship is engaged in tracing out in the New Testament itself the various streams and traditions which went to the making up of the developing theology of the Church. To later times the Middle Ages may seem to be dominated by the commanding figure of Thomas Aquinas; in point of fact there were in his day many other possibilities of interpretation; a perfect synthesis of mediaeval thought is an invention of later ages.

So it is in the modern world. We have seen the many convergences that have produced the ecumenical movement, and determined ecumenical progress up to the present time. It has also been necessary to draw attention to new lines of division, which run right across denominational boundaries, and in no way correspond to the old confessional divisions of the past. In this short survey there has been no space to discuss the immense growth in recent years of the forces of 'conservative evangelicalism', which have also organized themselves internationally, and presented to the world what they believe to be another and far sounder form of ecumenism.[71]

Some careful definition is needed, if we are to be clear what we are talking about.

Professor G. Thils of Louvain, in a small book, *La "Théologie Oecuménique"—Notion—Formes—Démarches** (Louvain, 1960), has attempted to wrestle with the question in all its complexity. He first deals briefly with 'ecumenical theology' as the theology of the World Council of Churches as seen by itself and as seen by others. Here much remains to be done but many of the fundamental questions have been posed. But this is very far from covering the whole field. Theology can be classed as ecumenical only if it involves an 'existential confrontation'. This means that the Christian who takes the ecumenical situation seriously will find himself led more and more inevitably to a critical 'reflection' which must be exercised upon his own church, upon the other churches, and upon their relationship to the Church of Jesus Christ itself. "And since the same question is being asked of all the faithful who have been called to the alert in each one of the churches, he will find himself participating with these others in an ecumenical dialogue, of transcendent value in proportion to the extent to which those who take part are really engaged" (p. 25). Professor Thils then goes on to consider "ecumenical theology as a 'dimension' present in all theology (pp. 47-60), and finally as a 'particular discipline' within the world of theology" (pp. 66–80).

The structure of this chapter has been planned to correspond to its title, and to suggest that the ecumenical dimension, like the missionary dimension, is relevant to every part of theological study. There is a certain danger in the proliferation of Ecumenical Institutes and chairs of Ecumenical Theology. It should be the aim of every professor of the subject to work himself out of a job by his success in ensuring that no part of theology shall be taught out of relation to the ecumenical dimension. After all, the Bible itself begins with the whole of humanity and ends with the gathering together of the nations of the world to the light of the City of God; it would be hard to state a more fully ecumenical programme than this.

* *Ecumenical Theology: The Idea—Forms—Approaches.*

This means that, for the future, no theological student should be trained only in the traditions of that section of the Body of Christ to which he happens to belong. As long as we live in separate churches, part of the training must be given in confessional seminaries in which the student becomes familiar with the liturgical and spiritual traditions of the church in the ministry of which he is to serve. But the greater part of the training should be given in a far freer atmosphere, in which the student is exposed to teachers who come from Christian confessions, or even from religions, other than his own, and to fellow-students from the greatest possible variety of churches.

In the future, in churches which accept the ecumenical vocation, no man or woman should be allowed to enter the service of the Church, if unable to accord assent to a brief list of ecumenical affirmations:

1. We must start with acceptance of the fact that Christians of other observances really are Christians, however improbable this may seem.
2. From this it follows that there is no Christian confession, and no individual Christian in the world, from whom we have not something to learn.
3. We may be sure that we possess the essentials of the Christian faith; but none of us lives by the fullness of the deposit which has been committed to us.
4. The end result of the ecumenical encounter may be to help us to rediscover our own forgotten treasures.
5. Ecumenical encounter must be existential; that is, it must be carried out under conditions of honest speaking and humble listening.
6. There is no place for rigid dogmatism, for uninformed criticism, for levity, or for superficiality.
7. The aim is not agreement at all costs, but the manifestation of the truth of God.
8. The end of ecumenical illumination is ecumenical obedience.
9. No Christian, and no confession, can hope to emerge unmodified from genuine ecumenical encounter.
10. No one should engage in the ecumenical adventure,

unless he is fully convinced that inevitable losses will be far more than compensated for by the resultant gains.

It may be felt that this is somewhat thin and inadequate as a summary of the results of sixty years of ecumenical endeavour, and as the starting-point for future ecumenical exploration. This view is likely to be taken only by those who have not made themselves familiar with the documents of the early days. It is vitally important not to claim agreement where no agreement really exists, and not to boast of progress which has not actually been attained. But, only when the difficulties of the early days are considered in the light of the things that we regard as self-evident today can the length of the journey already travelled and the extent of ecumenical success be justly apprehended. Much more might have been achieved, given deeper humility and a more adventurous faith. Nevertheless the convinced ecumenist may feel that he is justified in setting up his modest Ebenezer, and in claiming that "hitherto hath the Lord helped us".

For further reading

At every point reference must be made to R. Rouse and
S. C. Neill, *A History of the Ecumenical Movement 1517–1948*,
S.P.C.K., London, 1967², with its revised and enlarged
bibliography. For recent developments *The Ecumenical Review*
(1948) is full of information. Since 1964 we have also the
Journal of Ecumenical Studies, with valuable abstracts of all
important publications. For a general survey of the theme see
W. M. Horton, *Christian Theology: an Ecumenical Approach*,
Harper, New York, 1955.

For bibliographies in English:
Paul A. Crow Jr., *The Ecumenical Movement in Bibliographical
Outline*, National Council of Churches, New York, 1965, and
J. S. Lescrauwet M.S.C., *Critical Bibliography of Ecumenical
Literature*, Bestel Centrale V.S.K.B., Nijmegen, 1968.

Appendix

LANGUAGE STUDY AND THEOLOGY

ADVANCED STUDY and research in virtually every field of human knowledge involve some knowledge of languages other than one's own if there is to be adequate appreciation of the contributions being made throughout the world to the particular subject; the days when Latin provided a universal means of communication for the western world are gone, and though English, French and German provide an entry into much of the learned literature, much is published in other languages. The scholar needs to be multi-lingual.

For the more advanced stages of theological study this clearly applies. But Christian (and other) theological study involves the use of many texts whose original language is not that of any modern western community. Traditionally, it has appeared essential that every student of theology should be able to read at least his Bible in the original languages; Hebrew and Greek have in the past been a compulsory component of all self-respecting theological degrees, and not infrequently Latin has been almost equally emphasized. It is often asked today how far this is to be viewed as a realistic requirement at a time when the knowledge of Latin in schools is decreasing, and when study of Greek before the university level is even more rare. Can it be reasonably expected that within the compass of a theological study which involves so many disciplines the burden of learning two or three ancient languages should be borne? And how far is it to be viewed as an essential, when the texts—not only biblical—are increasingly available in translation?

The first questions may be answered more readily than this last. Given a relatively limited period of study, the imposition of a disproportionate burden of language study will inevitably mean that some other aspects of theology will be squeezed out. The reasonable policy here is to provide for a measure of specialization which will permit a fuller and more intensive study of the biblical (or other) languages alongside alternatives which allow of little or even no such linguistic study. Most theological courses in Great Britain and in the United States are organized so as to meet different types of need.

But the question how far such study is essential is a more difficult one. It is not simply a question of how much time is available; it is a question of what is the aim of such linguistic study. It is sometimes maintained that whereas the student of modern western languages or of oriental languages will be willing to learn them for their own sake, the student of theology learns languages simply as tools. There is truth in this, though it is not to be pressed too rigidly. For the reading of texts in a foreign language can never be simply to support exegesis; it must always in some measure involve entry into the culture which the language expresses. This is very evidently true for the ancient languages, for whereas we may visit France and Italy and see the culture there at first hand (more adequately with at least some knowledge of the language), our access to ancient Israel or first century Palestine and the Graeco-Roman world of the early Church is limited to the documentation, literary and archaeological, which is available to us. The exegesis of biblical texts involves more than knowledge of the meaning of words and understanding of syntax; it demands an appreciation of a whole rich way of life.

To a large extent this may be mediated through the translations of ancient texts and through the general books written about them by experts in the particular fields. But it may be doubted if this is enough. How much knowledge of a language is necessary for there to be real entry into the life and thought of the people? Of this no precise measure is available. It has been argued that even a year's study of Hebrew at least enables the reader of a biblical commentary to appreciate points of detailed discussion which depend on the meanings or forms of words, and to understand the nature of textual problems with their implications for exegesis. The same could equally well be said of New Testament Greek. It may be more reasonably urged that such an introductory course, if it is well taught and makes use of adequate methods of language teaching, will encourage some to go on and explore the richness of the language. But it may also be said that of those who study Hebrew and/or Greek for three years in a theological degree only a few will afterwards look at the original texts. Probably this is true, though it is equally true of many areas of study to which years are devoted at school and college and which seem afterwards to find no direct use. The assessment of such a point is one for educationalists and not simply for theologians. Perhaps a more useful point is the recognition that the study in depth of even a short section of biblical text in the original enables so much fuller an entry into the nature of the material and its inter-pretation that thereafter the approach to the text, in translation and with commentaries, will be all the more sensitive to the problems and more alert to the values.

The adequacy of translations is another point at which no generalization is possible. The study of the variety of good translations of the Bible now available is in itself a useful introduction to the problems of exegesis. It is also a warning that no translation will ever entirely convey the original, though it may well make a contribution to its fuller under-standing. For many texts, both ancient and modern, transla-tions are less good, or non-existent; dependence on an in-different or inaccurate translation will lead to misunderstanding and mis-statement.

The student of theology has to make a compromise here as in other matters. But at least he must be aware of the reasons for language study. He must be aware too that this is not simply the concern of the biblical scholar. The theology of the patristic age cannot be fully understood without Greek and Latin; the mediaeval world remains inaccessible at many points without Latin, for much remains untranslated. The great theologians of a later day, in spite of the wealth of translated books which flood the modern book market, are often to be known fully only with knowledge of the language in which they write. The investigation of religions other than the Christian inevitably reaches a point at which the study of the texts in translation is not enough; no one can be a real expert in Islam without at least some sound knowledge of Arabic, and the same is true of many other areas.

Notes and References

CHAPTER 1. CHRISTIAN THEOLOGY: ITS NATURE AND SCOPE

1. See Plato, *Republic*, Book 11, 379; Aristotle, *Metaphysics*, Book VI, 1026a; Augustine, *The City of God*, Book VI, Chapter 5.

2. For introductory accounts of the career and work of those mentioned, and of others, consult *The Oxford Dictionary of the Christian Church*, (ed. Cross), Oxford University Press, 1957.

3. An abbey founded even earlier (*c.*410) on the island of Lerinium (now St. Honorat) off Cannes became an important centre of monastic scholarship, and continued until the time of the French Revolution.

4. For an example, see the quotation from Arthur Frey in Brunner, *Revelation and Reason*, trans. Wyon, Westminster Press, Philadelphia, 1946, and S.C.M., London, 1947, pp. 377 f.

5. E.g. *The Reasonableness of Christianity* (Locke), *Christianity not Mysterious* (Toland), *Demonstration of the Being and Attributes of God* (Clarke), *Christianity as old as Creation* (Tindal), *Discourse on Freethinking* (Collins).

6. See Schleiermacher, *On Religion: Speeches to its Cultured Despisers*, Harper Torchbooks, New York, 1958; *Brief Outline on the Study of Theology*, John Knox Press, Richmond, Virginia, 1966; *The Christian Faith*, T. and T. Clark, Edinburgh, 1928, Chapter 1. A concise summary of Schleiermacher's *On Religion* is given in Healey, *Religion and Reality*, Oliver and Boyd, Edinburgh and London, 1965, pp. 16–19.

7. The alarm bell, warning the churches of their danger and recalling them to what he believed was the right path, was sounded by Karl Barth in his *Epistle to the Romans*, published in 1918. He discarded the first edition in favour of a revision made three years later. The first translation into English was done by Hoskyns from the sixth edition (Oxford University Press, 1933, and since reprinted). There are a number of introductions to and outlines of Barth's massive contribution to Christian theology, but perhaps as good a beginning as any can be made by reading his own *Evangelical Theology: An Introduction*, Weidenfeld and Nicolson, London, 1963.

8. The words quoted are taken from G. F. Woods, *Contemporary Theological*

Liberalism, A. and C. Black, London, 1965, and H. G. Wood, "The Function of a Department of Theology in a Modern University", reprinted in his *Jesus in the Twentieth Century*, Lutterworth, London, 1960. To these inaugural lectures may be added one by M. F. Wiles, *Looking into the Sun*, Church Quarterly Review, vol. 1, no. 3 (January 1969). See also *Theology and the University*, ed. Coulson, Helicon Press, Baltimore; Darton, Longman and Todd, London, 1965.

9. See e.g. D. M. Mackinnon, *Borderlands of Theology and Other Essays*, Lutterworth, London, 1968; J. B. Lippincott, Philadelphia, 1968.

10. With an article, or in the plural ('the Faith', 'a faith', 'faiths'), reference is usually to an organized body of religious beliefs, practices and institutions: this usage is well illustrated, for example, in Chapter 8. The word is sometimes used (especially by Eastern Orthodox or Roman Catholic writers) to signify assent to doctrines promulgated on the unquestionable authority of the Church. 'Faith', along with cognate words, is frequently used (as often in the Bible) in the sense of trust or confidence in God, emphasizing the affective aspect. Sometimes it is used in the sense of venturesome commitment, with an emphasis on the volitional aspect of faith. In the sense of a total interpretation of the universe and mankind in terms of the being and purposes of God the emphasis is on the intellectual aspect of faith. One popular use of 'faith' is ruled out from serious theological discussion altogether, namely, mere credulity, or illogical belief in the improbable.

11. The Greek translation of the Old Testament (the Septuagint) appears to have been virtually completed in the second century B.C. In those versions which have survived, the Greek word for 'Lord' (*kyrios*) is found where the Hebrew reads JHVH, the sacred name for God which Jews would not utter when reading their Scriptures aloud. The surviving versions, however, are not earlier than the Christian era. In recent years it has been argued that, in such passages, it was Christian copyists of the Septuagint who put in the word *kyrios*. Professor Moule kindly drew my attention to this discussion. Even so, when taken in conjunction with some passages in the New Testament, it is clear that the phrases 'Jesus is Lord' and 'the Lord Jesus Christ' imply sometimes, if not always, an early conviction among Christians of his 'divinity', his 'oneness with God'.

12. (i) Fresh experience of God changed the beliefs of Old Testament prophets which they had shared with predecessors and contemporaries. The disciples of Jesus, as a result of their confrontation with him, had to change some of their beliefs (and it is clear they did not do so all at once) about God and Jesus himself. Paul is another striking example. (ii) Examples of beliefs which adversely restrict living faith are equally numerous. The incident (inserted in Chapter 8 of John's Gospel) of Jesus, the Pharisees, and the adulteress is a classical case. Beliefs tenaciously held by certain sects provide modern examples.

13. The work of some of the Old Testament prophets is an obvious example. The new insights and personal influence upon the Christian community of Peter, of Paul, of Luther, of Pope John XXIII, may be cited among so many.

14. This is made plain in the treatment of 'the ecumenical dimension in theology' in Chapter 13 of this book. It appears prominently also in other chapters, especially those on the study of applied theology (Chapter 10) and of worship (Chapter 11). In Chapter 7 is a discussion of what remains for many a fundamental issue: the need for a continuing common enterprise in the discussion of Christian doctrine, and for agreement about the terms on which further work in such an enterprise may be based.

15. In traditional use, 'dogma' signifies a belief or principle divinely revealed and authoritatively defined by the Church, and therefore to be assented to by its members without question (cf. p. 156). The term is also used more widely as equivalent to a doctrine regarded as an essential articulation of Christian faith. Dogmatics would then be used as a title for the systematic exposition and discussion of all such doctrines by those who profess such faith. Some writers however (e.g. Macquarrie, *Principles of Christian Theology*) prefer not to use the term 'dogmatic theology' (see note 14, p. 330). The popular use of 'dogmatic' in the sense of groundless or unreasonable arrogance in expressing one's views would not be regarded by theologians as applicable to their work, and in fact would often be unjust. On the importance of Dogmatic Theology for inter-church relations, see p. 294 f.

CHAPTER 2. THE NEW TESTAMENT

1. The story is told in S. C. Neill, *The Interpretation of the New Testament: 1861–1961*, Oxford University Press, 1964; paperback, 1966.

2. See R. P. C. Hanson, *Tradition in the Early Church* S.C.M., London, 1962; M. F. Wiles, *The Making of Christian Doctrine*, Cambridge University Press, 1967.

3. See C. F. D. Moule, 'The Individualism of the Fourth Gospel', *Novum Testamentum* 5 (1962), pp.171 ff.; also *id.* 'The Influence of Circumstances on the Use of Eschatological Terms', *Journal of Theological Studies* n.s. 15, 1964, pp.1 ff.

4. A well-known representative of this view is H. **Conzelmann**, *The Theology of St Luke*, Harper, New York, 1960.

5. B. Lindars, *New Testament Apologetic*, S.C.M., London, 1961, has developed this method with great skill.

6. The relevant articles in Bible Dictionaries should be consulted, e.g. in J. Hastings' *Dictionary of the Bible*, revised edition, T. and T. Clark, Edinburgh, 1963; *The Interpreter's Dictionary of the Bible*, 4 vols., Abing-

don Press, New York,1962; *Theological Dictionary of the New Testament*, Eerdmans, Grand Rapids, 1964–, translated from *Theologisches Wörterbuch zum Neuen Testament*, eds. G. Kittel and G. Friedrich, Kohlhammer, Stuttgart; 1933–. See also the articles in *Peake's Commentary on the Bible*, Nelson, Edinburgh, 1962, and the New Testament Theologies listed at the end of the chapter.

7. See the Introductions mentioned at the end of the chapter.

8. For the 'Tübingen School' see S. C. Neill as in n.1, ch. 2; for statistical tests of style see A. Q. Morton and J. McLeman, *Paul, the Man and the Myth. A Study in the Authorship of Greek Prose*, Harper and Row, New York, 1966, which adds only Philemon to the epistles allowed by the Tübingen School to be authentic.

9. For speculation since the date of Kümmel's *Introduction*, see C. F. D. Moule, 'The Problem of the Pastoral Epistles: A Reappraisal', *Bulletin of John Rylands Library* 47, 1965, pp. 430 ff.

10. See K. Aland, 'The Problem of Anonymity and Pseudonymity in Christian Literature of the First Two Centuries', *Journal of Theological Studies* n.s. 12, 1961, pp. 1 ff.; D. Guthrie, *New Testament Introduction: the Pauline Epistles*, Tyndale, London, 1961, pp. 282 ff.

11. See S. C. Neill, as in n. 1; and W. R. Farmer, *The Synoptic Problem*, Macmillan Co. of New York 1964; *id.*, 'The Lachmann Fallacy', *New Testament Studies* 14, 1967–8, pp. 441 ff.; and other literature referred to in these works.

12. For the origin of the symbol, see W. F. Howard, *Expository Times* 50, 1938–9, pp. 379 ff.

13. B. H. Streeter, *The Four Gospels. A Study of Origins*, Macmillan, London, [4]1930.

14. See references and a critique by G. M. Styler, 'The Priority of Mark', Excursus IV in C. F. D. Moule, *The Birth of the New Testament*, A. and C. Black, London, 1962, pp. 223 ff.

15. See note 11. For a radical critique of method, H. Palmer, *The Logic of Gospel Criticism*, Macmillan, London, 1968.

16. For a brief survey of the immense literature, see A. M. Hunter, *According to John*, S.C.M., 1968.

17. Unless this verse refers only to the attestation of the immediately preceding verses: see C. H. Dodd, *Historical Tradition in the Fourth Gospel*, Cambridge University Press, 1963, p. 12.

18. J. L. Martyn, *History and Theology in the Fourth Gospel*, Harper and Row, New York, 1968, represents a skilful attempt to distinguish and disentangle two layers of reference in the Gospel—the traditions behind the writer, and the situation contemporary with him.

19. F. V. Filson, *A New Testament History*, S.C.M., London, 1965; W. Förster, *Palestinian Judaism in New Testament Times*, Oliver and Boyd Edinburgh, 1964; B. Reicke, *The New Testament Era*, Fortress Press Philadelphia, 1968.

20. See S. C. Neill, as in n. 1; and index of W. G. Kümmel's *Introduction*, as at the end of the chapter.
21. For surveys, see J. Doresse, *The Secret Books of the Egyptian Gnostics*, 1960; W. C. van Unnik, *Newly Discovered Gnostic Writings*, S.C.M., London, 1960; R. McL. Wilson, *Gnosis and the New Testament*, Blackwell, Oxford, 1968; J. M. Robinson, 'The Coptic Gnostic Library Today', *New Testament Studies*, 14, 1967–8, pp. 356 ff.
22. For a survey (to its date) see J. T. Milik, *Ten Years of Discovery in the Wilderness of Judaea*, S.C.M., London, 1959. For the thought of the Dead Sea Sect, see chapter 4 of the present volume, with references.
23. P. E. Kahle, *The Cairo Geniza*, Oxford University Press, ²1959. See also Chaim Rabin, *The Zadokite Documents*, Oxford University Press, ²1958.
24. See A. Deissmann, *Bible Studies*, T. and T. Clark, Edinburgh, ²1909; id., *Light from the Ancient East*, Hodder and Stoughton, London, 1927; J. H. Moulton, *A Grammar of New Testament Greek*, vol. i, T. and T. Clark, Edinburgh, 1908; J. H. Moulton and G. Milligan, *The Vocabulary of the Greek Testament Illustrated from the Papyri and Other Non-Literary Sources*, Hodder and Stoughton, London, 1930. But, for the distinctively semitic influences, J. H. Moulton and W. F. Howard, *A Grammar of New Testament Greek*, vol. ii, T. and T. Clark, Edinburgh, 1929, M. Black, *An Aramaic Approach to the Gospels and Acts*, Oxford University Press, ³1967, and M. Wilcox, *The Semitisms of Acts*, Oxford University Press, 1965. For a warning against over estimating the affinity between the non-biblical papyri and biblical Greek, J. H. Moulton and N. Turner, *A Grammar of New Testament Greek*, vol. iii, T. and T. Clark, Edinburgh, 1963. The most useful N. T. grammar is *A Greek Grammar of the New Testament and Other Early Christian Literature*, translated from the 10th ed. of A. Debrunner's famous German work 1959, and edited with considerable additions by R. W. Funk, Cambridge University Press, 1961. The best N. T. Dictionary is W. F. Arndt and F. W. Gingrich, *A Greek-English Lexicon of the New Testament and Other Early Christian Literature*, Cambridge University Press, 1957. See also the big *Theological Dictionary* noted in n. 6 above.
25. See R. McL. Wilson as in n. 21, pp. 6 ff.
26. For information and texts, see: J. W. Bowker, *Targums and Rabbinic Literature: an Introduction to Jewish Interpretations of Scripture*, Cambridge University Press, 1969; M. McNamara, *The New Testament and the Palestinian Targum to the Pentateuch*, Analecta Biblica 27, Rome, 1966; H. L. Strack, *Introduction to the Talmud and Midrash*, reprinted, Harper Torchbooks, New York, in association with the Jewish Publication Soc. of America 1959; G. Vermes, *Scripture and Tradition in Judaism*, Studia Post-biblica 4, Brill, Leiden, 1961; H. Danby, *The Mishnah*, Oxford University Press, 1933. Note also the historical importance of other Tannaitic literature (i.e. to *c.* A.D. 200, especially the *Tosephta*

(or complement to the Mishnah), of which an edition with German translation is being issued under the direction of K.-H. Rengstorf at Münster. (I am specially indebted to Mr. W. Horbury for advice and help in this note.)

27. See references in D. S. Russell, *The Method and Message of Jewish Apocalyptic*, S.C.M., London, 1964. The problem of the dating of sources has a close bearing on the debate about interpretation of 'The Son of Man' in the Gospels (see p. 102), and also on the question of the influence on Christianity of the mystery religions.

28. A valuable introduction to the influence of Hellenistic Judaism and related thought on the N.T. is C. H. Dodd, *The Bible and the Greeks*, Hodder and Stoughton, London, 1935. For an attack on certain assumptions about the distinctiveness of Hebrew and Greek ways of thought, see J. Barr, *The Semantics of Biblical Language*, Oxford University Press, 1961. For a discussion of Barr's thesis, and the application of philological study to certain words, see D. Hill, *Greek Words and Hebrew Meanings: Studies in the Semantics of Soteriological Terms*, Cambridge University Press, 1967. See, further, S. Lieberman, *Greek in Jewish Palestine*, Jewish Theological Seminary of America, New York, 1942; *id., Hellenism in Jewish Palestine*, Jewish Theological Seminary of America, New York, Texts and Studies 18, ²1962.

29. See B. Reicke as in n. 19; and L. Goppelt, *Jesus, Paul and Judaism*, Nelson, London/New York/Toronto, 1964.

30. See C. D. Morrison, *The Powers That Be*, S.C.M., London, 1960; C. F. D. Moule, *The Birth of the New Testament*, A. and C. Black, London, 1962, Ch. VII.

31. See E. A. Judge, *The Social Pattern of Christian Groups in the First Century*, Tyndale Press, London, 1960; *id.,* 'The Conflict of Educational Aims in New Testament Thought', *Journal of Christian Education*, 9, 1966, pp. 32 ff.; and background books as in n.19.

32. Out of an enormous literature, see, as well as the Introductions mentioned at the end of the chapter, R. Bultmann, *The History of the Synoptic Tradition*, Blackwell, Oxford, 1963; M. Dibelius, *From Tradition to Gospel*, Ivor Nicholson and Watson, London, 1934; V. Taylor, *The Formation of the Gospel Tradition*, Macmillan, London, 1935; and a brief review (to its date) by C. F. D. Moule, 'Form Criticism and Philological Studies', *The London Quarterly and Holborn Review*, April 1958, pp. 87 ff.

33. See O. Cullmann, *The Early Church*, S.C.M., London, 1956, pp. 59 ff., and *id., Salvation in History*, S.C.M., London, 1967, p. 106.

34. On the use of the Scriptures in the N.T., see C. H. Dodd, *According to the Scriptures*, Nisbet, London, 1952; E. E. Ellis, *Paul's Use of the Old Testament*, Oliver and Boyd, Edinburgh, 1957; B. Lindars, as in n. 5; J. Barr, *Old and New in Interpretation: A Study of the Two Testaments*, S.C.M., London, 1966.

35. H. Riesenfeld, *The Gospel Tradition and its Beginnings: A Study in the Limits of Formgeschichte*, Mowbray, London, 1957; B. Gerhardsson, *Memory and Manuscript: Oral Tradition and Written Transmission in Rabbinic Judaism and Early Christianity*, Gleerup, Lund, ²1964.

36. See C. H. Dodd, *The Parables of the Kingdom*, Nisbet, London, revised ed., 1961; J. Jeremias, *The Parables of Jesus*, S.C.M., London, 1963; G. V. Jones, *The Art and Truth of the Parables*, S.P.C.K., London, 1964; E. Linnemann, *Parables of Jesus: Introduction and Exposition*, S.P.C.K., London, 1966; C. W. F. Smith, *The Jesus of the Parables*, Westminster, Philadelphia, 1948.

37. The story has been told many times. See among many others, H. Anderson, *Jesus and Christian Origins: A Commentary on Modern Viewpoints*, Oxford University Press in New York, 1964; C. E. Braaten, *History and Hermeneutics*, vol. 2 of *New Directions in Theology*, ed. W. Hordern, Westminster Press, Philadelphia, and Lutterworth, London, 1968; J. H. Reumann, *Jesus in the Church's Gospels*, Fortress Press, Philadelphia, 1968.

38. Eusebius, *Ecclesiastical History*, 3.39.15.

39. See K. Stendahl, *The School of St. Matthew*, Gleerup, Lund, 1954; E. P. Blair, *Jesus in the Gospel of Matthew*, Abingdon, New York, 1960; D. R. A. Hare, *The Theme of Jewish Persecution of Christians in the Gospel According to St. Matthew*, Cambridge University Press, 1967.

40. See C. H. Dodd, 'Behind a Johannine Dialogue', *More New Testament Studies*, Manchester University Press, 1968, no. 4; J. L. Martyn, as in n. 18.

41. See O. Cullmann, as in n. 33.

42. See C. F. D. Moule, 'The Intention of the Evangelists', in *New Testament Essays in mem. T. W. Manson*, ed. Higgins, Manchester University Press, 1959; reprinted in *The Phenomenon of the New Testament*, S.C.M., London, 1967, as Appendix II; and A. W. Mosley, 'Historical Reporting in the Ancient World', *New Testament Studies*, 12, 1965–6, pp. 10 ff.

43. See C. F. D. Moule, 'The Use of Parables and Sayings as Illustrative Material in Early Christian Catechesis', *Journal of Theological Studies*, 3, 1952, pp. 75 ff.

44. Survey by J. Rohde, *Rediscovering the Teaching of the Evangelists*, S.C.M., London, 1968. For the value of redaction-criticism in connection with the study of the Old Testament, see pp. 73 f. of the present volume.

45. See C. F. D. Moule, as in n. 14, *passim*; and, as an example from one epistle, J. C. Hurd, *The Origin of I Corinthians*, S.P.C.K., London, 1965.

46. 'Situational ethics' has become something of a cliché, and there are plenty who oppose what seems like a sort of antinomianism. But it is vital to distinguish between principles and the specific duties arising from them in given circumstances; and the N.T. certainly affords

evidence of varied decisions as to specific action in varying circumstances. See also Chapter 12 in this present volume.

47. K. Aland, *The Problem of the New Testament Canon*, Mowbray, London, 1962; F. L. Cross, *The Early Christian Fathers*, Duckworth, London, 1960, Ch. IV; F. V. Filson, *Which Books Belong in the Bible? A Study of the Canon*, Westminster, Philadelphia, 1957; B. F. Westcott, *A General Survey of the History of the Canon of the New Testament*, Macmillan, London, ⁴1875. Also R. P. C. Hanson, as in n. 2.

48. C. L. Mitton, *The Formation of the Pauline Corpus*, Epworth, London, 1955; G. Zuntz, *The Text of the Epistles: A Disquisition upon the Corpus Paulinum*, British Academy, London, 1953; E. J. Goodspeed, *New Solutions to New Testament Problems*, University of Chicago Press, 1927; *id., The Meaning of Ephesians*, University of Chicago Press, 1933; *id., The Key to Ephesians*, University of Chicago Press, 1956; J. Knox, *Marcion and the New Testament*, University of Chicago Press, 1942; *id., Philemon among the Letters of Paul*, Abingdon, New York, ²1959; *id.*, 'Acts and the Pauline Letter Corpus', in L. E. Keck and J. L. Martyn (eds.), *Studies in Luke-Acts in hon. P. Schubert*, Abingdon, Nashville, 1966, pp. 279 ff.

49. O. Cullmann, *The Early Church*, as in n. 33, pp. 39 ff.

50. A noteworthy attack on 2 Peter is E. Käsemann's essay, 'An Apologia for Primitive Christian Eschatology' in *Essays on New Testament Themes*, S.C.M., London, 1964, pp. 169 ff.; but see E. M. B. Green, in *Tyndale New Testament Commentaries*, Tyndale Press, London, 1968, *in loc.*

51. See n.14, C. F. D. Moule, *op. cit.*, chap. IX.

52. B. M. Metzger, *The Text of the New Testament: its Transmission, Corruption and Restoration*, Oxford University Press, ²1969, is an excellent introduction, containing bibliography.

53. See nn. 24 and 28.

54. From the immense literature, the following, mostly from recent times, may be mentioned: E. C. Hoskyns and F. N. Davey, *The Riddle of the New Testament*, Faber, London, 1931; paperback 1959; H. W. Bartsch (ed.), *Kerygma and Myth*, S.P.C.K., London, 1953, vol. ii, 1962; J. Knox, *The Church and the Reality of Christ*, Harper and Row, New York, 1962; C. E. Braaten and R. A. Harrisville (eds.), *Kerygma and History*, Abingdon, New York, 1962; H. Anderson, as in n. 47; C. E. Braaten and R. A. Harrisville (eds.), *The Historical Jesus and the Kerygmatic Christ*, Abingdon, New York, 1964; E. Käsemann, 'The Problem of the Historical Jesus', Essay I in *Essays on New Testament Themes*, as in n. 50; J. M. Robinson and J. B. Cobb (eds.), *The New Hermeneutic*, vol. ii of *New Frontiers in Theology*, Harper and Row, New York, 1964; Van A. Harvey, *The Historian and the Believer*, Macmillan Co. of New York, 1966; S.C.M., London, 1967; C. K. Barrett, *Jesus and the Gospel Tradition*, S.P.C.K., London, 1967;

O. Betz, *What do we know about Jesus?*, S.C.M., London, 1968; D. T. Rowlingson, *The Gospel Perspective on Jesus Christ,* Westminster, Philadelphia, 1968. Surveys: H. K. McArthur, 'A Survey of Recent Gospel Research', *Interpretation* 18, 1964, pp. 39 ff.; *id., The Quest through the Centuries,* Fortress Press, Philadelphia, 1966; C. E. Braaten, *History and Hermeneutics,* as in n. 37; F. G. Downing, *The Church and Jesus,* S.C.M., London, 1968; J. Reumann, as in n. 37.

55. See Chapters 1, 7, 9–13.
56. See also literature in nn. 37 and 54.
57. A useful, if difficult, introduction is provided by *The New Hermeneutic,* as in n. 54. Easier is C. E. Braaten, *History and Hermeneutics,* as in n. 37.
58. For an analysis of the problem, see especially H. K. McArthur, *The Quest through the Centuries,* as in n. 54.

CHAPTER 4. INTER-TESTAMENTAL LITERATURE

In the following notes, references to Qumran documents are abbreviated as follows: CD=Damascus Document; 1 QH=Hymns of Thanksgiving; 1Qp Hab=Habakkuk Commentary; 4 Qp Nah=Nahum Commentary; 1 QS=Rule of the Community; 1 QSa=Rule of the Congregation.

1. Tobit 1: 18; 14: 10. The oldest extant recension of the Ahiqar story is in Aramaic (fifth century B.C.), among the Elephantine papyri; cf. A. E. Cowley, *Aramaic Papyri of the Fifth Century B.C.,* Clarendon Press, Oxford, 1923, pp. 204 ff.
2. Sir. 24: 23; Baruch 3: 9–4: 4.
3. Wisdom 10: 1 ff., especially 11: 5 ff.; 15: 18 ff.
4. Cf. Isa. 55: 11; Ps. 107: 20.
5. Wisdom 18: 15.
6. Gen. 5: 22, 24; cf. Wisdom 4: 10 ff.; Heb. 11: 5 f.
7. Ex. 24: 10.
8. Esther 4: 14.
9. E.g. I Macc. 3: 18 f.; II Macc. 7: 11. Cf. 'Heaven rules' in Dan. 4: 26 as an alternative to 'the Most High rules' in verses 17, 25, 32.
10. Testament of Levi 18: 13.
11. It appears in *Pirge 'Aboth* 5: 23, in a saying ascribed to R. Judah ben Tema (earlier second century A.D.); cf. Matt. 6: 1, etc.
12. Cf. J. Jeremias, *The Central Message of the New Testament,* S.C.M., London, 1965, pp. 9 ff.
13. Josephus, *Antiquities,* xiii. 172.
14. 1 QS iii. 18 ff.
15. Josephus, *Jewish War* ii. 164 f.; *Antiquities* xiii. 173.
16. Josephus, *Jewish War* ii. 162 f.; *Antiquities* xiii. 172; xviii. 13.
17. R. Aqiba (*c.* A.D. 100) in *Pirge 'Aboth* 3: 19.

18. Acts 5: 38 f. Cf. the dictum of R. Yohanan the sandal-maker (a pupil of Aqiba): "Every assembly which is for the sake of heaven will in the end be established, and one which is not for the sake of heaven will in the end not be established" (*Pirqe 'Aboth* 4: 14).

19. Cf. Mal. 3: 16 f. for an early reference to them (*c.* 450 B.C.).

20. So R. Hillel (*c.* 10 B.C.) could say "No *'am har-'ares* ('member of the people of the land', i.e. ignoramus) is pious" (*Pirqe 'Aboth* 2: 6; cf. John 7: 49).

21. *Pirqe 'Aboth* 1: 1.

22. Mark 7: 3, 5.

23. Jubilees 1: 9, etc.

24. Aqiba in *Pirqe 'Aboth* 3: 19.

25. Testament of Issachar 5: 2; cf. Testament of Gad 6: 3 ff.

26. Tobit 4: 15.

27. Wisdom 9: 17.

28. Psalms of Solomon 17: 42.

29. *Martyrdom of Isaiah* 5: 14. (This book is a Jewish work with Qumran affinities, incorporated in the later Christian *Ascension of Isaiah,* 1: 1–3: 12; 5: 1b–14.)

30. IV Ezra (= II Esdras) 14: 22.

31. 1 QS iii. 18 ff.

32. CD ii. 12.

33. 1 QH xii. 11 f.

34. 1 QH vii. 6 f.

35. 1 QH ix. 32.

36. 1 QS iii. 7 f.

37. 1 QS iv. 20 f.

38. J. A. T. Robinson, "The Baptism of John and the Qumran Community", *Harvard Theological Review* 50, 1957, pp. 175 ff., reprinted in *Twelve New Testament Studies,* S.C.M., London, 1962, pp. 23 ff.

39. 1 QS ix. 3–5. For the echo of Hos. 14: 2b at the end of this quotation cf. Heb. 13: 15.

40. CD v. 11 f.; cf. vii. 3 f. (also 1 Cor. 3: 16 f.; 6: 19, where, however, the Holy Spirit who is polluted is the Spirit of God).

41. Wisdom 2: 24.

42. 1 Enoch 6: 1–8: 4; 10: 7 f.; Jubilees 5: 1–3.

43. Sir. 25: 24.

44. IV Ezra (=II Esdras) 7: 11, 118. This outcry against Adam is but one expression of the pessimism of this apocalypse, reflecting the outlook of the period following A.D. 70: the times are late and evil, and while many have been created, few will be saved (8: 3).

45. II Baruch 54: 19.

46. Dan 4: 27.

47. Tobit 12: 9.

48. Sir. 3: 3 f.

49. IV Ezra (=II Esdras) 7: 77; 8: 26–36.
50. II Baruch 14: 12.
51. Cf. S. Schechter, *Some Aspects of Rabbinic Theology*, Black, London, 1909, pp. 170 ff.; A. Marmorstein, *The Doctrine of Merits in the Old Rabbinical Literature*, Oxford University Press, 1920.
52. Matt. 3: 9/Luke 3: 8; cf. John 8: 33, 39.
53. IV Macc. 13: 12; Leviticus Rabba 29: 8; cf. H. J. Schoeps, *Paul*, Lutterworth, London, 1961, pp. 141 ff.
54. II Macc. 7: 38.
55. IV Macc. 6: 28 f.
56. II Macc. 17: 22–18: 4.
57. Isa. 52: 13–53: 12.
58. Cf. M. Black, "Servant of the Lord and Son of Man", *Scottish Journal of Theology* 6, 1953, pp. 1 ff.; F. F. Bruce, *Biblical Exegesis in the Qumran Texts*, Tyndale, London, 1960, pp. 56 ff.
59. 1 QH iv. 30 f.
60. 1 QS x. 12 f.
61. 1 QS xi. 3–15.
62. *Luthers Werke* (Weimar edition), 54, 1928, p. 186.
63. Rom. 4: 2.
64. 1 QH ix. 14–16.
65. 1 QH iv. 35–38.
66. 1 Qp Hab. viii. 1–3 (on Hab. 2: 4b).
67. E.g. 1 QH ii. 15, 32; 4 Qp Nah. i. 2 (on Nah. 2: 11), 7 (on Nah. 2: 12), ii, 2 (on Nah. 3:1), 4 (on Nah. 3: 3), iii. 3 (on Nah. 3: 6), 6 f. (on Nah. 3: 7).
68. Cf. Isa. 26: 19; Dan. 12: 2.
69. Mark 12: 18 ff.
70. Eccl. 3: 18 ff.; 9: 1–10.
71. Sir. 44: 1 ff.
72. Sir. 41: 4.
73. II Macc. 7: 11.
74. Heb. 11: 35.
75. II Macc. 12: 44.
76. Wisdom 3: 1 f.
77. IV Macc. 7: 18 f.; cf. 16: 25.
78. Luke 20: 38.
79. Cf. T. W. Manson, "Sadducee and Pharisee", *Bulletin of the John Rylands Library*, 22, 1938, pp. 153 ff.; *The Servant-Messiah*, Cambridge University Press, 1953, pp. 19 f.
80. Acts 23: 8.
81. Tobit 12: 15; cf. Luke 1: 19; Rev. 8: 2.
82. 1 Enoch 20: 1–8.
83. The *Amesha Spentas;* cf. J. H. Moulton, *Early Zoroastrianism*, Williams and Norgate, London, 1913, pp. 110 ff., 252, 293 ff.; R. C. Zaehner,

The Dawn and Twilight of Zoroastrianism, Weidenfeld and Nicolson London, 1961, pp. 45 ff.

84. Tobit 3: 8.
85. Acts 12: 15; cf. Matt. 18: 10 (see J. H. Moulton, *op. cit.,* pp. 254 ff.; R. C. Zaehner, *op. cit.,* pp. 146 ff.).
86. Deut. 32: 8 (LXX, RSV); cf. Dan. 10: 13, 20, 21; 11: 1; 12: 1; Hebrew Testament of Naphtali 8: 4 ff.
87. Cf. Jubilees 2: 2; IV Ezra (=II Esdras) 8: 21 f.; II Enoch 11: 4 f.; III Baruch 6: 13; 8: 4; Rev. 16: 5.
88. Cf. Haggai 2: 20 ff.; Zech. 6: 12 f.
89. Ps. Sol. 17: 8.
90. Ps. Sol. 17: 23–36.
91. Luke 2: 11 (similarly Lam. 4: 20, LXX).
92. Cf. P. Winter, "Magnificat and Benedictus—Maccabaean Psalms?", *Bulletin of the John Rylands Library,* 37, 1954–5, pp. 328 ff.
93. Luke 1: 69.
94. Luke 1: 32 f.
95. Gen. 49: 10.
96. Num. 24: 17.
97. II Sam. 7: 11b–16.
98. Amos 9: 11 f.
99. Isa. 11: 1.
100. 4Q *Patriarchal Blessings,* line 3.
101. E.g. 1 QSa ii. 12.
102. 1 QS ix. 11; CD xii. 23 f., xx. 1; 1 QSa ii. 12 ff.
103. Ezek. 44: 3; 45: 7, 16 ff.; 46: 2 ff.; 48: 21 f.
104. 1 QS ix. 11; cf. 4Q *Testimonia* 5 ff.
105. Cf. J. Macdonald, *The Theology of the Samaritans,* S.C.M., London, 1964, pp. 362 ff.
106. Acts 3: 22 f.; 7: 37; cf. Mark 9: 7 ("listen to him") with Deut. 18: 15 ff.
107. *Clementine Recognitions* i. 16 f., 44 ff., v. 10; *Clementine Homilies* ii. 4 ff.
108. Cf. M. de Jonge, *The Testaments of the Twelve Patriarchs,* Van Gorcum, Assen, 1953.
109. Testament of Judah 21: 2–5; cf. Testament of Naphtali 5: 1–3.
110. Testament of Levi 8: 14.
111. Testament of Reuben 6: 11 f.
112. 1 Enoch 37–71.
113. I Enoch 48: 10; 52: 4 (the Anointed One); 39: 6 (the Elect One); 38: 2 (the Righteous One).
114. I Enoch 48: 2 f.
115. Cf. M.D. Hooker, *The Son of Man in Mark,* S.P.C.K., London, 1967, pp. 33 ff.
116. IV Ezra (=II Esdras) 13: 1–53.
117. IV Ezra (=II Esdras) 7: 28 f.; 12: 32 f.

118. E.g. I Enoch 10: 17 ff.
119. E.g. II Baruch 44: 8 ff.
120. E.g. IV Ezra (=II Esdras) 7: 28 ff., where the messianic age of 400 years' duration is followed by a week of universal death; then the righteous enjoy eternal bliss in "the paradise of delight".

CHAPTER 5. THE STUDY OF CHURCH HISTORY

1. P. Willmott, *Adolescent Boys of East London*, Pelican Books, 1969, p. 87.
2. N. Sykes, *The Study of Ecclesiastical History*, Cambridge University Press, 1945.

CHAPTER 6. CREEDS AND CONFESSIONS OF FAITH

Note: bibliographical details of books listed at the end of the chapter are omitted here.

1. J. N. D. Kelly, *Early Christian Creeds*, 2nd edn., p. 26.
2. But if we take Philip's preceding words, "If you believe with all your heart, you may" as an indirect question, then this rudimentary creed becomes interrogatory!
3. A. Harnack, *The Apostles' Creed*, p. 33.
4. J. N. D. Kelly, *Early Christian Creeds*, pp. 411–420.
5. But Harnack considered Eusebius' creed as his own composition: *The Apostles' Creed*, pp. 40–41.
6. A. Harnack, *Konstantinopolitanisches Symbol* in *Realencyklopädie* XI, p. 15.
7. J. N. D. Kelly, *Early Christian Creeds*, p. 229.
8. A. E. Burn, *The Nicene Creed*, p. 14.
9. F. J. A. Hort, *Two Dissertations*, pp. 73–115.
10. F. Loofs, *Athanasianum* in *Realencyklopädie* II, p. 178.
11. G. Morin, *L'Origine du Symbole d'Athanase* in *Journal of Theological Studies*, vol. XII (1911), pp. 161 ff., and 337 ff.
12. A. E. Burn, *The Athanasian Creed*, pp. 28 ff.
13. F. J. Badcock, *The History of the Creeds*, pp. 226 ff.
14. *Op. cit.*, p. 231.
15. D. Waterland, *Works*, pp. 197–220.
16. *Op. cit.*, p. 337 ff.
17. J. N. D. Kelly, *The Athanasian Creed*, p. 123.
18. Given in *English Reformers*, ed. T. H. L. Parker, S.C.M., London & Philadelphia, 1966, pp. 20–33.
19. *Calvin: Theological Treatises*, ed. J. K. S. Reid, S.C.M., London & Philadelphia, 1954, p. 90.
20. P. Schaff, *The Creeds of the Evangelical Protestant Churches*, pp. 94–95.
21. *Op. cit.*, p. 90.

22. P. Schaff, *Op. cit.*, p. 95.
23. *Op. cit.*, pp. 89–90.
24. F. Kattenbusch, *Symbol* in *Realencyklopädie*, XIX, p. 197, p. 201.
25. *Ibid.*, pp. 201 f.

CHAPTER 7. THE STUDY OF CHRISTIAN DOCTRINE

1. See the discussion by David Jenkins in *Theology and the University*, ed. Coulson, Helicon Press, Baltimore; Darton, Longman & Todd, London, 1965, pp. 151 and 157.
2. Cf. K. Barth, *Church Dogmatics*, I i, The Doctrine of the Word of God, p. 323.
3. K. Barth, *id.*, p.l.; P. Tillich, *Systematic Theology*, vol. 1, p. 1. This insistence on 'theology as a function of the Church' need not necessarily involve the view that it is an exclusively confessional activity. In between his denial that doctrine is either purely historical or purely phenomenological (see previous note), Barth includes a third denial: 'nor yet just the clearing up and exposition of the faith as the dogmatician in question thinks it right to proclaim it personally.' It is difficult to define just what is involved here. (Some might claim that Barth's denial could be turned against Barth himself.) It is essentially a reminder that Christian doctrine, even when strongly individual in character, must not be out of touch with the living reality of the Christian community.
4. K. Barth, *op. cit.*, p.1.
5. Tillich, *op. cit.*, p. 68.
6. Barth, *op. cit.*, p. 339.
7. Tillich, *op. cit.*, p. 45.
8. *Ibid.*, pp. 8 and 69–71.
9. Barth, *op. cit.*, p. 2.
10. See T. F. Torrance, *Karl Barth, An Introduction to his Early Theology 1910–31*, S.C.M., London, 1962, p. 188, from which these phrases descriptive of Barth's method are taken.
11. G. Wingren, *Theology in Conflict*, Oliver and Boyd, Edinburgh, 1958, p. 27.
12. G. Eberling, "Discussion Theses for a Course of Introductory Lectures on the Study of Theology", in *Word and Faith*, S.C.M., London, 1963, pp. 427 and 432.
13. Useful bibliographies of this discussion will be found in K. Rahner, *Theological Investigations*, Helicon Press, Baltimore; Darton, Longman & Todd, London, vol. 1, pp. 39–41; *A Catholic Dictionary of Theology*, Nelson, London, 1967, p. 189.
14. For this reason J. Macquarrie uses the term 'symbolic theology' as a substitute for 'dogmatic theology' despite its traditional usage

(see p. 319) to refer to the theology of creeds (*Principles of Christian Theology*, p. 36).

15. K. Barth, *From Rousseau to Ritschl*, S.C.M., London, 1959; P. Tillich, *Perspectives on Nineteenth and Twentieth Century Protestant Theology*, S.C.M., London, 1967.
16. E.g. K. Barth, *Anselm: Fides Quaerens Intellectum*, S.C.M., London, 1960; P. Tillich, *A History of Christian Thought*, S.C.M., London, 1968.
17. The best example of a recent study of this kind which brings out well the problems of method involved is J. McIntyre, *The Shape of Christology*, S.C.M., London, 1966.

CHAPTER 9. PHILOSOPHICAL THEOLOGY

1. F. R. Tennant, *Philosophical Theology*, 2 vols. Cambridge University Press, 1928–30; re-issued 1968.
2. Tertullian, *De Praescriptione Haereticorum*, C. 7.
3. J. Hick (ed.) *Faith and the Philosophers*, Macmillan, London, 1964, pp. 159–200. Cf. Dowey's reply 'But is it Barth?' and other contributions in the succeeding pages.
4. Much the same estimate of Barth is found in Paton, *The Modern Predicament*, where he speaks of "the theological veto". For the sake of clarity I must add that I regard this as a mis-representation of Barth's position. Indeed I should say that one of the most valuable aspects of Prof. T. F. Torrance's excellent book on Barth's early theology, *Karl Barth : An Introduction to his early Theology*, S.C.M., London, 1964, is the way Prof. Torrance sees Barth's theology as developing by means of an essentially philosophical struggle with Realism and Idealism.
5. John Wisdom, *Paradox and Discovery*, Blackwell, Oxford, 1965, pp. 1 ff.
6. Plato, *Republic*.
7. See in *The Philosophy of G. E. Moore* articles by M. Lazerowitz and John Wilson.
8. Russell, *Our Knowledge of the External World*, p.3.
9. *Ibid.*, p. 33.
10. J. Wilson, *Philosophy and Psycho-analysis*, p. 145. I have not attempted to give any adequate summary of the development of philosophy in recent years because this story—especially in its relation to theology—has been told several times. See, for instance, H. J. Paton, "Fifty Years of Philosophy", *Contemporary British Philosophy* (ed. Lewis) Third Series, and his *The Modern Predicament;* also H. D. Lewis, "Survey of Recent Work in the Philosophy of Religion", *Philosophical Quarterly*, April and June 1967, and I. T. Ramsey "Empiricism and Religion", *The Christian Scholar*, June 1956.
11. F. Waismann, "How I see Philosophy", *Contemporary British Philosophy*, Third Series, p. 471.

12. On St. Anselm see Barth, *Anselm: Fides Quaerens Intellectum*, S.C.M., London, 1960, G. A. Koye, *L'idée de Dieu dans la philosophie de St. Anselm*. Prof. E. L. Mascall rejects this view of Anselm in the appendix to *He Who Is*, Darton, Longman and Todd, London, 1966. On St. Thomas few books are more instructive than Victor White, *God the Unknown*, but a fuller discussion is A. E. Sillem's most valuable book, *Ways of Thinking about God*. Valuable also are the two books by Prof. Mascall on the proofs—*He Who Is* and *Existence and Analogy*.

13. Kant, *Critique of Pure Reason*, C 618–658.

14. Fortunately there are several discussions which are easily consulted— e.g. H. D. Lewis, *Philosophy of Religion*, Van Nostrand, London, 1965; E. L. Mascall, *opp. cit.*, E. A. Sillem, *op. cit.*

15. For a discussion of this and related points see my *Subjectivity and Paradox*, Blackwell, Oxford, 1957.

16. Cf. R. M. Hare, "Theology and Falsification", *New Essays in Philosophical Theology* (eds. Flew and Macintyre), S.C.M., London, 1955; N. Malcolm, "Is it a Religious Belief that 'God Exists'?" *Faith and the Philosophers* (ed. J. Hick); H. H. Price, "Faith and Belief", *ibid.*; H. H. Price 'Belief "In" and Belief "That" ', *Religious Studies*, vol. I, no. 1, pp. 1–21.

17. St. Mark 5: 6–7.

18. R. B. Braithwaite, *An Empiricist's View of the Nature of Religious Belief*, Cambridge University Press, 1955, reprinted in I. T. Ramsey (ed.) *Christian Ethics and Contemporary Philosophy*, S.C.M., London, 1966, pp. 53–74.

19. Cf. G. E. Moore's reference to 'theological naturalism' in *Principia Ethica*, Cambridge, 1903, pp. 113f.

20. This topic has been discussed recently by B. F. Porter in his book *Deity and Morality*. There he argues that 'God is good' is analytically true because names can have a content of meaning (pp. 121–133).

21. Ronald Hepburn, *Christianity and Paradox*, Watts, London, 1958, p. 16.

22. *ibid.*, p. 17.

23. St. Thomas Aquinas, *Summa Contra Gentiles*, Bk. I c. 34. Cf. *Summa Theologica* I a Q. 13.

24. Crombie, "Possibility of Theological Language", *Faith and Logic* (ed. Mitchell), Allen and Unwin, London, 1957.

25. I. T. Ramsey, *Religious Language*, S.C.M., London, 1957, *Models and Mystery*, Oxford University Press, 1964.

26. Paul Tillich, *Systematic Theology*, vol. 1.

27. I. T. Ramsey, *Religious Language*, p. 62.

28. I. T. Ramsey, *Models and Mystery*, p. 44.

29. See *Systematic Theology* I pp. 217, 265, 304 et passim. I have discussed this in my *Paul Tillich : An Appraisal*, S.C.M., London, 1963, and again in *Religious Studies*, vol. 1, pp. 89–93.

30. J. L. Austin, *How to do Things with Words,* (ed. J. O. Urmson), Oxford, 1962.
31. Cf. D. D. Evans, *The Logic of Self-Involvement,* S.C.M., London, 1963, pp. 27–40.
32. D. M. Mackinnon, *Borderlands of Theology,* Lutterworth, London, 1968, p. 69.
33. *Ibid.,* p. 75.
34. L. Wittgenstein, *Lectures and Conversations on Aesthetics, Psychology and Religious Belief,* Blackwell, Oxford, 1966, pp. 53 ff.
35. J. Calvin, *Institutes* Book III c. xxi.
36. Cf. I. T. Ramsey's paper "Hell" in *Talk of God,* Royal Institute of Philosophy Lectures, Volume 2, Macmillan, 1969, pp. 207–25.

CHAPTER 10. THE STUDY OF APPLIED THEOLOGY

Full reference is made in the list of books at the end of the Chapter to works marked*.

1. Greeves, however, defends the use of 'cure of souls': cf. F. Greeves,* pp. 4–8.
2. This image is exemplified in Carrington's reference to 'the work of the Eastern Shepherd, ... from which the whole conception of pastoral ministry has been derived' (W. L. Carrington, *Psychology, Religion and Human Need,* Epworth, London, 1957, p. 4.). The very title of a recent book suggests a completely different orientation: P. F. Rudge, *Ministry and Management,* Tavistock Publications, London, 1968.
3. Second Vatican Council, *De Ecclesia* II.15: cf. E. H. Peters (Ed.), *The Constitution on the Church of Vatican Council II,* Darton, Longman and Todd, London, 1965, p. 90. See further pp. 305 f. of the present volume.
4. O. S. Tomkins (Ed.), *The Third World Conference on Faith and Order held at Lund,* S.C.M., London, 1952, p. 33.
5. W. A. Visser't Hooft (ed.), *The Evanston Report, 1954,* S.C.M., London, 1955, p. 84.
6. Cf. S. C. Mackie (ed.), *Ministry I,** pp. 10–15.
7. *De Ecclesia* II: *op. cit.*
8. The 'People-next-door' campaign of the British Council of Churches in 1967 demonstrated both a latent enthusiasm for involvement in mission by laymen, and a failure to carry this enthusiasm into further action once the campaign was over: cf. K. Sansbury, R. O. Latham & Pauline Webb, *Agenda for the Churches,* S.C.M., London, 1968.
9. Cf. e.g., 'All Christian ministry is a sharing in Christ's service to God, the Church and the world. All Christians are called to participate in it. . . A "professional" or separated ministry can never be a substitute for this': *Conversations between the Church of England and the*

Methodist Church (The Anglican—Methodist Report), Church Information Office and Epworth Press, London, 1963, p. 21. 'This total ministry Christ shares with the people of God as a whole': D. L. Edwards (ed.), *Unity begins at Home*, Report of the first British Faith and Order Conference at Nottingham, S.C.M., London, 1964, p. 67. 'A recovery of a true doctrine of the laity has brought with it the recognition that ministry is the responsibility of the whole body and not only of those who are ordained': P. C. Rodger (ed.), *The Montreal Report*, S.C.M., London, 1963, p. 62.

10. Statement of the *Second Consultation on Theological Education in S. E. Asia, 1965* S. C. Mackie (ed.), *Ministry II*,* p. 33.

11. For convenience we distinguish between *kērygma*, the proclamation offered to those outside the Church, and *prophēteia, didachē and paraklēsis*, utterances addressed to those within the Church. But a warning has been given not to distinguish between *kērygma* and *didachē* too rigidly, and that warning probably applies equally to the other 'Church-directed' utterances: cf. C. F. D. Moule, *The Birth of the New Testament*, Black, London, 1962, p. 130.

12. The German language brings out the correlation of *Wort* and *Antwort* more clearly than the English.

13. Not surprisingly, the training of such ministers has been heavily biased towards homiletics: cf. e.g. John Oman, *Concerning the Ministry*, S.C.M., London, 1936, reprinted 1963.

14. This is the ideal portrayed by Richard Baxter in his classic *The Reformed Pastor*, London, 1656 (ed. J. T. Wilkinson, Epworth, London, 1939).

15. Gibson Winter,* pp. 129 and 130; Bishop J. A. T. Robinson has well summarized his thesis in *The New Reformation?* S.C.M., London, 1965, pp. 64–66.

16. Reference to the ministry of worship is not developed further here in view of its treatment in Chapter 11.

17. The correspondence between the *kingly* role of Christ and the office of *overseer* in the Church is developed by S. C. Mackie (ed.), *Ministry I*,* p. 14.

18. Acts 15 and Galatians 1–2 portray Paul's attitudes to the authority of the Jerusalem 'pillars' in different lights. He had no doubt of his own authority (cf. Galatians 3–6), although he clearly recognized that this did not include any power of coercion (2 Corinthians 10).

19. Canon Law is a subject for study in its own right, exercising the talents of lawyers, historians and theologians. As an introduction, cf. E. W. Kemp, *An Introduction to Canon Law in the Church of England*, Hodder, London, 1957; E. Garth Moore, *An Introduction to English Canon Law*, Clarendon, Oxford, 1967.

20. Cf. the military imagery of both the Jesuits and Salvationists.

21. Cf. the work of the missionary societies founded between 1792 and

1804. William Carey charged his friends, when he set off for India, 'I will go down the mine if you will hold the rope', and was not disappointed.

22. The work of Christian Aid, nationally and internationally, demonstrates that these churches are capable of effective co-operative work in the contemporary world-scene.

23. This question has been explored, with no claim to definitive results, in S. C. Mackie (ed.), *Ministry I—VI*;* cf. also *The Shape of the Ministry*.*

24. Cf. *A Tent-making Ministry*, Department of World Mission and Evangelism, New York, 1962, published also in *International Review of Missions*, January 1963, pp. 47 ff.; cf. also L. Vischer in D. M. Paton (ed.),* pp. 36 ff.

25. Cf. J. A. T. Robinson, *op. cit.* pp. 56 f.

26. Cf. I Corinthians 14.

27. 'On Luther's presuppositions, in place of the sacerdotal hierarchy of mediaeval Christendom the Pastor suffices . . . He conceived the Church as a *Pastorenkirche*'. J. S. Whale, *The Protestant Tradition*, Cambridge University Press, 1955, p. 113.

28. 'Should such a ministry fail, the apostolic Church, which is the Body of Christ in space and time, would disappear with it'. K. E. Kirk (ed.), *The Apostolic Ministry*, Hodder, London, 1946, p. 40.

29. Cf. K. Carey (ed.)*.

30. Cf. e.g. the evangelization of Europe in the Dark Ages, the colonization of the New World in the sixteenth and seventeenth centuries, and the missionary expansion in Africa and Asia in the nineteenth century.

31. Frank Lake,* p. 323: his italics.

32. R. A. Lambourne,* p. 120.

33. Speaking of the 'collusion' which 'is, psychodynamically speaking, a feature of all human relationships', Lambourne says, 'Where the collusion is satisfactory to everybody the psychiatrist, *but not the pastor*, is out of a job'. R. A. Lambourne,* footnote to p. 68, our italics.

CHAPTER 11. THE STUDY OF WORSHIP

1. A. S. Herbert, *Worship in Ancient Israel*, Lutterworth, London, 1959; W. O. E. Osterley, *The Jewish Background of the Christian Liturgy*, Clarendon, Oxford, 1925; H. H. Rowley, *Worship in Ancient Israel*, S.P.C.K., London, 1967.

2. A. J. B. Higgins, *The Lord's Supper in the New Testament*, S.C.M., London, 1952; J. Jeremias, *The Eucharistic Words of Jesus*, 3rd ed., S.C.M., London, 1966.

3. W. Rordorf, *Sunday*, S.C.M., London, 1968.

4. Fuller details about the second and third centuries will be found in J. H. Srawley, *Early History of the Liturgy*, C.U.P., Cambridge, 1913.

5. G. Dix, ed., *The Treatise on the Apostolic Tradition of St. Hippolytus of Rome*, corrected by H. Chadwick, S.P.C.K., London, 1968.

6. J. Wordsworth, ed., *Bishop Serapion's Prayer Book*, S.P.C.K., 2nd ed., London, 1910.

7. F. L. Cross, ed., *St. Cyril of Jerusalem's Lectures on the Christian Sacraments*, S.P.C.K., London, 1951.

8. R. H. Cresswell, *The Liturgy of the Eighth Book of the Apostolic Constitutions*, S.P.C.K., London, 1921.

9. Ambrose, *St. Ambrose "On the Mysteries" and the Treatise "On the Sacraments"*, trans. T. Thompson and J. H. Srawley, S.P.C.K., London, 1919.

10. References are collected in F. van der Meer, *Augustine the Bishop*, Sheed and Ward, London, 1961, pp. 397–402.

11. A. A. King, *The Rites of Eastern Christendom*, Catholic Book Agency, Rome, 1947; F. E. Brightman, *Liturgies Eastern and Western*, Clarendon, Oxford, 1896.

12. J. A. Jungmann, *The Mass of the Roman Rite*, Benziger, New York, 1951–55; A. A. King, *Liturgies of the Religious Orders*, Longmans, London, 1955; *id.*, *Liturgies of the Primatial Sees*, Longmans, London, 1957; *id.*, *Liturgies of the Past*, Longmans, London, 1959; S. J. P. Van Dijk and J. H. Walker, *The Origins of the Modern Roman Liturgy*, Darton, Longman and Todd, London, 1960.

13. F. Procter and W. H. Frere, *A New History of the Book of Common Prayer*, Macmillan, London, 1941; C. W. Dugmore, *The Influence of the Synagogue on the Divine Office*, O.U.P., London, 1944.

14. J. G. Davies, *The Secular Use of Church Buildings*, S.C.M., London, 1968; R. W. Muncey, *A History of the Consecration of Churches and Churchyards*, Heffer, Cambridge, 1930; J. Wickham Legg, *English Orders for Consecrating Churches in the Seventeenth Century*, Henry Bradshaw Society 41, London, 1911.

15. G. Ellard, *Ordination Anointings in the Western Church before 1000 A.D.*, Med. Acad. of America, Cambridge, Mass., 1933; W. K. Lowther Clarke, ed., *Liturgy and Worship*, S.P.C.K., London, reprint 1943.

16. W. K. Lowther Clarke, *op. cit.*; O. D. Watkins, *Holy Matrimony*, Rivingtons, London, 1895.

17. W. K. Lowther Clarke, *op. cit.*

18. A. A. McArthur, *The Evolution of the Christian Year*, S.C.M., London, 1953; W. Rordorf, *op. cit.*

19. J. G. Davies, *The Origin and Development of Early Christian Church Architecture*, S.C.M., London, 1952; *id.*, *The Architectural Setting of Baptism*, Bartie & Rockcliff, London, 1962; *id.*, *The Secular Use of Church Buildings*, S.C.M., London, 1968; R. Krautheimer, *Early Christian and Byzantine Architecture*, Penguin Books, Harmondsworth, 1965.

20. H. A. Wilson, *The Gelasian Sacramentary*, Clarendon, Oxford, 1894;

id., *The Gregorian Sacramentary under Charles the Great*, Henry Bradshaw Society 49, London, 1915.

21. M. Andrieu, *Les Ordines Romani du Haut Moyen Age*, Spicelegium Sacrum Lovaniense, Louvain, 5 vols., 1931–61.

22. J. Julian, *A Dictionary of Hymnody*, rev. ed., Murray, London, 1907; C. Northcott, *Hymns in Christian Worship*, Lutterworth, London, 1964.

23. J. G. Davies, *Holy Week: A Short History*, Lutterworth, London, 1963; C. P. N. Jones, ed., *A Manual for Holy Week*, S.P.C.K., London, 1967; J. W. Tyrer, *Historical Survey of Holy Week*, Alcuin Club 29, S.P.C.K., London, 1932.

24. H. Norris, *Church Vestments*, Dent, London, 1949; C. E. Pocknee, *Liturgical Vesture*, Mowbray, London, 1960.

25. G. W. O. Addleshaw and F. Etchells, *The Architectural Setting of Anglican Worship*, Faber, London, 1948; A. Bieler, *Architecture in Worship*, Oliver & Boyd, Edinburgh, 1965; A. L. Drummond, *The Church Architecture of Protestantism*, T. & T. Clark, Edinburgh, 1934.

26. L. D. Reed, *The Lutheran Liturgy*, Muhlenberg, Philadelphia, 1947.

27. E. E. Yelverton, *The Mass in Sweden*, Henry Bradshaw Society 57, London, 1920.

28. J. M. Barkley, *The Worship of the Reformed Church*, Lutterworth, London, 1966; W. D. Maxwell, *John Knox's Genevan Service Book, 1556*, Oliver & Boyd, Edinburgh, 1931; *id.*, *An Outline of Christian Worship*, O.U.P., London, 1939; Y. Brilioth, *Eucharistic Faith and Practice*, S.P.C.K., London, 1939.

29. F. Procter and W. H. Frere, *op. cit.*; F. E. Brightman, *The English Rite*, Rivingtons, London, 1915; W. J. Grisbrooke, *Anglican Liturgies of the Seventeenth and Eighteenth Centuries*, Alcuin Club 40, S.P.C.K., London, 1958; B. Wigan, *The Liturgy in English*, Alcuin Club 43, S.P.C.K., London, 1962.

30. E. Lewis, *Prayer Book Revision in the Church of Wales*, Provincial Council for Education, Penarth, 1958.

31. J. C. Bowmer, *The Sacrament of the Lord's Supper in Early Methodism*, Dacre, London, 1951; *id.*, *The Lord's Supper in Methodism 1791–1960*, Epworth, London, 1961.

32. Horton Davies, *Worship and Theology in England: From Watts and Wesley to Maurice, 1690–1850*, O.U.P., London, 1961; *id.*, *Worship and Theology in England: From Newman to Martineau, 1850–1900*, O.U.P. London, 1962; *id.*, *Worship and Theology in England: The Ecumenical Century, 1900–1965*, O.U.P., London, 1965.

33. G. D. Kilpatrick, *The Origins of the Gospel according to St. Matthew*, Clarendon, Oxford, 1946.

34. O. Cullmann, *Early Christian Worship*, S.C.M., London, 1953.

35. F. L. Cross, *I Peter: a Paschal Liturgy*, Mowbray, London, 1954.

36. J.-D. Benoit, *Liturgical Renewal*, S.C.M., London, 1958; O. Casel, *The Mystery of Christian Worship*, Darton, Longman & Todd, London,

1962; J. D. Crichton, ed., *The Liturgy and the Future,* Fowler Wright, Tenbury Wells, 1966; E. B. Koenker, *The Liturgical Renaissance in the Roman Catholic Church,* University Press, Chicago, 1954; G. Hebert, ed., *The Parish Communion,* S.P.C.K., London, 1937; The Priests of St. Séverin and St. Joseph, *What is the Liturgical Movement?* Burns and Oates, London, n.d.; M. H. Shepherd, ed., *The Liturgical Renewal of the Church,* O.U.P., Oxford, 1960: J. H. Srawley, *The Liturgical Movement,* Mowbray, London, 1954; O. Rousseau, *Progress of the Liturgy,* Newman, Westminster, 1951.

37. G. Cope, ed., *Making the Building Serve the Liturgy,* Mowbray, London, 1962; F. Debuyst, *Modern Architecture and Christian Celebration,* Lutterworth, London, 1968; P. Hammond, *Liturgy and Architecture,* Barrie & Rockcliff, London, 1960; W. Lockett, ed., *The Modern Architectural Setting of the Liturgy,* S.P.C.K., London, 1964.

38. E. Lewis, *Prayer Book Revision in the Church of Wales,* Provincial Council for Education, Penarth, 1958.

39. J. D. Crichton, *op. cit.*

40. T. S. Garrett, *Worship in the Church of South India,* rev. ed., Lutterworth, London, 1965.

41. G. Cope, J. G. Davies and D. A. Tytler, *An Experimental Liturgy,* Lutterworth, London, 1958.

42. T. Wieser, ed., *Planning for Mission,* Epworth, London, 1966.

43. J. G. Davies, *Worship and Mission,* S.C.M., London, 1966.

44. N. Goodall, ed., *The Uppsala 68 Report,* World Council of Churches, Geneva, 1968; A. van den Heuvel, *The Humiliation of the Church,* S.C.M., 1967; J. F. White, *The Worldliness of Worship,* O.U.P., New York, 1967; *Worship in the City of Man,* The Liturgical Conference, Washington, 1966.

45. Space prevents the discussion of such other important topics as indigenization and liturgical arts.

46. J. G. Davies, *The Secular Use of Church Buildings,* S.C.M., London, 1968.

CHAPTER 12. CHRISTIAN ETHICS

1. J. Burnaby, *Amor Dei,* Hodder & Stoughton, London, 1938, p. 49.

2. *Ibid.,* p. 29.

3. E. Gilson, *The Christian Philosophy of St. Thomas Aquinas,* Victor Gollancz, London, 1957, p. 264.

4. It is true that on Gilson's interpretation "charity never leaves a moral virtue as it finds it" (*ibid.,* p. 349); but it is difficult to see that Aquinas can consistently have meant more than that supernatural grace restored to human nature the stability which St. Thomas, unlike many other mediaeval theologians, considered to have been disturbed by the Fall, which none the less consisted essentially of the loss of an original

338

justice, a *donum superadditum,* and which did not therefore directly affect human nature.

5. The Shorter Catechism, which was formulated along with the Confession of Faith by the Westminster Divines (see p. 145), declares in the answer to its first question that "man's chief end is to glorify God, and to enjoy him for ever" and, in the answer to its second question, that "the word of God, which is contained in the scriptures of the Old and New Testaments, is the only rule to direct us how we may glorify and enjoy him".

6. J. Calvin, *Institutes of the Christian Religion,* S.C.M., London, 1961, Book III: VI, 1.

7. *Ibid.,* Book II: VIII, 1.

8. *Ibid.,* Book III: VII, 4; cf. Book III: XII, 1.

9. John, 6: 29.

10. Luke 24: 26.

11. K. Barth, *Church Dogmatics,* Vol. II, Part 2, T. & T. Clark, Edinburgh, 1957, p. 513; cf. *The Knowledge of God and the Service of God,* Hodder & Stoughton, London, 1938, pp. 143 f.

12. *Grundlegung* translated in T. K. Abbott, *Kant's Theory of Morals,* Longmans, Green and Co., London, 1927, p. 55.

13. J. S. Mill, *Utilitarianism,* Dent, London, 1931, Ch. II.

14. H. H. Henson, *Christian Morality,* Oxford University Press, Oxford, 1936, p. 3.

15. P. L. Lehmann, *Ethics in a Christian Context,* S.C.M., London, 1963, p. 262. The word 'internal' is worth noting and contrasting with the external relationship (see below) posited by Brunner and Bonhoeffer between the 'orders' and 'mandates' respectively and the Christian life.

16. K. Barth, *Church Dogmatics,* Vol. II, Part 2, p. 513.

17. *Ibid.,* p. 509.

18. *Ibid.,* p. 517.

19. *Ibid.,* p. 524.

20. E. Brunner, *The Divine Imperative,* Lutterworth, London, 1937, p. 53.

21. *Ibid.,* p. 59.

22. *Ibid.,* p. 55.

23. R. Bultmann, *Theology of the New Testament,* Vol. I, S.C.M., London, 1952, p. 325.

24. E. Brunner, *The Divine Imperative,* p. 86.

25. Professor P. L. Lehmann's suggestion that Christian ethics is "the disciplined reflection upon the question and its answer: What am I, as a believer in Jesus Christ and as a member of his church, to do?" (*Ethics in a Christian Context,* p. 45; cf. p. 25) might also meet the case.

26. R. Niebuhr, *An Interpretation of Christian Ethics,* S.C.M., London, 1941, p. 79.

27. Cf. R. M. Hare, *The Language of Morals,* Oxford University Press, London, 1952, pp. 195 f.

28. Cf. *ibid.*, p. 69.
29. E. Brunner, *The Divine Imperative*, p. 35. It seems, however, no more plausible to say that the function of ethics is to *erect* a moral standard than it would be to maintain that the purpose of theology is to *create* a religion.
30. *Ibid.*, p. 345.
31. *Ibid.*, p. 347.
32. R. G. Smith, *The New Man*, S.C.M., London, 1956, p. 45.
33. *Ibid.*, p. 55.
34. D. Bonhoeffer, *Ethics*, S.C.M., London, 1960, p. 61.
35. P. L. Lehmann, *Ethics in a Christian Context*, p. 117.
36. *Ibid.*, p. 159.
37. Cf. *ibid.*, p. 121.
38. Cf. W. G. Maclagan, *The Theological Frontier of Ethics,* George Allen & Unwin, London, 1961, p. 72.
39. E. Brunner, *The Divine Imperative*, p. 355.
40. P. L. Lehmann, *Ethics in a Christian Context*, p. 152.
41. Visser 't Hooft and J. H. Oldham, *The Church and Its Function in Society*, George Allen & Unwin, London, 1937, p. 210.

CHAPTER 13. THE ECUMENICAL DIMENSION IN THEOLOGY

1. The authority on this is John McNeill, *Unitive Protestantism: The Ecumenical Spirit and Its Persistent Expression,* John Knox Press, Richmond, Vir., 1964.[2]
2. See especially P. S. Allen, *Erasmus: Lectures and Wayfaring Sketches,* Oxford, 1934, ch. 4: "Erasmus on Church Unity".
3. On the "Fundamental Articles", and on Bishop A. C. Headlam as a modern representative of this point of view, see S. C. Neill, *The Church and Christian Union,* O.U.P., London, 1968, pp. 383–6, and R. C. D. Jasper: *Arthur Cayley Headlam,* O.U.P., London, 1960.
4. A significant statement of this experience is to be found in the Report of Section I at the Amsterdam Assembly of the World Council of Churches in 1948. See *The First Assembly of the World Council of Churches,* S.C.M., London, 1948, pp. 51–57. Note especially p. 56: "Even when the parts seem to be similar they are set in a context which, as yet, we find irreconcilable with the whole context of the other".
5. New edition with introduction and commentary by G. R. Geiselmann, Olten, Köln, 1908. See *Oxford Dictionary of the Christian Church,* p. 912, with bibliography. It is to be noted that this book of Moehler was translated into English (1843), and was one of the few German books known to J. H. Newman.
6. The Disruption is best studied in H. Watt, *Thomas Chalmers and the Disruption,* Nelson, Edinburgh and New York, 1943.

7. It was the intention of Thomas Campbell (1763–1854) whose famous *Declaration and Address* appeared in 1809, to unite all Christians on the basis of a return to the faith of the New Testament. But, as nearly always happens in such cases, the movement ended in the formation of a new denomination, known in America as the Disciples of Christ, in Britain and elsewhere as the Churches of Christ. See W. E. Garrison and A. T. De Groot, *The Disciples of Christ. A History*, Bethany Press, St Louis, 1964.[2]

8. On the Old Catholics, see C. B. Moss, *The Old Catholic Movement, its Origin and History*, S.P.C.K., London, 1964.[2]

9. For the early period the authority is G. Bardy, *La question des langues dans l'église ancienne*, Vol. I, Paris, 1948, especially chapter 2: "La Latinization de l'Église d'Occident".

10. The form in which the *Apology* is familiar to most modern readers is the translation by Anne, Lady Bacon, one of the most brilliant pieces of translation in the English language.

11. Books I–IV of the *Treatise on the Laws of Ecclesiastical Polity* were published in 1594; Book V in 1597, Books VI and VIII in 1648 and Book VII in 1662.

12. It was finally translated by a group of scholars under the direction of Professors H. R. Mackintosh and J. S. Stewart, and appeared in 1928. Mackintosh's own posthumous book, *Types of Modern Theology*, 1937, which has deservedly gone through edition after edition, introduced the theological public to Schleiermacher, as well as to Kierkegaard and Karl Barth, a genuinely ecumenical service. On Schleiermacher, see also pp. 18, 270f., 317.

13. The Edinburgh Series of nine volumes contains the best survey of the general world missionary situation ever produced, and is still invaluable as source material. It is to be noted that the distinguished German scholar F. Siegmund-Schultze sharply contests this account of the origin of the ecumenical movement, and attaches far more significance to the work of the World Alliance for Promoting International Friendship through the Churches. See his review of the German translation of the *History of the Ecumenical Movement* in *Ökumenische Rundschau* 1959, pp. 13 ff.

14. Pietism is a convenient general term for all the movements, from 1675 onwards, which have stressed the need for a personal experience of conversion, and for the gift of the Holy Spirit with a view to holiness of life.

15. Warneck (1834–1910) produced an immense *Missionslehre* in five volumes, and in 1896 became the first professor of missions in a German university, Halle. His prophetic quality is shown in the remarkable proposal that he put before the Missionary Conference held in London in 1886, in which he foreshadowed almost exactly the International Missionary Council as it came into being 33 years

later. As far as I am aware, the ecumenical character of the missionary journals has not previously been noted by writers on ecumenical themes.

16. Warneck never understood the distinction between 'evangelization', the preaching of the Gospel, and 'conversion', acceptance of the Gospel, which was quite clear to those who used the slogan. John R. Mott constantly made use of the phrase, but I do not think that it was invented by him. The phrase fell from popularity in the period after the First World War.

17. A full-scale biography of John R. Mott (1865–1954) is in preparation. The existing lives are entirely inadequate as a picture of the life and activity of this many-sided man. B. Mathews: *Ambassador of Christ: the Story of John R. Mott*, S.C.M., London, 1950, is lively and readable. Mott's own addresses and papers have been published in six volumes, Association Press, New York, 1946–7. The quiet influence of J. H. Oldham (1874–1969) has spread to every corner of the ecumenical field. When a full-scale biography appears, much light will be shed on a great many dark corners.

18. On Nikolai (Kasatkin) see S. C. Neill, *A History of Christian Missions*, Harmondsworth, Pelican Books, 1965, pp. 445–7.

19. This particularly affected the American Board of Commissioners for Foreign Missions, the liberal point of view being especially represented by the Andover Seminary. The particular issue was whether one who believed in 'the second chance' after death could be accepted for missionary service under the Board.

20. The first missionary of the *Verein* was the distinguished Sinologist, E. Faber, who came over from the Rhenish Mission, and whose book, *Introduction to the Science of Chinese Religion*, had been reviewed in the *Evangelisches Missionsmagazin*, 1880, p. 175.

21. See E. Sharpe: *Not to Destroy but to Fulfil*, Gleerup, Lund, 1965.

22. The Provincial Synod of Anglican bishops in India in 1900, while generally approving the principle of 'comity' in the mission field, claimed the right to minister to Anglicans wherever they might be, and "deprecates any such territorial agreements in the future". See R. P. Beaver: *Ecumenical Beginnings in Protestant World Mission: A History of Comity*, Nelson, Edinburgh, 1962, pp. 273 ff.

23. The story of this development is told in full by T. Tatlow, *The Story of the Student Christian Movement*, London, 1933, chapters 9 and 21. On the part played by Canon Tatlow in the preparations for Edinburgh 1910, see R. Rouse and S. C. Neill, *A History of the Ecumenical Movement 1517–1948*, pp. 405–07.

24. The best introduction to the thought of F. D. Maurice is still A. R. Vidler, *The Theology of F. D. Maurice*, London, 1948. But the two-volume *Life* by Maurice's son (London, 1884) is still indispensable.

25. For brief biographies and bibliographies for these writers, consult

Lexikon für Theologie und Kirche, Evangelisches Kirchenlexikon, and *Die Religion in Geschichte und Gegenwart.*[2]

26. The first notable work of Walter Rauschenbusch (1861–1918), *Christianity and the Social Crisis,* appeared in 1907, one year before the setting up of the Federal Council of the Churches in the U.S.A. Rauschenbusch was a better theologian, and a more deeply biblical Christian, than has often been supposed. The weakness of the theorists of the Social Gospel was that, conditioned by the individualism of their times, they failed to realize the significance and the power of *structures* in the ordering of human life. See B. Y. Lands, *A Rauschenbusch Reader,* Harper, New York, 1957. P. A. Carter, *The Decline and Revival of the Social Gospel,* Ithaca, Cornell U.P., 1957.

27. At last we have an adequate biography of Söderblom—B. G. M Sundkler: *Nathan Söderblom: his Life and Work,* Lutterworth Press, London, 1968. The short life prefixed to Söderblom's Gifford Lectures, *The Living God,* Oxford, 1931, by his son-in-law Yngve Brilioth, who was later to become Archbishop of Uppsala, is still valuable. In the complex system for the election of a Swedish Archbishop, Söderblom was brought on to the short list of three to be submitted to the King only by the casting of lots to decide a tied vote in one of the dioceses; if the lot had fallen the other way, he could not have become archbishop. See Sundkler, *op. cit.,* pp. 101–04.

28. The story of COPEC is briefly set out in E. Shillito, *Christian Citizenship. The Story and the Meaning of C.O.P.E.C.,* London, 1924. William Temple, at that time Bishop of Manchester, was Chairman, and Canon C. E. Raven Secretary, of the Conference.

29. One of the leaders in this movement was Allen Baker, whose son Noel Baker carried on the same concern for peace and international goodwill. See E. B. Baker and P. J. N. Baker, *J. Allen Baker,* London, 1927.

30. One of the earliest ecumenical movements, the *Evangelical Alliance* of 1846, was, like the World Alliance, a movement of interested individuals. The influence of its conferences and their reports was considerable through the nineteenth century; but it made no claim to speak in the name of the churches. The revolutionary character of the change here recorded, and the strong resistance to it encountered in many quarters, are often forgotten by those who have grown up in the ecumenical atmosphere subsequent to 1925. It was at this point that ecumenical theology became essentially a theology of *the Church.*

31. The full text of these utterances can be found in G. K. A. Bell (ed.), *The Stockholm Conference 1925. The Official Report of the Universal Christian Conference on Life and Work held in Stockholm, 19–30 August 1925,* Oxford and London, 1926.

32. At the very first meeting of the Commission, the Continentals laid down the principle that the Christian hope can only be eschatological,

and relates only to the 'second coming of Christ', a term the meaning of which they were unable to define to the satisfaction of the Americans Cf. p. 37.

33. J. Moltmann, *The Theology of Hope*, S.C.M., London, 1967.

34. This slogan is often attributed to Söderblom himself; but, though it entirely expresses his mind, it seems to have originated with Söderblom's friend, Dr. Kapler, President of the Federation of Evangelical Churches in Germany. See B. G. M. Sundkler, *Nathan Söderblom*, p. 340. Kapler was a layman and a lawyer, not a theologian.

35. It is to be regretted that there is as yet no adequate biography of Brent. A. C. Zabriskie, *Bishop Brent, Crusader for Christian Unity*, Philadelphia, 1948, is good as far as it goes: but there was more to Brent than is shown in this short biography. See also S. C. Neill, Brent Centenary Lecture, in *Canadian Journal of Theology*, 1962. No biography at all exists of the remarkable layman Robert Halliwell Gardiner, who kept Faith and Order in existence through the difficult years between 1910 and 1924, when he died. It is understood that a full biography is in preparation.

36. The most famous of these was the Colloquy of Ratisbon in 1541, the last serious attempt made in the Empire to bring Roman Catholic and Protestant views into accord with one another. There had been a number of others across the centuries, but on the whole with diminishing rather than increasing returns.

37. The Orthodox, greatly hampered by linguistic difficulties, never really understood what the conference was about, and wished to guard themselves against even the appearance of being committed to some proximate union of the churches, of a kind that the conference had never dreamed of. The Orthodox habit of handing in separate statements was not broken until the Third Assembly of the World Council of Churches at New Delhi in 1961.

38. E. Molland, *Christendom: The Christian Churches: their doctrines, constitutional forms and ways of worship*, Mowbray, London, 1959.

39. P. Manhold, *Ökumenische Kirchenkunde: Lebensformen der Christenheit heute*, Kreuz-Verlag, Stuttgart, 1962.

40. The progress of Faith and Order can be followed in the admirable selection of documents published by Lukas Vischer under the title, *A Documentary History of the Faith and Order Movement, 1927–1963*, World Council of Churches, Geneva, with a thoughtful introduction by the editor.

41. This attitude was modified after 1952. In that year S. C. Neill was asked by Faith and Order to produce a book on current movements for union, *Towards Church Union 1937–1952*, S.C.M., London, 1952; and from that date onwards the *Ecumenical Review* has published periodical surveys of the progress of movements for corporate unions, supplied by the Faith and Order Division of the World Council of Churches.

A brief and useful study is J. E. Skoglund and J. R. Nelson, *Fifty Years of Faith and Order: an Interpretation of the Faith and Order Movement*, Bethany Press, London, 1964.

42. A complete list of all known negotiations up to 1948 was published in the *History of the Ecumenical Movement*, 1954, pp. 496–505.

43. C. E. Silcox, *Church Union in Canada: its Causes and Consequences*, Institute of Social and Religious Research, New York, 1935.

44. B. F. M. Sundkler, *The Church of South India: The Movement towards Union 1900–1947*, Lutterworth Press, London, 1954.

45. There is one outstanding study of the processes of church union within a single confession—R. Sjolinder, *Presbyterian Reunion in Scotland 1907–1921*, Almgrist and Wilsell, Stockholm, 1962.

46. The raw materials for such a judgement have been brought together in G. K. A. Bell, *Documents on Christian Unity*, 4 Vols, O.U.P., London, 1924, 1930, 1948, 1958. The first two volumes are out of print, but the more important documents have been reprinted in *Documents on Christian Unity: A Selection 1920–1930*, 1958.

47. Kraemer followed up his first great book by a number of others, notably *Religion and the Christian Faith*, Lutterworth, London, 1948; *The Communication of the Christian Faith*, Philadelphia, 1956; *Why Christianity of all Religions?*, Lutterworth, London, 1956; *World Cultures and World Religions: The Coming Dialogue*, Lutterworth, London, 1960. But he made little modification in the absoluteness and rigidity of his early position. We now have an excellent story of Kraemer's early development in G. F. Hallencreutz, *Kraemer Towards Tambaram, A Study in Hendrik Kraemer's Missionary Approach*, Gleerup, Lund, 1966.

48. A careful study of the theology of some of these thinkers has been made by H. Wagner, *Erstgestalten einer einheimischen christlichen Theologie in Südindien*, Hamburg, 1961. A lengthy study of P. Chenchiah has been made by D. A. Thangaswamy, *The Theology of P. Chenchiah*, Madras, 1966. Reference may be made also to the work of Bishop A. J. Appasamy, *The Christian Task in Independent India*, S.P.C.K., London, 1951.

49. As an exceptionally valuable guide to the reader, we may mention Charles J. Adams (ed.), *A Reader's Guide to the Great Religions*, The Free Press, New York, 1965; E. C. Dewick, *The Christian Attitude to Other Religions*, C.U.P., Cambridge, 1953, is clear and well-informed, with a slight bias in the liberal direction. A simple introduction to the idea of dialogue between the religions is S. C. Neill, *Christian Faith and Other Faiths*, O.U.P., London, 1968.[2]

50. This view of Gogarten's is most readily accessible to English readers in in A. T. van Leeuwen, *Christianity in World History: The Meeting of the Faiths of East and West*, Lutterworth, London, 1964. Much confusion has been caused by the use of the term 'secularization'. The correct

term is 'desacralization'. A secularized world would be one in which God was no longer recognized as being at work at all.

51. R. O. Latham, *God for All Men: The meeting of the Commission on World Mission and Evangelism of the World Council of Churches at Mexico City*, December 8 to 19, 1963, Edinburgh House Press, London, 1964.

52. *The Uppsala Report: Official Report of the Fourth Assembly of the World Council of Churches, Uppsala July 4–20, 1968* World Council of Churches, Geneva, 1968.

53. A brief popular account of some of the men who made the ecumenical movement in modern times is S. C. Neill, *Men of Unity*, S.C.M., London, 1960, out of print, but available in many libraries.

54. A fairly full account of the processes through which the council came into being is *The Ten Formative Years*, World Council of Churches, Geneva, 1948. The report of the constitutive Assembly of 1948 is *The First Assembly of the World Council of Churches*, S.C.M., London, 1948. The best general account of ecumenical development is N. Goodall, *The Ecumenical Movement: what it is, and what it does*, O.U.P., London, 1961.

55. On this see also S. C. Neill, *The Church and Christian Union*, Oxford University Press, London, 1968, pp. 173–4. Van Dusen's book also contains a most valuable chronology of all the important events in ecumenical history.

56. *The Universal Church in God's Design*, pp. 177–95. Of course there is no one identifiable theology of the movement; but it is possible to speak again in terms of convergence, different people from many starting-points finding their way to a common concern.

57. This document is reprinted in full in L. Vischer, *A Documentary History of the Faith and Order Movement 1927–1963*, World Council of Churches, Geneva, 1963, pp. 167–77.

58. *The New Delhi Report: The Third Assembly of the World Council of Churches, 1961*, S.C.M., London, 1962. The crucial statement on the nature of the unity we seek is on p. 116.

59. The Russian church accused the World Council of having lost its interest in questions of faith and order, and of seeking to win for itself a political kingdom by the use of American financial power.

60. The authority on all this is R. Slenczka, *Ostkirche und Ökumene: die Einheit der Kirche als dogmatisches Problem in der neueren ostkirchlichen Theologie*, Vandenhoech and Ruprecht, Göttingen, 1962.

61. L. A. Zander, *Vision and Action*, Gollancz, 1952.

62. Especially *L'Orthodoxie*, Delachaux and Niestlé, Neuchâtel, 1959. See also N. Zernov, *The Russian Religious Renaissance of the Twentieth Century*, Darton, Longman and Todd, London, 1963.

63. See N. Nissiotis, "The Witness and Service of Eastern Orthodoxy" in *Ecumenical Review*, 14, 1962, pp. 190 ff. Dr Nissiotis is at present Director of the Ecumenical Institute, Château de Bossey.

64. The text of *Mortalium Animos* is conveniently to be found in G. K. A. Bell, *Documents on Church Unity, II. A Selection 1920–1930*, O.U.P. London, pp. 188–200.

65. R. Aubert in *Twentieth Century Christianity*, ed. S. C. Neill, Collins, London, 1962,² pp. 32–80. Professor Aubert takes as his main illustration the liturgical movement, but what he says is equally applicable to the ecumenical movement.

66. Eng. trans: *Divided Christendom: a catholic study of the problem of reunion*, G. Bles, London, 1939.

67. See S. C. Neill, *The Church and Christian Union*, O.U.P., London, 1968, Chapter 1: "The Rediscovery of the Church".

68. A long list of writers on this subject can be compiled. The most important is Karl Rahner, whose Essays have been brought together in the four volumes of his *Theological Investigations*, Helicon Press, Baltimore; Darton, Longman and Todd, London. The best known is Hans Küng, who combines lucidity of thought with such liberality of spirit that some readers have wondered how long he will be allowed to continue to publish, even in the relaxed atmosphere which has followed upon the second Vatican Council.

69. The literature on the council is already a shoreless sea. It is generally agreed that the best day to day account is that contained in the four volumes published under the pseudonym Xavier Rynne. A distinguished account by an observer is that of Douglas Horton, *Vatican Diary 1964*, United Church Press, Philadelphia, 1965.

70. Editions and translations of the council documents are manifold. For detailed study of the history and theological significance of the various documents perhaps the most satisfactory work is the stately two volume addition to the *Lexikon für Theologie und Kirche*, Herder, Freiburg, 1967. Here the experts seem to have brought together all that even the most exacting student could wish to know.

71. A useful introduction to this large subject is provided by J. De F. Murch, *Co-operation without Compromise*, Eerdmans, Grand Rapids, 1956. A far more destructive wing of anti-ecumenical activity is represented by C. McIntire, *Modern Tower of Babel*, N. J., Collingwood, 1949 and *Servants of Apostasy*, N. J., Collingwood, 1955.

Index

Titles of books in the Bible, and names mentioned only in
NOTES AND REFERENCES, are not included in this Index.

354